D0502605

Portrait of

LIVERPOOL

HOWARD CHANNON

ILLUSTRATED
AND WITH MAP

ROBERT HALE & COMPANY

UNIVERSITY OF VICTORIA
LIBRARY
Victoria, B. C.

DA 690
L8 CH8
1972

© *Howard Channon 1970 and 1972*
First published in Great Britain November 1970
Second edition February 1972

ISBN 0 7091 3025 2

Robert Hale & Company
63 Old Brompton Road
London S.W.7

FOR

TIM AND JOYCE

who will see what becomes
of the place

Printed and bound in Great Britain by
C. Tinling & Co. Ltd., London and Prescot

CONTENTS

ILLUSTRATIONS

PICTURE CREDITS

Liverpool Daily Post and *Echo:* 1, 2 and 3, 4b, 5a, 5b, 7,
8, 10, 18, 19, 24b; Liverpool Corporation: 9a, 9b, 13b, 14a,
14b, 20, 23a; Liverpool University: 16b, 21, 22; Royal
Liverpool Philharmonic Society: 12.

PREFACE

FUNDAMENTAL changes have occurred since this book was first printed in 1970. In December of that year, the Mersey Docks and Harbour Board, which a few months before had been anticipating nationalisation, became insolvent with debts of at least £93 million; and, because the new Government decided that its 'no help for industrial lame ducks' policy included lame docks, all quays south of the Pier Head (described in Chapter Five) will close before the end of 1972. Thus a large downtown area will have to be found new purpose but what this will be had still to be determined at the time this book again went to press. Plans for a £100 million office complex, to be known as 'Aquarius City', to cover two of the south-end docks, were abandoned at about the same time that the port authority announced it could no longer pay its bills.

The Mersey's future rests almost entirely upon the success of £40-million docks at Seaforth which are outside Liverpool's present boundaries. Meanwhile the Docks Board's bond-holders, many of whom had invested modest life-savings in the port, are the principal victims of the financial catastrophe; so the effects upon business in the city, where rates were swingeingly increased in 1971, have been serious.

At the time of writing, the port remains economically in jeopardy though, parallel with the first half-year of Mr. John Cuckney's energetic chairmanship of the new regime, there were encouraging trends. Millions were invested by millers in new buildings by the Seaforth docks and this faith in the port should encourage more to be put into the enterprise once money is flowing freely, particularly as there are definate prospects that the long period in which labour unrest bedevilled the port, where there were too many employers, is now coming to an end. Obviously it is no accident that this improvement coincided with a metamorphosis of dock management, for so many years far from efficient. But blame for the plight of the port also lies with successive governments. Statute prevented the Docks Board putting more than £100,000 a year aside for depreciation in the period up to 1936. By 1941 the port had been devastated by bombs; and ever since, between periodic promises of nationalisation, governments have persistently neglected an authority striving to reconstruct through decades of escalating interest charges.

The dock labour force increased in 1971 but, with factories closing and firms contracting, unemployment in Liverpool emphatically worsened. The city has far more unskilled and semi-skilled people than most other parts of Britain and is losing its qualified young men and women at a higher rate. Therefore it was a bitter disappointment when the present Government declined to make Merseyside one of its 1971 special development areas. Its refusal to treat the second Mersey tunnel as a motorway was a further blow, coming so soon after aid to the city's languishing airport had also been rejected.

The first tube of the second tunnel was opened in mid-1971 by the Queen and her visit stimulated long overdue improvements in the city centre, bringing rosebeds to Lime Street and trees to the newly-flagged Williamson Square which lost its cobbles and Victorian urinal after many years of campaigning and complaining.

The Royal Court Theatre, which in mid-1970 seemed doomed, was in mid-1971 made safe for at least three more years. The Exchange Hotel closed but bigger hotels were well on the way to completion. The riverside railway station, once famous, shut down and demolition at Central Station began. But an underground railway for the city was assured with Government grants of £8 million pledged.

There was prospect of positive action to counter the deplorable pollution of the Mersey which receives 50 million gallons a day of untreated sewage flushed into Liverpool Bay where a proportion of Manchester's discard is also dumped.

New stars rose in the Merseyside soccer firmament—players like University graduates Steve Heighway and Brian Hall, of Liverpool F.C., and David Johnson, of Everton, all three local boys made good. But the shadow over the future of the Grand National at Aintree lengthened.

Socially and economically, Liverpool is inextricably a segment of Merseyside. I have had to extricate it for the purpose of this book because it is not possible, in a single volume of reasonable size, adequately to portray the whole of an area wherein more than 1,500,000 live and which the Government wants a metropolitan council to administer from 1974. When such a metropolis is created, those with homes in its Liverpool District will be a Merseyside minority.

I have skipped early history in order to look, in some detail, at the period of the slave trade and privateers and at nineteenth-century poverty in Liverpool because I believe this helps one more readily to appreciate some attitudes and difficulties in the present-day city. I have drawn from Gomer Williams's book *The Liverpool Privateers*, published in 1895, which, in my view, is the standard reference work concerning the slave trade by ships from the Mersey as well as the adventures of raiders at sea.

My thanks go to: Liverpool Daily Post and Echo Ltd., for allowing me to publish their photographs and extracts from several articles of mine which appeared in the *Liverpool Echo*; Liverpool Corporation, the Royal Liverpool Philharmonic Society, and Liverpool University for permission to reproduce their photographs; Pete McGovern and Spin Publications, Jackie and Bridie and Galliard Ltd., and Stan Kelly and Heathside Music Ltd. for leave to use words from their songs; Frank Shaw for his expert help with Scouse; the Society of Authors, as the literary representative of the Estate of John Masefield, for permission to quote his words; and Mr. Arthur Behrend for allowing me to extract from his book *Portrait of a Family Firm*.

Woolton,   HOWARD CHANNON
Liverpool

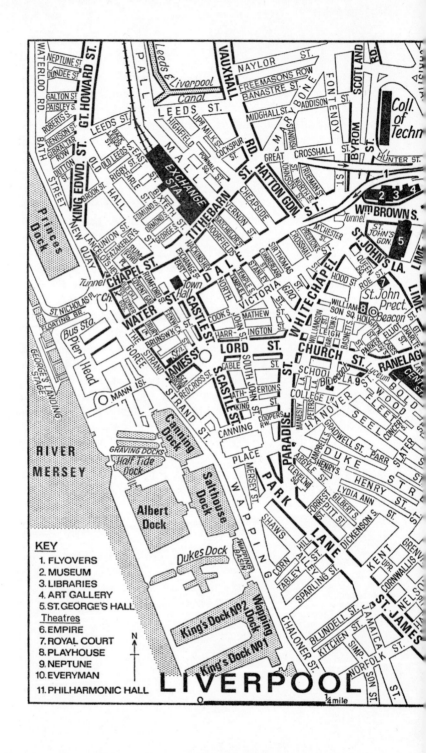

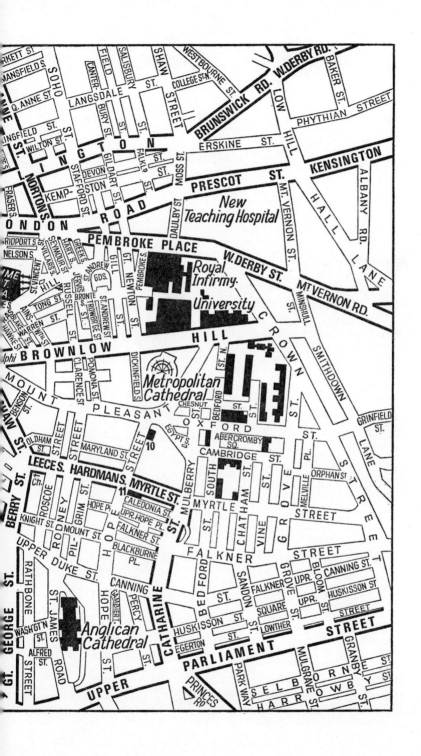

We speak with an accent exceedingly rare,
Meet under a statue exceedingly bare;
And if you want a Cathedral we've got one
to spare. . . .

Pete McGovern
('In Me Liverpool Home',
Spin Publications)

ONE

CHANGE AND CHALLENGE

THIRTY years ago I fell in love with Liverpool, and here I am, so help me, still made up with it (as a Merseysider would say) and ready to shout 'Ee-aye-addio', even though, as with a cherished wife after her silver wedding, virtues are taken for granted while shortcomings increasingly strain indulgence.

There are times when I am exasperated by aspects of the city and by the conduct of Liverpudlians, times when they embarrass me in front of my visiting friends, times, indeed, when I am repelled or alarmed; and yet, when I go to other cities in England, cities that are glossier, better ordered and emphatically more prosperous than Liverpool, I find them by comparison to be un-flavoured, their citizens almost anonymous beside the salty wacker and his missus, his judy that was.

The one city in which I would expect a Liverpudlian to find his element is Dublin, 65 miles nearer the Mersey than London is, closer to it than are Tyneside, Clydeside and Cardiff. He would certainly be more at home here than in Manchester which is but forty minutes' ride from Lime Street Station and now almost attached to Merseyside by umbilical brick as well as the cord of the Ship Canal. By the Liffey are the extremes in grandeur and meanness, elegance and gracelessness, foresight and folly that have always been commonplace in the 'Pool; and here are inhabitants who have some of the pungency, the inborn acuity, the exuber-ance, the extravagance, the slovenliness, the spontaneous hospit-ality and the bellicose resentment of criticism from strangers that are all traits of the wacker.

Do not suppose, however, that these characteristics are entirely a consequence of Irish corpuscles in the Liverpudlian blood. They were in development in the second half of the eighteenth century, that lusty era of privateers and slave ships when the port was growing into one of the greatest in the world; and this was long before that hungry human tide crossing the Irish Sea (Protestant Orange as well as the Catholic Green) reached its spate.

Welsh influences have been at least as profound. There are five columns of Murphys and some 200 O'Briens in the Liverpool telephone book, but the Joneses occupy thirty-six columns and the Williamses twenty-two. If the Irish brogue remains an everyday sound in the city's streets so does the cadence of English as it is spoken in the Principality; and to overhear a conversation in the Welsh language beneath those naked genitals of the Epstein man striding out on a ship's prow over a department store's main entrance opposite windows of the Adelphi Hotel, is unremarkable for it is the mother tongue of many of the wives who cross two tidal rivers every Thursday to shop in the 'Pool.

There are a dozen or more churches in the city where the notice boards are in Welsh and there are hundreds of Liverpool natives who can, at very least, sing '*Hen Wlad Fy Nhadau*' and '*Ar Hyd Y Nos*' in the words of their forefathers and with equal fervour. The National Eisteddfod has been held thrice on Merseyside, where there are more of Welsh ancestry, it is said, than in the whole of North Wales; and the Liverpool Welsh Choral Union is one of the great choirs of Britain.

But in the shops, in the pubs and on the buses Liverpudlians also hear the languages of Europe, Asia and Africa because those who speak them sail regularly into the Mersey. A great many Liverpudlians have themselves been at sea or are the sons and daughters of seafarers, among whom were Scandinavians, Dutch, Chinese, Malays, Indians and Arabs. With the cargoes of fruit and onions, sherry and port into the Mersey came Spanish and Portuguese merchants as well as seamen.

The advent of steam and the lengthening of the ribbon of docks brought a great Yorkshireman, Jesse Hartley, and many Scots. The expanding commerce attracted Jews (there was a synagogue nearly 200 years ago), and many more, nineteenth-century refugees from Europe on their way to America, stayed in the port instead of sailing from the Mersey.

Two centuries of trading with the world have made Liverpool a cosmopolitan city, the least provincial in outlook and the most mature in attitudes to colour and race (though this is not to say that it is free from prejudice).

Since the last war the Mersey has lost almost all its transocean passenger liners to the Solent, Cunard's former headquarters have been bought by the Prudential; and boat trains no longer pull into the Riverside Station, linked to the half-mile-long floating landing stage for in 1971 this was closed. But with the departure of the liners new leviathans have arrived, carriers of oil to replenish those tanks laid in great clutches on both banks of the river, and to feed those refineries sprouting imitations of rocket launching pads beyond the Cheshire shore; and, although there are now very large industries in and around their city that have nothing to do with the sea, Liverpudlians have stayed infatuated with ships and sailors, taking ferry trips or promenading the decks built a few years ago athwart the Pier Head just to spot ensigns, house flags and ports of registration and to focus cameras on tugs sallying forth from the landing stage to dance attendance upon some new arrival from a faraway place that blared for their company.

Liverpudlians, the laughter of gulls in their ears and the smells from quaysides in their nostrils, never tire of a view downhill from the commercial heart of the city, the point where the dignified Town Hall steps out of line and, as it were, into the street. This is a vista of the Mersey through a canyon built by banking, shipping and insurance; and it is so blinkered by tall office blocks that one large vessel in the portion of river visible becomes the undisputed focal point of a living picture.

It was as a sailor, and when close to the Town Hall, that I fell in love with the city on 3rd September 1940. It was not love at first sight. In childhood I traipsed with a school party round a Cunarder, as a youth I gawped into the mouth of the Mersey Tunnel newly burrowed below the river; but these visits left the impression of a city brutally big, much too begrimed and much too busy ever to appeal to the bumpkin I was then rather proud to be.

Yet on that first anniversary of war, when I had arrived to join a destroyer, the city was about its business with such brisk purposefulness and such *élan* as to generate an exhilaration I found wholly irresistible. That evening I had a 1s. 6d. dinner at a table that had upon it a crisp, linen cloth, polished cutlery and a vase of

fresh chrysanthemums (few of the country's best hotels were by
that time able to run to a daily change of flowers); and I was
waited upon by a girl who was pretty and nicely turned out and
who talked to me as though I were an acquaintance of a valued
friend of her family. I was in the dining room of the Angel Club,
its name—a singularly happy one—taken from an hotel handed
over to ladies of Liverpool so that they could provide meals and
beds for Servicemen; and it was in complete contrast to the run
of canteens up and down the country staffed by volunteers who
were so often either patronising or grudging as they stood by wet
counters slopping tea into chipped mugs and doling out doorstep
sandwiches and jaw-tiring wads.

The 'angels' (as they were inevitably known) ran the club on
the assumption that everyone in uniform came from a comfortable and orderly home. The place became talked about all over
the world and so, I think, did the State Restaurant, conveniently
almost next door, with the tables ringing a dance floor. I was
there on that first night, too, met in the entrance hall and escorted
without ostentation to a seat in the middle of a family group.
This, as I discovered, was a practice established almost at the outbreak of war. The 'Angel' (which survived the bombs) and the
'State' (which, unhappily, did not) were my first experience of
Merseysiders on their mettle as hosts; and when they are this they
have few equals and no superiors for generous hospitality and
relaxed friendliness.

Near the end of that year I stood in the crowded foyer of the
Empire Theatre watching flames rise from the long roof of St.
George's Hall, across Lime Street, as though from a monster
cauldron. About me many were in tears, believing that one of the
city's greatest treasures was doomed; and yet they trooped back
into the theatre, although German bombers were still overhead,
and were able to laugh at an impromptu show that went on until
the small hours. By then it was evident that, although grievous
internal wounds had been inflicted, St. George's Hall was still
largely in one piece; but the flames from the rooftop that night
were as though from a beacon signalling in advance the holocaust
of the following May.

I was in the city in that fearful week of 1941 when the port came
close to being put wholly out of action. I walked along some of
the scores of fissured streets where gas and water mains were

ruptured, where sleep-starved rescue teams toiled and scrabbled among rubble that had been homes—streets where people, some very young, some very old, drifted in trauma through a haze of smoke and dust and stench from burst sewers. I saw tortured bodies of carthorses that had been dragged from blazing stables, then abandoned in heaps because there were humans to extricate. I saw shambling cows, released by bombs from back street byres (there were scores of them in Liverpool at that time) and bellowing to be milked. I saw a baby's body in the splintered debris of its cradle.

I saw some of the many hundreds in Liverpool and in adjoining Bootle who had lost a home and everything in it, those frantic for news of a loved one, those in anguish because they had received it. I saw a shawled woman—she clutched the handle of a cage in which a canary twittered (presumably her only possession to survive)—sitting on a pile of bricks and sobbing with joy because she had just heard that her married daughter and her grand-daughter were alive after another night of savagery. The remains of some 500 of the 1,300 who died during that week lie in a communal grave at Anfield Cemetery marked by a memorial which has no cross because many of the victims were not of the Christian faith. Fewer than half of those in this resting place, were, in fact, identified.

Having been a spectator through those May days of agony and the nights of terror, having seen a great swath mown by the Luftwaffe through the centre of the city, familiar and esteemed buildings like the great classical Customs House erased and large segments of older suburbs obliterated or left in semi-destruction, I had in my heart, as well as in my memory, a special place for Liverpool and its people which would have stayed if I had never set foot in the place again. As it happened, I left a few days after the blitz with others of the crew of a destroyer that had been badly mauled; and I visited the port only three or four times, then briefly, between that week of devastation and January 1952, when I returned to Liverpool to work and to be a ratepayer.

There were then, on all sides, still spoilheaps from the war and many a void from which these had been cleared. But the people of the sadly shabby city had picked themselves up and dusted themselves down and, although a great many of them dwelt in squalor, they had recovered their ebullience. The Punch and Judy Professor's brightly painted portable theatre was back on the Plateau beneath the noble temple front at the southern end of St. George's Hall—an incongruity that few corporations, jealous of dignity, would countenance but has been allowed in Liverpool and, somehow, looks right in a city of numerous contrasts no less emphatic—for example, the daytime shack from where newspapers were sold on the opulent threshold of the Adelphi Hotel; and the taxi-drivers' hut that stared the Playhouse in its made-up face until 1971.

In Clayton Square and by Central Station were 'the flower ladies' with basketed blooms, coaxing and scolding and thanking customers in terms from an especial thesaurus. In tatty back ways off nearby Elliot Street, barrow boys—and girls—shouted their wares; and in Church Street, outside 'Woolies' ' (the first established in Britain), pavement salesmen despatched mechanical toys under the feet of shoppers and occasionally departed in haste, balloons flying, when the approach of a 'scuffer' was signalled by their look-out.

There were still many horses in the main streets in 1952 and, as well as the heavy brigade, a cavalry of light vanners were in the employ of British Railways. They emerged every few minutes from the cavern of the big, shabby parcels depot in Whitechapel fighting for the bit; then, given their heads when the way was clear, high-tailed it over a cobbled route, ending with a canter up the steep slope which led them under the great arch into Lime Street Station.

Tramcars were also still running, mostly the stately, bosomy kind that Liverpudlians called 'Green Goddesses'. And along the waterfront, so much of it then in half-ruin or temporarily patched, the antique rolling stock of the Overhead Railway, having escaped from the dark and dripping tunnel of a terminal at Dingle, pursued an elevated and leisurely way northward to a platform at Seaforth, where passengers could transfer to an electric train to Southport; so that, in school holidays and at weekends, the paraphernalia of the beach was in evidence in the sedate old coaches, and a docker in a hurry to alight at one of the waterfront stations was liable to trip over a child's bucket and spade.

From the Overhead trains there were exciting glimpses of ships and lighters loading and discharging alongside 40 miles of quay;

and across the bustling river a view of the distinctive, if not particularly prepossessing, towers above the fairground at New Brighton (now destroyed), beyond them the prominent dome of a church on a hill. The prospect from the opposite windows was dominated for a part of the journey by the majestic tower, topped by a gracious coronet, of the Anglican Cathedral which the sun, when westward, tints pink.

So, in 1952, although Liverpool was badly scarred and dishevelled and nearly every public building had a face grimed with soot and was disfigured by a nævus of pigeon droppings, it had a vigorous, bouncy personality. Comparatively speaking, it was poverty-stricken, having had nothing like a fair share of the immediate postwar boom; yet it was confronted with a mammoth rebuilding task: domestic (100,000 homes were far below modest standards of decent living), commercial and civic. In this reconstruction, particularly during the fifties, cardinal blunders were made, some of them heartbreaking in their lack of flair in a city where, certainly in the nineteenth century, civic and commercial leaders planned with panache.

The biggest mistake—the biggest, because it is unlikely to be rectified in this century—was to restore Lord Street as a corridor thoroughfare, the Corporation being apparently oblivious to the tremendous annual increase in traffic and the inevitability of this artery being seized, within a decade, by vehicular thrombosis. The first row of premises rushed up, virtually on foundations of those the Luftwaffe knocked down, were as repulsive as any then being built in the country, though they are matched by another dreadful post-war block in Church Street (Lord Street's continuation).

I found it at the time almost beyond belief that councillors, conferring inside the elegant Town Hall and surrounded by examples of handsome thinking by their Victorian and Edwardian predecessors, could have sanctioned erection of what is, to all appearances from the street, a high wall of reconstituted stone with apertures in it for windows. One almost wept at such poverty of imagination in the city where was conceived, by sublime civic visionaries, the noble grouping of buildings—sessions house, art gallery, roundel reading room, libraries, museum and technical college—to present a frontage so wonderfully in keeping with the magnificence of nearby St. George's Hall.

Consider the opportunity there was, after the war, to design on an even grander scale than this in Lord Street. From Derby Square —the first summit reached coming from the river—down to Church Street the entire right-hand flank had been razed; and on the far side of this swath of destruction those buildings which remained more or less intact were, with a few exceptions, ripe for demolition. The premises spared by the Luftwaffe on the same side of James Street (Lord Street's riverward continuation from Derby Square) were similarly unprepossessing. So there might have been laid here a substantial sector of what could have become, in due time, one of the best-looking High Streets in the world, the new buildings having a broad frontage of lawns, with occasional groups of trees, which would have swept uphill from the waterfront, downhill and then uphill again, for a truly regal mile to the skeletonised St. Luke's, its tower a permanent monument, graced with flower beds, to recall the 1941 blitz.

The scholarly Bluecoat Chambers, built three years after the death of Queen Anne and one of the centres of the city's cultural life, could have been open to this grand parade. Instead it has been left in a nasty alley with ill-visaged neighbours and screened from the mainstream of Church Street by an overpowering block of shops and offices, erected in 1955; and though this is less ugly than that first section of Lord Street's post-war façade and the earlier post-war frontage in Church Street, there is nothing about it to gratify the eye.

Later additions to Lord Street, occupying spaces between where that apertured 'wall' ends and Derby Square, are more prepossessing but still far from compelling; and no sooner was this reconstruction complete and the street thereby restored irrevocably to its pre-war width, than the predicted traffic jams materialised. Not only Lord Street and Church Street were congealed— the entire shopping centre and business quarter of the city became immobilised from Pier Head to the inner suburbs, so that on some evenings a great many people found it quicker to walk home from work than go by bus or car. The spectacle of a great city brought to a halt, every street packed with stationary vehicles, was frightening; and when it was repeated half a dozen times or more in a month, as was the case in Liverpool at the beginning of the sixties, it was almost beyond endurance.

Nearly always the cause of this hypertension was to be found in the Mersey Tunnel, where it needed but a brief sequence of trivial incidents—two or three forgetful drivers running out of petrol and a punctured lorry tyre, for example—to begin a cumulative congestion affecting first the approaches to the Tunnel, then spreading to every street. Going home by car, particularly if home was 'over the water' on the Wirral Peninsula (and the Tunnel therefore the only way to get there), became an early evening nightmare. On those occasions, mercifully few, when two or three drivers, suddenly possessed by a demon, pressed their horns and the madness afflicted a thousand other frustrated motorists, life between five o'clock and six-thirty became scarcely bearable even for those who took refuge in restaurant and pub waiting for the tourniquet on the traffic to ease.

Such a phase was doubtless inevitable in Liverpool because, even if there had been the foresight there was not the finance for massive road improvements needed; but if expert guidance had been heeded at the beginning of the sixties and a decision made then to bridge the Mersey with six traffic lanes from the high land south of the city centre to an equivalent altitude on the Wirral side, Liverpool would by now be within sight of permanent liberation from paralysis by motor car.

The city fathers were not to blame for this opportunity lost— they favoured such a bridge, but opposition from authorities on the Cheshire side of the river was obdurate. Eventually it was agreed again to burrow under the Mersey (north of the existing tunnel) but so timorously that the project was immediately dubbed 'The Mousehole'. The first tube of the new tunnel, with two traffic lanes, opened in 1971 and a second tube was expected to be in use by 1975.

Meanwhile the position in the city has been to an extent improved by various expediencies—a revised traffic distributory system and a pattern of one-way streets among them—and by the costly provision of new approach roads at the Birkenhead entrance to the Tunnel and by flyovers at the Liverpool end. There are new vehicular arteries under construction and planned (they are discussed in the final chapter of this book), but for the time being Lord Street and Church Street still have too heavy a burden of traffic and they reek of diesel fumes.

Extraordinarily, behind Lord Street's post-war façade the wide open spaces left by the bombs still remained as 1970 entered, the only development on them a pinchbeck patch of lawn and shrubs, almost hidden from the main thoroughfare and where a band plays on summer days to entertain those who go there to eat lunch-time sandwiches and toss morsels to the pigeons. The remaining acres are a car park by day and a vacuum by night; and the cost of this undeveloped land in terms of rates lost to the city must by now be astronomic. Plans to fill the void have shuttled between the Corporation and Whitehall and private developers almost for a decade and still there is no visual evidence of progress though the construction began in the spring of 1970, on an adjoining site, of a 200-bedroom hotel.

In another central zone, ruins made by 1941 bombs still rise above ranks of parked cars. Not until mid-1970, five years after a public inquiry, was Ministerial sanction given for offices to be built on these devastated acres, the proposals remaining all this time in Whitehall pending trays and pigeon-holes while private developers marked time, some of them inevitably losing interest because of the procrastination. It is hard to believe that similar sites would have been allowed to lie so shabbily fallow, year after year, in London.

This particular area of neglect is almost in front of Exchange Station, a terminus that has lost much of its former main-line importance but is used daily by very large numbers travelling between home and work on the electric trains that run along the coast to Southport and inland to the market town or Ormskirk with stations serving some Liverpool suburbs, the adjacent boroughs of Bootle and Crosby and rapidly expanding towns and villages beyond. Diesel services also connect Exchange with a number of the Lancashire industrial towns (from which Liverpool draws a fair amount of labour), although a deal of this traffic was switched some years ago to the Lime Street railhead.

In the period of the Beeching amputations—this coinciding with the time when road-traffic congestion in central Liverpool was at its worst—British Railways went so far as to hint that all the suburban lines out of Exchange might be discontinued and the station closed. This suggested transfer of thousands of daily travellers from railway to road would have been a catastrophe for the already grossly overloaded centre of the city.

Ferry across the Mersey
(overleaf) The waterfront and city centre

There was a loud outcry; but, more important, this threat, coming as it did when the heart of Liverpool was periodically being stopped by its traffic, turned attention to the train as the means of getting home quickly at the end of the day's work. City office workers who lived by the Dee at West Kirby and in seaside towns served by the Southport line were at their tea-tables before citizens of Liverpool, with homes only 3 or 4 miles from the centre, had, on some evenings, moved by bus or car a few yards along Lord Street. The lesson was reinforced by experiences in a prolonged bus strike in the city when many turned to the train for the first time to get to and from jobs and shops.

If only this realisation that travelling to and from work by train could add hours a week to leisure had come a few years earlier and saved the Overhead Railway! What a profound mistake it was to allow the elevated track to be dismantled. Certainly it was losing money, certainly it was antiquated, certainly it would have cost a great deal of money to bring up to date; but if it had been taken over by the Corporation and modernised over a period of years it would have become of enormous worth as a line of commuter communication. It was already attached to the Southport line at Seaforth in the north; and in the south it could have been connected, without great difficulty, to the line running from Central Station through environs of Liverpool and areas just beyond the city boundaries where thousands of homes were to be built in the next few years.

But the unique Overhead and its shack-like stations had been destroyed by the time the planners at last came up with a suburban railway system—a line looping the periphery of the city, one end of it at Central Station and the other at Exchange. No sooner had this scheme been announced than British Railways decided to withdraw all services from the upper level of Central Station, thus closing a suburban line that was part of the proposed loop. After protracted discussions, the Corporation agreed to meet half the running expenses of the suburban line, and so, in 1970, here was a large station beneath an arched roof of glass existing solely for a not very frequent service using a single platform, the other bays serving as a car park.

Central Station has below-stairs platforms, though, where the Mersey Railway—the earliest burrower under the river—terminates; and these are as busy as at any London Underground

Dockland scene
The 206,000-ton Melo in the Mersey

Station, and so are those, reached by lifts from James Street, where trains halt before running under the river to Birkenhead and from there to both New Brighton and Deeside, linking with lines serving other parts of Wirral suburbia, Chester and North Wales.

There is now a Merseyside Passenger Transport Authority which, as well as running buses and ferries, is charged with developing that loop through the outer Liverpool environs and also providing, with British Railways, a link in the city centre between the bottom tier of Central Station and new underground stations at Lime Street (the terminus of the electric line from Euston) and Exchange. Unquestionably this would be a great asset (one of its results would be to permit increased frequency of Mersey Railway trains, at present impossible because of the full stop at Central); but, although this has been promised by the mid-seventies, the average Liverpudlian (if he is discussing the matter with another native and not some carping stranger from the South) is cynical, 'Gerroff wi' yer,' he'll comment, 'Why it took 'em sixty years to clean up the Pier Head.'

And, of course, it did. The dramatic trinity there—the Royal Liver Building (its towers the permanent perches of the great Liver Birds), the offices of the Mersey Docks and Harbour Board (their pillared dome taken from one of the rejected designs for the Anglican Cathedral) and the Italianate former headquarters of Cunard—was completed before the end of the 1914–18 war to compose one of the most impressive waterfront groups in the world, and, miraculously, it escaped destruction by last war bombs. There were plans to make a riverside worthy of the port at this point years before the foundation stone of the nine-storey Liver Building (first of the trinity) was laid in 1908.

They remained on paper, and so did more schemes drawn up before the First World War and again before the Second World War. The vast, windy plain between the trinity of buildings and Georges Landing Stage (from which ferries depart to Birkenhead and Wallasey) stayed a mournful expanse of cobbles, tarmac and asphalt, a terminus first for trams and then for buses, their waiting passengers given shelters that were very nearly as mean as the shacks and shanties nearer the landing stage.

In 1965 a transformation was at last achieved with a two-tier promenade running alongside the landing stage, the lower deck serving as a bus station concourse. Lawns were laid, traffic-free piazzas made and subways provided to bus station platforms. Obviously this is a very great improvement; yet, one feels that it could have been much better, a more imposing foreground for those three palaces of commerce. Hutches where the subways descend are paltry and in diarrhoea colours; and, because Liverpudlians are like small boys who invariably scuff new shoes the day after putting them on, there is already an indefinable air of shabbiness about the bus station corridors and of the adjacent sunken gardens.

Since the inhabitants of this city are about the least tidy in the country there is inevitably litter—no sooner is one scattering swept up than fresh deposits of paper, wrappers and packets are made. Late at night the concourse, and the area about it, are haunted by a variety of unsavoury characters, drunks, deadbeats, addicts and young men seeking a flimsy excuse for a punch-up; and the city's greatly understrength police force—its officers on this particular patrol frequently accompanied by dogs—is hard put to keep such riffraff under surveillance. The memorial, overlooking the river, to men of the Merchant Navy who died in the last war, has been defaced time and again.

The top deck gives a bracing view of the river and of Liverpool Bay beyond the Mersey's mouth. It is an especial delight to dine in the restaurant, which is part of the promenade building, and from one's table watch the lights of merchantmen and ferries moving above the dark moat.

It was a mistake to make Pier Head a starting point for so many bus routes as though the ferries were still the only way home for those who live 'over the water' (though on a fine day, particularly when there is a wind to whip up white horses, they are certainly the most exhilarating means of getting to and from work). But this plateau is on the rim of the city so that nearly every bus route from it is through shopping streets and the commercial quarter, adding substantially to traffic congestion.

A reader without knowledge of Liverpool may be pardoned if, by now, he has assumed that little worthwhile was achieved in the quarter of a century after the Second World War and that most of the things that ought to have to be done were left undone. But such a conclusion would be false. I have thus far been dwelling

upon the shortcomings (not, by any means all of them) to which
the opening paragraph of this chapter referred. It is time I turned
to some of the virtues.

The City Council's wisest and most fruitful decision was taken
early in the sixties when Mr. Graeme Shankland, the eminent
town planner, was appointed to signpost ways and means to give
the city a new core with the vitality and originality of those
designs produced by inspired Victorians. So, in 1964, came the
Shankland Plan, a cohesive set of patterns for each quarter of the
half moon of the central area which the master draughtsman
enclosed within an inner motorway. The plan swept away dingy,
out-dated warehouses and other property cleft by labyrinthine
streets. It proposed for those on foot a series of elevated routes
called 'walkways' as well as pedestrian precincts; and it found
bright purpose at last for Williamson Square and Queen Square,
each containing a theatre and an open space, but for decades,
before as well as after the war, reprehensibly neglected.

The Shankland concepts appealed to the Liverpudlians because
they had humanity as well as functional symmetry. They recognised the architectural jewellery not only of nineteenth-century
civic buildings—like St. George's Hall and the complementary
group of art gallery, libraries and museum—but of such Victorian
structures as the colonnaded warehouses of Albert Dock and the
classical Albany, where offices surround a white-faced courtyard
spanned by a bridge of cast iron. But Shankland was also sensitive
to the attractions of narrow byways such as Leather Lane and
Hackins Hey with little shops, pubs and cafés, survivals from the
eighteenth century; to the warm animation of open-air stalls, of
Paddy's Market and Tatters' Market, those lively bazaars of
secondhand wear and wares; and to the stimulation and colour
that barrow traders and flower-sellers bring to a city.

In 1971 the Shankland Plan is still far from fulfilment. Some
amendments have, indeed, been made to it and doubtless there
will be more; but the broad principles are being followed and
for as long as this is true so will there be prospects of a city that
will be such a pleasure to visit, for business and for leisure, that
those aberrations of the fifties in Lord Street and Church Street
will be readily excused. There have been some distressing post-
Shankland errors—for example, the replacement of the imposing
frontage of the Cotton Exchange (a neighbour of the Albany)

with a glassy-eyed monster and dreadful new buildings in James Street, but mistakes have been fewer than in the years before Shankland, and the losses have been more than balanced by the gains.

Soon after approval of the Shankland Plan, the Corporation coined a slogan to head its publicity ... 'City of Change and Challenge'. The changes have been spectacular in the past five years and should be at least as emphatic in the next. The challenge, as I (and, I am sure, many Liverpudlians) see it, is to preserve in the city not only the best from the past in terms of stone and brick and mortar but the homeliness and cordiality as exemplified by that Punch and Judy stand leaning against the pillars of St. George's Hall, noted on the day I came to Liverpool to live.

These endearing qualities are under dire stress now that so many thousands who lived in the city have been decanted (to employ one of the objectionable words of modern town planning) into overspill (to use another) beyond Liverpool's boundaries at the price of profound social upheaval and grave psychological damage. It is in this respect, more than any other, that the challenge has yet to be met with inspiration.

Just outside the perimeter of the city's centre there were, in 1971, voids left by bulldozers bigger than those left by bombs. Eventually they will be covered with new homes and new roads; and some of the acres now strewn with brick-ends, household discard, abandoned cars and other refuse will turn green and become parkland. But for the time being these broad wildernesses, bare but for an occasional thin quilt of stunted weeds, are an utterly depressing mess in the daylight, and by night they become fields of operation for vandals who see to it that street lamps and public telephone boxes stay useless. Only the bold venture into these no-man's-heaths when darkness falls. They are desert refuges— the equivalent of the 'bad lands' in cowboy films—for car thieves, wage-snatchers and other rogues of whom Liverpool, alas, has well above an average share.

The citizens who dwelt in the homes which once occupied these zones were ejected (and I do not think that is too strong a word) either into the drawers of tall filing cabinets, more than 150 of them sprouting in every part of Liverpool, or into immense estates beyond, or just within, the city boundary. On these estates there is often a profound monotony, and it is made the more repellent by unkempt squares and roadside verges where the grass grows tall and traps the flying litter.

Admittedly the houses here, like the many-storeyed homes in tower blocks, are infinitely more sanitary than the property from which their occupants came, property often in the last stages of decay; but the Liverpudlian is, by heritage, a homogeneous creature intensely neighbourly, happiest in animated streets with corner shops and small pubs and doorstep gossip. Life is alien to him inside one of the new 'Mersey mountains', as they have been called—even if you can see into Wales from the higher windows; and he is hardly less uncomfortable in the privet privacy of a far-flung new suburbia with achingly long avenues where wayside trees are constantly vandalised.

Social malaise created by this massive shift of population has been, and continues to be, serious, despite all the efforts (and they have been painstaking if uninspired) by the Corporation and various voluntary organisations to generate a sense of community and strengthen lines of communication between Them (the local authority and welfare services) and Us (those who dwell in the tiers of the twenty-two-storey and shorter towers and in the new townships, paying far more rent and bus fares than they did before the move and—though no doubt irrationally—resenting it).

There is a corrosive bitterness inside most of those who either owned or were on the way to owning the houses they occupied in areas which came under the blight of slum clearance. In so many cases they saw not only their homes vanish but their capital, the compensation they received being trumpery and not nearly sufficient to serve as a building society deposit so that they could again hope to be masters of their four walls. They protested, often with justice, that they had made their houses, if not palaces, at least comfortably habitable; but the scale of the clearances was too big to permit occasional dwellings in long terraces to escape the demolition men, so neat little homes vanished with the hovels.

Their occupants were obliged to become tenants of 'the Corpy'; and reluctant tenants, with a deep sense of grievance, they may well remain until the end of their days.

Of course, these are problems of nearly every large town in 1971; but they have been overwhelming in Liverpool because the task of rehousing has been overwhelming. The last word in that slogan 'City of Change and Challenge' was not intended to have any reference to making scores of thousands shifted to the outskirts feel at home, part of the Liverpool weft, essential figures in the Liverpool scene. But that is what it ought to have been about.

A considerable proportion of Liverpool Corporation's tenants are not Liverpool ratepayers; their local authorities are Whiston, Huyton (pronounced 'High-ton) and Kirkby (pronounced 'Kairbee') District Councils. There has also been a substantial migration, with Liverpool Corporation sponsorship, to the boroughs of Ellesmere Port and Widnes—on Merseyside but upriver—to the new towns of Skelmersdale and Runcorn and to the greatly expanded Winsford in mid-Cheshire; and, of course, there has been a big voluntary exodus to privately developed estates in and near the seaside towns, in inland Wirral and in the Lancashire interior—places like Maghull and Rainford, villages before the war, towns now.

So, although Liverpool remains the second largest provincial city in England and Wales, its population has been declining for a number of years. The tide is likely to turn, however. There is room for many hundreds of homes on those empty sites within 2 or 3 miles of the centre of the city and none of them, thank God, will be in tower blocks for the Corporation decided, in the autumn of 1969, that it had finished with filing cabinets. It also decided—and how fervently many Liverpudlians wish that this had been possible a decade earlier—to do all that was possible to persuade landlords and owner-occupiers to renovate, and thus save from the bulldozers, the thousands of houses still standing that are below standard. A further important decision was to slow down the movement to overspill zones.

I believe that when the houses go up on those empty lands from which the heart of the city is so easily reached—the houses of a new Everton, a new Anfield, a new Toxteth, a new Edge Hill—they will be in great demand as long as they evoke that feeling of togetherness that was so apparent in the old back streets and, indeed, in the mean courts (for it was the structures in them that were abhorrent, not the inhabitants). I believe there will be a clamour to live in these houses from those who are now domiciled in Kirkby, Speke, Cantril Farm, Knowsley, Croxteth, Halewood, Huyton and other places just within, or just beyond, the city bounds and who are too far away, for their liking, from pavements thronged with shoppers, from theatres, from concerts, from beat clubs, from the river—in short, from as they see it (and why not?) life.

And I believe that by the time these houses are built and occupied there will be a heart to the city they can be proud of and that will be the envy of their friends who live elsewhere. For in all the muck and the mess and the empty spaces among the towering cranes and ascending walls, notwithstanding Lord Street's excrescences and those elsewhere, I see the shape of such a city forming.

In the past five years Liverpool has added two prominences to its central skyline as viewed from both Cheshire and inland Lancashire—the Metropolitan Cathedral of Christ the King, crowning the high level of Mount Pleasant and Brownlow Hill; and the Beacon, a 450-foot lance thrust into the ground with, for its cross-guard, a restaurant that is perched to display through gyrating windows a panorama extending from summits of Snowdonia to bulwarks of the Pennines and, northward, out to sea.

The Roman Catholic Cathedral, 115 years in conception but only four and a half years in gestation, was as theatrical in its construction as it is completed—a huge church in the round, tent-like roof capped with a lantern tower and set upon this a circle of thorn-sharp, inverted poniards held by filigrees and thus making a crown which is symbolic of the poignant diadem worn by the Saviour on the Cross and has the nobility, yet also the compassion, that the Crucifixion inspires.

When it was in embryo, a frame of ribs in gaunt outline— particularly stark at night above the lights of the temporary factory inside the skeleton—Liverpudlian wags irreverently nicknamed it 'Paddy's Wigwam' and 'the Mersey Funnel', but those sobriquets are stale now. For this is a building of world significance, if not universally acclaimed certainly universally discussed; and by marvellous circumstance it commands one entrance to a long street named Hope while at the other, on St. James's Mount, is the elder Cathedral, the Church of Christ, the largest Anglican church in the world, almost certainly the last great anthem in gothic, begun in the early years of this century, due to be completed in 1975.

These two twentieth-century mansions of God, one in sandstone and the other in concrete, are so utterly different in appearance and yet are as apposite as dissonances in a great work of music. They are symbiotic, connected by a street with a name they make yet more meaningful—and especially here in Liverpool where, in the past, there was so much strife between the faiths—because they are used from time to time for non-denominational purposes so that Catholics enter the Anglican Cathedral of Christ and Protestants go to the Metropolitan Church of Christ the King.

Jackie and Bridie, who compose as well as sing modern Liverpool folk tunes—and one girl is a Catholic, the other Protestant—put it in these simple terms:

> One is old and one is new,
> A Street called Hope between the two;
> Each one leading to the other,
> When every man can call you brother. . . .
>
> Let two Cathedrals prove it's right
> That hope's not to divide but to unite.*

Another modern folk song is of the Orange and the Green and is rattled off by the Spinners to audiences containing those who have roots in Northern Ireland and those whose forbears were from the South. To have done this years ago would have been to incite a riot; but it is not like that any more, as was shown in 1969–71 when fratricidal explosions in Belfast and Londonderry produced not a reverberation in Liverpool, long rid of its equivalents of Bogside and the Shankhill Road.

Orange Day is still massively celebrated with a long and boisterous procession through the centre of the city, innumerable King Billys and escorts of children in party frocks and Sunday school suits, heading concertina and pipe bands as they march to Exchange Station to entrain for Southport. But it has become a summer day out rather than an annual demonstration to flaunt the Battle of the Boyne in the face of the Catholics; and one testimony of this is the participation in it of children with brown and black faces whose parents made a much longer voyage of migration than the one across the Irish Sea.

While nearly all Liverpudlians, Catholic or otherwise, accept and many warmly admire the Metropolitan Church, they are less well-disposed towards the 450-foot Beacon, which, like the

* Jackie and Bridie, *Songs for Singing Folk*, Galliard Ltd., 1969.

C

Cathedral-in-the-round, is a part of the profile appearing in Corporation advertisements above that motto of the sixties, 'City of Change and Challenge', and is far too prominent a feature to be ignored. Some of its critics, however, do not take into account its practical function, which is to disperse, high above the city, fumes from the centralised boiler rooms heating the whole of the St. John's Precinct, a complex of covered market, shops, hotel, ballroom, restaurants and multi-floored car park, faced in white and black and at a Lime Street corner with Elliot Street. The only alternative to the Beacon would have been a series of much smaller chimneys which would have added nothing attractive to the architectural furniture.

The Beacon's ruff, the restaurant with revolving windows, is indubitably a gimmick; yet it does make the concrete pillar more acceptable as a dominant factor in the Liverpool scene, and the picture window views to distant hilltops and marine horizons assuredly catch the breath for they are at least as spectacular as those from London's taller Post Office Tower.

St. John's Precinct—uncompleted in mid-1970, many months after the target date—occupies the site of buildings from which hung a broad battery of flashing neon advertisements that, certainly at night, immediately captured the attention of every new arrival emerging from Lime Street Station. This view has completely altered; and a single-storey row of shops has taken the place of a scruffy hugger-mugger that partly hid from Lime Street a majestic arc of the station's roof. The row ends in a too-large exclamation mark in glass called Concourse House, staring across Lime Street at the white, striped black, Precinct, which in turn stares at the Graeco-Roman south façade of St. George's Hall; and these stares, it seems to me, are hostile and therefore alien to Liverpool's tradition and Liverpool manners.

To reach the Precinct from the station the pedestrian goes via a subway. When citizens were invited to suggest a name for this underground route hundreds of them plumped spontaneously for 'Sub-Lime Way'. Thwarted by timorous city councillors who chose the singularly dull 'Market Way' rather than accept an example of Liverpool's wry sense of fun, they now know it unofficially, and for obvious reasons, as 'The Tunnel of Love'.

Those renewing acquaintance with Liverpool after several years will recognise Lime Street because St. George's Hall—face cleaned so that its stone is now honey-brown in street lights instead of soot black and pigeon-dirt grey—identifies it, notwithstanding all the changes. But such a visitor might very well inquire, 'What ever happened to Scotland Road?' because, although this thoroughfare is still there, few marks remain from its lurid past when it had more than seventy pubs with doss-houses and sleazy shops. Byrom Street, its portal, is now beneath the scissors of fly-over roads and pedestrian ways, and beyond them rises, in considerable bulk, a new College of Technology, part of a Polytechnic. Then there are open spaces due to be landscaped, approach roads to the second Mersey tunnel and blocks of flats climbing to Everton Brow, from where, when night falls, lights from the tiered homes appear to be in the sky and are like a constellation.

Other districts on the fringe of the city centre have changed or are changing just as radically. Part of Islington, once a considerable centre of small wholesale businesses dealing in clothes, fancy goods and hardware, has been gutted to make room for the inner motorway. On Mount Vernon's slopes, formerly slum-ridden, stand the tall blocks of a teaching hospital, and these look across the roofs of a large new comprehensive school to the many buildings the University has built in the last ten years, trailing the green ribbon of a campus from Brownlow Hill to Abercromby Square which is still graciously Georgian. Only a fragment—a few cafés, provision shops and Asian seamen's hostels—remains of the prewar Chinatown. New buildings occupy the site of the Customs House. All these changes have been for better; but one for the worse, to my mind, has been on the Exchange Station flank of Tithebarn Street, where overpowering office blocks have been substituted for the Silkhouse Lane quarter in which the buildings and flagged passages had a Dickensian flavour so strong that it needed no stretch of imagination to sketch in elderly, whiskered clerks, their coat lapels powdered with snuff, and gigs and cabs waiting in the evening beneath gas lamps (which, in fact, survived into the 1960s).

Those who occupied these buildings when they were in their heyday—and this lasted until after the First World War—were people whose homes were in the city and who knew the city and cared about it. Nowadays a high proportion of the nine-till-five dwellers in the commercial sector, including the most influential, appear daily, Monday to Friday, from three warrens—James Street and Central (Low Level) stations and the Mersey Tunnel— to which they return at the end of the day's work. Like the thousands who train-ride in each morning from stations along the Southport and Ormskirk lines, with a fleeting glimpse of the city *en route*, they know only the core of Liverpool and even parts of that only slightly. Take them outside the core's circumference and, generally speaking, they are in strange territory. Though, in the main, from Liverpudlian stock and with Liverpudlian traits, they have no feeling of being Liverpool citizens. They are much more concerned (and naturally enough) with the way in which their home towns are administered than with Liverpool's conduct of its affairs.

Of course, offices in the hearts of Birmingham, Leeds, Manchester and Sheffield are similarly populated by non-citizens; but it is because the river arbitrarily divides Merseyside politically that the early evening exodus from Liverpool through the rail and road tunnels is so much more definite than the commuting between centre and environs in other cities. Birkenhead, though in a different county, is nearer Liverpool's Pier Head than are Liverpool's Cathedrals; and there are suburbs of the city farther from the Town Hall than are Wallasey and Bebington, boroughs in Cheshire.

The Mersey is an impediment against the return from Wirral towns to Liverpool in the evening for social purposes because the Tunnels add shillings to the cost of a trip by car and the absence of late-night trains makes public transport an unsatisfactory alternative. In consequence the Wirral towns are gradually making their own social fabrics. Moreover, those with homes there, even though they may work in Liverpool, are increasingly turning to Chester both for weekend shopping and leisure activity, primarily because it is cheaper to drive there—with no tolls to pay—than to Liverpool and easier to park the car. Thus here is another aspect of that word 'challenge' in the Liverpool publicity slogan; and another reason why it is so important, for the economic health of the city as well as its social well-being, that those big blanks around the downtown area should be filled with homes at top speed. New shops were being built as 1971 entered and storey upon storey of offices were awaiting tenants; but there will be little business for additional shopkeepers or to attract firms to the new offices unless population returns to residential areas now in waste.

The 1970 change of Government resulted in a re-appraisal of the sweeping proposals for Merseyside made in the Redcliffe-Maud Report but nevertheless a fairly drastic reshaping of local authority boundaries appears inevitable; and it is, in my view, right that the river should become of no more consequence, as an administrative division, than the Thames is in London. The question is whether, when its Corporation becomes subservient to a new regional authority, Liverpool will remain indisputably the dynamo of Merseyside life.

I believe that it must do so if living on Merseyside is to continue to be rewarding. Even with a population of a million and a half there can be only one hub in the social round, only one mainspring of the region's arts. There are valid reasons why they should continue to be in Liverpool which for so many years has furnished —and in some instances at a disproportionate cost to the city's ratepayers—the means to enjoy leisure (the visual arts, music of every kind and all forms of entertainment) not only for Wirral and Lancashire boroughs but also for a part of North Wales.

I am not in love with Merseyside, I am in love with Liverpool. I believe it has infinitely more to offer, as a place in which to live as well as to work, than the rest of the region put together. I believe that, provided the guidelines of Graeme Shankland are followed, it can multiply attractions already so considerable: the excitement of the river; the grandeur of the Pier Head's trinity and of St. George's Hall and its civic neighbours; the drama of the two Cathedrals, the elegance of the Town Hall's salons and the Bluecoat courtyard; the humanity of byways like Old Churchyard and Hackins Hey; the surprise of Exchange Flags, a square in the commercial sector that was freed from vehicles long before 'pedestrian precinct' entered the town planner's phrasebook; and the bounty of a 4-mile length of mature parkland in the south ot the city which was preserved far in advance of national campaigning for green belts.

I am distressed by the violence in the streets, so much more disturbing than in the period when Scotland Road and the Dock Road and Chinatown were scenes of nightly rumpus and squalid delinquency, because nowadays no part of the city is immune from young hooligans, often armed with knives, who terrorise bus passengers and assault bus crews, pick quarrels at bus stops, waylay the elderly, torment schoolchildren and so frequently escape punishment. I am appalled at the insensate destructiveness of children, some of them very young, who wreck schools, dismember trees, smash every window of a house within hours of it becoming untenanted and cost the city an enormous sum in repairs and replacements.

I am depressed by the way gutters, road-island rose gardens and grass verges are no sooner cleared of their litter than this is replenished. And I am grieved by the discontent of many of the families obliged to inhabit the gross barracks of flats, built between the wars and since 1946, many of them so euphemistically named 'Gardens' when all they have is a quadrangle of dusty asphalt.

But I am exhilarated by the catholicism that could propagate, in a warehouse womb, the phenomenon of the Mersey Sound to echo round the world; and yet also fill the Philharmonic Hall for symphony concerts and make the Merseyside Youth Orchestra one of the most accomplished assemblies of teenage musicians in the kingdom. I am cheered by the energy and dedication that takes the theatre, lorry-borne, to back street children and encourages them to participate. I am refreshed by the appearance of one of the city's most recent commercial buildings, the block built in handsome Castle Street by an insurance company, the architecture capturing some of the appeal, without blatant imitation, of the century-old Oriel Chambers, a short distance away.

I admire the maturity of mind represented by the figure of a black Christ crucified on a new Methodist church in a district where numbers from the West Indies and Africa live; and I rejoice that this figure was created by an extrovert Liverpudlian who has been deck-hand and docker, Arthur Dooley, who you will meet in a later chapter.

I enjoy those pubs where, standing between a poet and a pansy, you can argue about renaissance music with an artist who spent his afternoon painting in the abstract; and I am still astonished at the Edwardian opulence of public houses like the 'Philharmonic' and the 'Vines'. I am heartened that a man devotes some of the fortunes from his football-pool promotion to sponsoring a biennial art competition, now world known, and not so much from a sense of duty but because he enjoys art as much as he does going to Goodison, one of the two great stadia of soccer where the wacker blows his top.

Above all, I am enchanted by the ebullience, the sharp humour, the inquisitiveness, the generosity, the extravagances, the ''allo, luv' and 'ta-ra well' of the Liverpudlian, maligned in print, lampooned by TV, endowed with Welsh fervour, Irish eccentricity, Lancashire gumption and a sailor's perception, his speech an especial and colourful brand of English that got its name from a stew.

There is so much still to be done in Liverpool and so much that ought not to have been done. But whenever I see Professor Codman's Punch and Judy stand against St. George's Hall it nourishes my now instinctive faith that, amid all the change, the challenge will be accepted and that it will come right in the end.

TWO

SUGAR, PLUNDER AND SLAVES

KING John put Liverpool on the map. Until his Charter of 1207 it was an obscure village, probably of fishermen, dominated by a castle of uncertain origin standing on the ridge that is now Derby Square and Castle Street. This overlooked a basin 1,000 yards long that was filled from the Mersey at high tide but at the ebb became a muddy creek; and south-eastwards, from the royal chase of Toxteth to a line of forest-clad hills, stretched marshes that had deterred Roman engineers from penetrating seawards from the road they built connecting Chester and Warrington. The village did not rate a mention in the Domesday Book, though this contained references to Childwall, Walton and West Derby, all three of which were to be absorbed by Liverpool in the nineteenth century.

John had Milford Haven as a supply port for his forces trying to extend the Pale of Ireland, but he was dissatisfied with it because it was vulnerable to forays by the recalcitrant Welsh. There were political objections against using Chester as an alternative; so he decided to develop 'Liverpul', offering inducements to all who would settle in the vicinity of the elbow made by the river and the tidal pool. A certain amount of trade with Ireland was gradually established and there was naval activity from time to time, but otherwise Liverpool remained of small consequence for another 500 years; and although from 1580 it had a town council of thirty-six, who co-opted life members as required, it did not become a separate parish until 1699.

Through the centuries there were two important families, the Stanleys of Liverpool Tower and the Molyneux who held the constableship of Liverpool Castle. Both survive today and

Liverpudlians have good reason to be grateful that they do for the substantial private parks of the Stanleys (Lord Derby at Knowsley) and the Molyneux (Lord Sefton at Croxteth) have prevented the city's spread to St. Helens, there to become embraced in the conurbation which extends westward from the foothills of the Pennines.

William Ferrers, Earl of Derby, succeeded Ranulf, Earl of Chester, as Lord of Liverpool; and when Thomas Lord Stanley crowned his stepson Henry VII at Bosworth Field the Earldom of Derby was resurrected. A hundred and fifty-nine years later, in 1644, the then Earl of Derby persuaded Prince Rupert to interrupt his march north and end the Parliamentarian hold on Liverpool. The Prince looked down on the little port from the heights of Everton and observed that it was 'a mere crow's nest which a parcel of boys might take'; but, in fact, the garrison withstood the much superior Royalist forces for eighteen days, delaying their northward advance and so perhaps contributing to their rout at Marston Moor.

In the next half century there was growth in Liverpool's importance due to developing trade with the West Indies and Virginia. Bristol was, of course, a far larger recipient of imports across the Atlantic, but the arrival in Liverpool of 'Mr. Smith, a great sugar baker from London' (who forsook the capital after the Plague) was significant. He founded the sugar refining that is today still an important Liverpool industry; and evidently the place prospered after his arrival because the high rates quoted by merchants in the port to victual troops and transport them to Ireland—for the Battle of the Boyne, as it was to turn out—shocked William III's advisers (William, himself, sailed from Hoylake at the mouth of the Dee).

At the beginning of the eighteenth century there were about seventy vessels entering and leaving the pool at high tide. In 1715 the basin was partly filled in and cut off from the Mersey and the country's first wet dock was constructed to be managed by Thomas Steers for £50 a year. It was not entirely a success because of persistent silting; but from it ships sailed in steadily increasing number to the West Indies for sugar and spice and to Virginia for tobacco and cotton. Some of the vessels were armed as a protection against Spanish marauders who plundered cargoes and brutally maltreated the crews while English men-o'-war lay impotently in Caribbean harbours. But in 1739 England and Spain were at war, five years later the French joined in and the privateers came into their own.

They had, in fact, been in existence for a century. There is a record of a privateer owned by Sir Thomas Stanley, son of the Earl of Derby, bringing a prize into the Mersey in 1563, and it is unlikely that this was the first; but in 1744 there were only four using Liverpool as a base—the *Old Noll* and the *Terrible* (each of twenty-two guns and 180 men), the *Thurloe* (twelve guns and one hundred men) and the *Admiral Blake*. The *Thurloe* captured a rich Martinicoman only to be seized, with her prize, by a French privateer; but the *Old Noll* then rescued the *Thurloe*, recaptured the merchant ship and drove off the Frenchman (thirty-six guns and 300 men) in a brilliantly resourceful action. There were still French guards in the *Thurloe* when she joined up with her rescuer, and they were among the first of many of their compatriots who were to languish in the Tower of Liverpool.

Rapidly the force of privateers expanded. In one of the additions, the diminutive *Ann Galley* (four guns and fourteen men), Captain Nemehiah Holland defeated a Frenchman with thrice his gunpower off the coast of Antigua in 1746 and this despite having been twice set on fire.

Soon afterwards Liverpool was thrilling to news of the exploits in the Mediterranean of Captain Fortunatus Wright, the Wallasey-born son of a Liverpool master mariner. He fitted out the brigantine *Fame* as privateer in Leghorn, and in 1746 alone she took sixteen French ships reputed to have been worth £400,000. Some of this fortune went to lawyers, for Wright was involved in expensive litigation after he had seized Turkish property aboard the French ship *Hermione*. After a spell in prison in Leghorn he renewed an association with William Hutchinson— one of the great names in Liverpool's maritime history—in buying and fitting out an old twenty-gun frigate, the *Leostoff*. Hutchinson was of rougher stock than Wright, who was the friend of Leghorn nobility. He was a Tynesider who first went to sea in colliers as cook's cabin boy and drawer of the crews' beer. He sailed to the East Indies as a fo'c's'le man and became desperately ill from the scurvy; but by the time of his first meeting with Wright he had learned to read and write and had mastered more than the elements of navigation. His first command was the *Swallow*, and this he handed over to Wright. The ship was taken while on a voyage from Lisbon to London and was ransomed at sea, Hutchinson being detained as security.

Wright was content to let his partner sail the *Leostoff* to the West Indies while he stayed in Leghorn, where in 1756 he built the *Saint George*. He collected a motley crew of Slavs, Venetians and Swiss and sailed from the port as protector of three English merchantmen, knowing that there lay in wait for him a French xebec, her commander intent on earning the knighthood and a fortune promised him for Wright's capture. The French ship had sixteen guns and more than 200 men who had spent nearly a month drilling for this encounter. Wright left Leghorn with only four guns and was able to buy another eight from vessels riding near the harbour entrance.

Once he had the xebec in sight Wright signalled his convoy to run for it and then turned to engage the Frenchman. In under an hour the guns of the xebec were silenced, her lateen sails were in shreds and her captain and eighty of the crew were dead. A letter from Leghorn to a Liverpool merchant said that Fortunatus could easily have taken the xebec, but when two other privateers appeared on the horizon, he sped away to protect his convoy and bring it safely back into Leghorn.

The *Saint George* continued to be the scourge of the French, operating now from Leghorn and now from Malta, though in both places Wright had to contend with bitter hostility from pro-French factions. In 1757 the polacca *Le Hirondelle* (twenty-six guns, 283 men) was built for the specific purpose of ridding the Mediterranean of Wright, but at their first encounter the Liverpool captain—now in the *King George*—soon had the Frenchman in disarray. Both vessels put into Malta to refit, and Wright was given a reception even more unfriendly than on his previous visits. To make matters worse he received warning that he would encounter a similar attitude if he returned to Leghorn. None the less it was for Leghorn he next set sail, escorting a French prize. Beyond a vague report that he had been seen at Messina, no further word of Wright was received, and it seems certain that he went down with the *King George* in a storm.

Meanwhile William Hutchinson had made several profitable voyages to the Caribbean in the venerable *Leostoff*. He left her to command one of the finest privateers then based on the Mersey, the *Liverpool* (twenty-two guns and 200 men), which had been fitted out by Henry Hardware and other merchants in the port. Her first prize was *Le Grand Marquis de Tournay*, taken in the Atlantic when returning to Bordeaux from St. Domingo and worth £20,000. Soon afterwards the *Liverpool* was set upon by French men-o'-war and she routed the lot.

However fortune was not always with Hutchinson. He told in his journal of the *Liverpool* coming upon a vessel soon after midnight when outward bound from Kinsale, the port on the south coast of Ireland often used by Mersey privateers. The *Liverpool* hailed the strange ship in French.

> Without answering [the journal continued] he made us feel the weight of his broadside and carried away our fore top-gallant mast . . . he ill-managed our sails and running rigging and wounded twenty-eight of our men. We soon found our mistake, the vessel proving to be His Majesty's ship *Antelope* in company with her prize, a French privateer. . . .

The *Liverpool* joined up with a fleet of men-o'-war but was obliged to leave because, as a result of the encounter with the *Antelope*, fever and flux raged on board. 'We buried six and had 103 sick,' stated Hutchinson's journal. One of those who died was a young volunteer, James Holt, a member of a Rochdale family who were later to become eminent in Liverpool shipping, commerce and philanthropy.

This was Hutchinson's last voyage as a private commander. He now turned his attention to an enterprise for supplying Liverpool with live fish brought in by cod smacks and stored in a large vessel moored in the river. But there was at the time a prejudice against fish caught by smacks and the project failed. In 1759 Hutchinson was appointed principal water bailiff and dockmaster of Liverpool and held this position for nearly forty years, a period which saw a vast expansion of the slave trade and the development of the port into one of the most important in the world.

His immediate task on becoming dockmaster was to protect the port against attack. At this time there were fast and well-armed French raiders operating in the Irish Sea, and their depredations on shipping had become painfully expensive to Liverpool merchants. The boldest of the enemy freebooters, who were virtually blockading Liverpool Bay towards the end of 1759, was

Captain Thurot in the *Marshal Belleisle*, and soon after Hutchinson took office word reached the port that this daring Frenchman intended to sail into the Mersey, guns blazing. Hutchinson offered to resume command of the *Liverpool* and sail out to engage the *Marshal Belleisle*; but though 207 seamen signed articles only twenty-eight turned up when the privateer was ready to put to sea. She was sold by auction very soon afterwards.

Hutchinson now raised volunteers to man armed ships and make a barrier across the Mersey. The walls of St. Nicholas's Church, near the waterfront, were buttressed and mounted with guns. Merchants were regimented under the mayor (Colonel Spencer) and divided into four independent companies, each man uniformed and armed at his own expense. The Lincolnshire militia marched to Liverpool from Manchester to give additional support; and French prisoners in the Tower of Liverpool were removed to Chester Castle. The high ground at Everton became thronged with people who evacuated their homes in the town below. Soldiers encamped on the ridge had orders to light a beacon immediately Thurot's fleet was sighted, and this was to be a signal for other hilltop fires to be lit as far north as Rivington Pike and as far south as the Wrekin. But they were not needed; for on 28th February 1760 a squadron of English frigates fell upon Thurot's privateers and took every one. Thurot died on the poop deck of the *Marshal Belleisle*, and 300 of his officers and men were either killed or wounded. The survivors joined their compatriots, returned from Chester Castle, in the now overcrowded Tower of Liverpool.

This red sandstone fortress, for so long owned by the Stanleys, stood close to where Water Street now runs. It was sold in 1737 to the Clayton family, who let it to the Corporation as a town gaol. It was far from comfortable, but the prisoners-of-war, who slept in hammocks, fared a deal better, it would seem, than English sailors captured by the French at that time. 'The most brutal savage would have shown more compassion,' declared one English account of the conditions.

> The captains . . . were put in a dungeon 40 feet underground and not permitted fire or candle. They had straw to lie upon but were obliged to pay dear for it. As to the provisions allowed them per day, it was three ounces of poor beef such if brought to our markets would be burnt. They were treated worse than we treat dogs.

Discipline in the Tower was lax, and there were numerous escapes (though not, it seems, by a subterranean passage said to have run from the Tower to a house in Chapel Street (which is parallel with Water Street). The French prisoners were subsequently transferred to new quarters in Great Howard Street and on Mount Pleasant, and a number of them were released on parole and allowed to go as far as Ormskirk and Wigan. Several found wives and there are present-day Liverpudlians descended from them.

In the second year of Hutchinson's superintendence, the threat from Thurot now removed, Liverpool surpassed Bristol in tonnage handled, and thus became second to London in importance as a port. In part this was because insurance rates, which were determined by the extent of losses to the enemy, were lower for Mersey-based ships so Liverpool merchants were able to undercut Bristol competitors. They also paid captains and seamen less than those sailing from the Avon, relying on the inducement of the crews' share in plunder from freebooting to attract all the manpower needed.

There were two docks in Hutchinson's charge to begin with, South Dock having been built to supplement the unsatisfactory Old Dock; but soon George's Dock was added. Salt from the Cheshire mines was an increasingly valuable export (South Dock was later renamed Salthouse Dock), being loaded as ballast for the slave ships bound for the Niger delta harbours of Bonny, Brass and Old and New Calabar, where it was used as barter for the human cargoes collected from the hinterland by Ijo chiefs.

Hutchinson wrote a valuable manual on seamanship and interested himself in tidal phenomena (his observations provided the data upon which Richard Holden and Sons based their tide tables, still in use in present times). Within four years of becoming Liverpool's dockmaster the former beer boy in Newcastle colliers had perfected reflecting mirrors for lighthouses, and he installed the first of them in a lighthouse overlooking the Mersey and Liverpool Bay from Bidston Hill on the Wirral. He founded the Liverpool Marine Society for the benefit of masters, their widows and children—one of the first charities in a port that was to become famous for pioneer philanthropy. Hutchinson also wrote a manual of guidance for privateer captains. Here is a passage from it:

I have observed among new fighting men there will always be something to show that natural instinct for self-preservation: and in order to keep their heads under shelter of the breastwork from the enemy's shot they fire their muskets at random up in the air. Seeing this, and to prevent the bad examples in fighting, I have made a feigned lunge at a man's breast with my drawn sword and have been obliged to threaten death to any man that should show such a bad example: though it must be allowed to be only a failing and not a fault among new undisciplined landsmen first called into action who, at seeing a man shot through the head above the breastwork, may show a little fear but, by practice, may prove brave afterwards.

When he took office as dockmaster, and in his studies of the tides, Hutchinson no doubt consulted observations made by a Liverpool tide surveyor named John Newton; and, indeed, he must have been acquainted with this extraordinary man whose story is perhaps the most astonishing of all from this period of Merseyside history.

Through the tortured early manhood of John Newton only two factors were constant: his love for Mary Catlett and the help he received from a Liverpool merchant named Manesty, an old friend of his father. He was born in London, the reckless and to an extent unprincipled son of a prosperous sea captain who persuaded Manesty to find the wayward boy a job in Jamaica. A few days before he was due to sail from Liverpool he visited relatives in Kent and met Mary Catlett, then aged 13, and fell in love with her. He stayed three weeks in Kent instead of the three days arranged and so missed his ship. The following year (1743) he returned to Kent and Mary, and this time fell into the clutches of a press gang who took him to the man-o'-war *Harwich* at the Nore.

Because of his father's influence he reached the quarterdeck as a midshipman after less than a month. The *Harwich*, bound for the East Indies, put into Plymouth where Newton was sent ashore with some of the crew to make sure they did not desert. Instead, he deserted himself. After two or three days he was picked up by soldiers, marched through the streets of Plymouth and then, aboard the *Harwich*, publicly stripped and whipped. Some of the officers, however, remained his friends and, because of their intercession, he was permitted by the captain to leave the *Harwich* at Madeira to join a slave ship commanded by an old acquaintance of his father and bound for Sierra Leone. He made an enemy of the master of the slave ship by lampooning him.

Newton then entered the service of a slave trader who had been a passenger in the ship; but he neglected to obtain a written agreement on wages and so found, that when he reached the trader's African base, he was little more than a slave himself. The trader was under the influence of a negress who shared his bed, and she took an instant dislike to Newton. When the young man became seriously ill the trader left him in the care of the woman, who treated him like a dog, requiring him to eat like one from a platter on the floor. Occasionally, when more magnanimous, she would feed him scraps from her own table. Other slaves were ordered from time to time to pelt Newton with stones, but when their mistress was out of sight they showed him pity.

The trader, on his return, rejected Newton's complaints of being ill-used; but when the young man accompanied him on his next voyage he accepted without question a tale that Newton had stolen goods from him during the night. As punishment, Newton was locked up on deck and obliged to live on a pint of rice a day and such fish as he could catch with a hook baited with the entrails of a fowl flung to him by the trader. Yet, in weeks of misery when he was often shaking with ague as the result of exposure, Newton spent many hours studying Euclid. When the trader returned to Africa, the young man would find a quiet spot on the beach, away from the tyranny of the negress, and there draw diagrams in the sand.

Throughout this time he wrote as regularly as he was able to Mary Catlett far away in Kent; and Manesty, the Liverpool merchant, must have had the ne'er-do-well often in mind, for he at last sent one of his slave ship captains to search for Newton and send him back to England. By the time the captain found him, Newton had entered the service of another slave trader and was unenthusiastic about returning home, even with prospect of seeing his beloved Mary. The captain persuaded him to change his mind by telling him (quite falsely) that he had been left a considerable legacy.

A full year of voyaging, in which the ship all but foundered, passed before Newton saw England and he spent the time studying mathematics and inventing profanities. He arrived in Liverpool in 1748, visited Mary Catlett and was then made mate of a new slave ship owned by Manesty. He sailed once more for Sierra Leone and from there transported slaves to Antigua and Charleston. He was back in the Mersey the following year and he and Mary Catlett were married at last. A few months later, in command of another of Manesty's slavers, *The Duke of Argyle*, Newton dropped anchor off the place where he had himself been all but a slave, and sent a longboat to bring to him the woman who had delighted in tormenting him. He wrote afterwards:

I desired the men to fire guns over her head in honour of her because she had formerly done so much good, though she had not meant it. She seemed to feel it like heaping coals of fire on her head. I made her some presents and sent her ashore. She was evidently most comfortable when she had her back to my ship. . . . I stepped on the beach and two black females were passing. The first who noticed me observed to her companion that 'there was Newton and, what do you think, he has got shoes!' 'Ay', said the other, 'and stockings, too!' They had never seen me before with either.

It is interesting, in view of his own indiscipline aboard the *Harwich*, to read Newton's observations on his supreme authority as a captain. He wrote to his wife:

I am as absolute in my small dominions (life and death excepted) as any potentate in Europe. If I say to one, 'Come', he comes; if to another, 'Go', he flies. . . . Not a man in the ship will eat his dinner till I please to give him leave—nay, nobody dares to say it is twelve or eight o'clock in my hearing till I think proper to say so first. . . . I would not have you judge from my manner of relating these ceremonies that I do not value them highly for their own sake; but they are old-fashioned customs and necessary to be kept up for without a strict discipline the common sailors would be unmanageable. But, in the midst of my parade, I do not forget—I hope I never shall—what my situation was on board the Harwich. . . .

In 1752 he took command of a new slaver, the *African*, and it was at about this time that he became a devout Christian, filled with remorse for his often vaunted atheism and the excesses of his earlier years—'A common drunkard or a profligate is a petty sinner to what I was,' he wrote. He was gravely ill during the voyage of the *African*, and back in Liverpool two years later, now captain of the *Bee*, he collapsed and was advised by his physicians

D

to abandon the sea. Again Manesty came to his help. Through the merchant's influence he was appointed tide surveyor, and he made profitable investments in the port.

But he was now seriously considering entering the ministry, though it was not until 1758 that he made his first attempt to do so and it was unsuccessful. For a time he spoke at dissenters' meetings; then, at last, he was ordained and there is a report of the former captain of slave ships 'ascending the pulpit of St. George's Church and preaching to a crowded and various auditory composed of the cream of slave-trading Liverpool'. He became curate of Olney (Bucks.) in 1764 and was there for sixteen years, becoming a close friend of William Cowper, with whom he produced the series known as 'The Olney Hymns'. Then he moved to a church in London and had the Lord Mayor as one of his parishioners.

He was now preaching and writing vigorously against the slave trade. 'I hope it will always be a subject of humiliating reflection to me,' he declared, 'that I was once an active instrument in a business at which my heart now shudders. . . . I did it ignorantly. I should have been overwhelmed with distress and terror if I had known, or even suspected, that I was acting wrongly.' He died, aged 82, in the year slave trading was abolished in English ships (1807), and himself composed the epitaph on a memorial in the church where he was rector: 'John Newton, once an Infidel and Libertine, a Servant of Slaves in Africa, was by the rich mercy of our Lord and Saviour, Jesus Christ, Preserved, Restored, Pardoned and Appointed to preach the Faith he had long laboured to destroy.'

When Newton left Liverpool for Olney there were ninety ships from the Mersey trading in slaves. This nefarious commerce had developed, so far as Liverpool was concerned, in less than forty years, although English participation in it dated back to the reign of Elizabeth I when Sir John Hawkins, against the express wishes of the Queen, seized Africans to sell to the Spanish. In 1709 there was only one slaver sailing from Liverpool, yet by 1753 there were seventy-three.

This growth had its roots in a highly prosperous trade in contraband cloth established between the port and the West Indies. Spain clamped a 300 per cent duty on the French and German cloth shipped to her colonists; and to evade this impost the islanders began regularly to run schooners and large canoes to Jamaica, where they were able to buy Lancashire cloth which was far cheaper and also of superior quality. Liverpool merchants were quick to cash in on this commerce despite the vigilance of the Costa Garda on the Spanish Main and their barbaric treatment of the crews of those vessels they intercepted (for example, the entire crew of the Liverpool ship *Ogden* were killed by guards, except for five boys, and the vessel was then sunk). The Grenville Treaty of 1747 abruptly ended the trade in contraband which had brought, at its zenith, a yearly return of about £560,000 to Manchester and an annual profit to Liverpool merchants which exceeded a quarter of a million. So the merchants switched to human cargoes.

At that time Bristol and London dominated the traffic in black ivory; but the merchants there paid their captains liberally and also gave their factors in the West Indies a 5 per cent commission on slave sales. Their rivals in Liverpool paid captains less and put their factors on a fixed salary so 'prime negroes' taken in Liverpool ships to the Caribbean could be sold about 12 per cent less than those carried in Bristol and London ships yet yield an equal profit. By the mid-1760s Liverpool had become the principal European centre of the slave trade.

An astonishing aspect of this eventful period was the emphatic distinctions made in contemporary descriptions of the crews of slave ships and those of privateers—the first, scoundrels, the second, heroes—though frequently they were the same men, the ships performing both functions. One account of the men who manned the privateers read:

> The captain is always some brave, daring man who fought his way into his position and his officers are selected for the same qualities. As for the men, what a reckless, dreadnought, dare-devil collection of human beings, half-disciplined but yet ready to obey every order, the more desperate the better. Your true privateersman is a sort of half-horse, half-alligator, with a streak of lightning in his composition—something like a man-o'-war's man but much more like a pirate—generally with a superabundance of whisker, as if he held with Samson that his strength was in the quantity of his hair. The daring privateer dazzled the eyes of the understanding and kindled wild and fierce enthusiasm on all sides.

But now read this note on 'the character of the seamen in the slave trade' by a slave ship captain:

> Many of the individuals were the very dregs of the community. Some of them had escaped from gaols, others were undiscovered offenders who sought to withdraw themselves from their country lest they should fall into the hands of the officers of justice. These wretched beings used to flock to Liverpool when the ships were fitting out and, after acquiring a few sea phrases from some crimp or other, they were shipped as ordinary seamen, though they had never been at sea in their lives. If, when at sea, they became saucy and insubordinate, which was generally the case, the officers were compelled to treat them with severity; and having never been in a warm climate before, if they took ill they seldom recovered though every attention was paid to them. Among these wretched beings I have known many gentlemen's sons of desperate character and abandoned habits.

Not all who went to sea in Liverpool privateers and slavers were men. 'Arthur' Douglas, who at 19 joined the privateer *Resolution* (in 1757), served in her for several months, going aloft and using arms, before her sex was discovered. She was on board when the *Resolution* was set upon by three French privateers which were beaten off only after an engagement lasting forty hours. 'Jack' Roberts, who drank grog and chewed tobacco, signed on as a member of the crew of the slave ship *Anne* but was found to be Jane Roberts, aged 18, before the vessel was out of home water bound for Bonny in the Niger delta and was 'landed with all possible gentleness'.

According to the mate of the *Anne* 'about this time several handsome young women committed themselves in the same way and some succeeded in probably eluding all discovery of their sex and made a voyage or two at sea'.

There were certainly many mothers, indeed grandmothers, and also babes in arms with a stake in the fortunes of the Liverpool ships, whether these were privateering or carrying slaves. It was the practice for husbands to buy shares for their womenfolk and children, including the newly-born, as well as for themselves, as soon as a vessel began building. Launches were therefore occasions attended by scores of shareholders of both sexes and all ages and it was the custom for them to inspect the new ship and take a trip up and down the river in her. Thus there were numbers of women and children aboard the privateer *Pelican* when, a few hours after her launch and with a band playing, she suddenly capsized off the Cheshire side of the Mersey with a loss of some seventy lives.

James Stonehouse, the son of the owner (and for many years master) of the slave ship *Mary Ellen*, recalled in his nineties memories of touring the ship as a youth with children who were part-owners.

> We took them on deck [he wrote] and showed them where a bloody battle had been fought. And did we not show them the very guns and muskets, the pistols, the cutlasses the shot-lockers and magazines and tell them how the lad scrubbing a brass kettle in the caboose had been occupied as a powder monkey and seen blood shed in earnest? And did we not, moreover, tell them that, if the forthcoming voyage was only successful and if the ships of the enemy were taken—no matter about the streams of blood that might run through the scuppers—how their little ventures would be raised in value many hundredfold? Would not young imaginations be excited and the greed for gain be potent in their hearts? No matter what woman might be widowed, parent made childless or child left without protector, if the gallant privateer was successful that was all they were taught to look for.
>
> Although a slave captain and afterwards a privateer, my father was a kind and just man, a good father, husband and friend. I have been told that he was quite a different man at sea, that there he was harsh, unbending and stern, but still just. How he used to rule the turbulent spirits of his crews I do not know but certain it is that he never wanted men when other Liverpool shipowners were short of hands.
>
> The men used to make much of me as a boy. They made me little sea toys and always brought my mother and myself presents from Africa such as parrots, monkeys, shells and articles of the natives workmanship. . . . on his return from a successful West Indian cruise, the mate of the *Mary Ellen*, a great big fellow named Blake and who was one of the roughest and most ungainly men ever seen, would insist upon my mother accepting a beautiful chain of Indian workmanship to which was attached the miniature of a very lovely woman. I doubt the rascal came by it very honestly.

From Stonehouse we have also a description, written in more enlightened times, of the Liverpool he knew as a boy.

Its streets were tortuous and narrow with pavements in the middle skirted by mud. The sidewalks were rough with sharp-pointed stones that made it a misery to walk upon them. I have seen houses with little low rooms suffice for the dwelling of a merchant or well-to-do trader, the first being content to live in Water Street while the latter had no idea of leaving his little shop with its bay or square window to take care of itself at night. I have seen Liverpool streets with scarcely a coach or a vehicle in them, save such as trade required, and the most enlightened of its inhabitants at that time would not boast of much intelligence; while those who constituted its lower orders were plunged in the deepest vice, ignorance and brutality.

Scarcely a town by the margin of the ocean could be more salty in its people than the men of Liverpool of the eighteenth century, so barbarous were they in their amusement, bullbaitings, cock and dog fightings and pugilistic encounters. What could we expect when we opened no book to the young and employed no means of imparting knowledge to the old, deriving our prosperity from two great sources, the slave trade and privateering? Swarming with sailormen, flushed with prizemoney, was it not likely that the inhabitants generally would take a tone from what they beheld and quietly countenanced?

Not only harlots, crimps, swindlers and footpads lay in wait for free-spending sailormen, home from the sea after months of privation and danger. The press gang also lurked ready to pounce upon any man or youth who had made himself unwary through drink. This was one description of Liverpool press gangs:

At their head was generally a rakish, dissipated but determined-looking officer in a very seedy uniform and shabby hat. And what followers! Fierce, savage, stern, villainous-looking fellows were they, as ready to cut a throat as eat their breakfast. Men scowled at them as they passed, the women openly scoffed at them, the children screamed and hid behind doors or fled round corners. And how rapidly the word was passed from mouth to mouth that there were 'Hawks abroad' so as to give time to any poor sailor who had incautiously ventured from his place of concealment to return to it. But woe upon him if there were no warning voice to tell him of the coming danger. He was seized upon as if he were a common felon, deprived of his liberty, torn from his home, his friends, his parents, wife or children, hurried to the rendezvous house, examined, passed, and sent on board the tender like a negro to the slave ship.

Sometimes the sailors and their friends would show fight and as the mob always joined them the press gang invariably got the worst of it in such battles. Sometimes, too, the press gangers would seize an American sailor or a carpenter and then there was sure to be a squall. If it was a carpenter, bells from the shipbuilding yards would boom out a warning and thousands would muster to set their companion at liberty. A press gangsman was occasionally tarred and feathered when caught alone.

Pool Lane (today South Castle Street), at the beginning of the eighteenth century a quiet, almost rural, byway, later became the scene of numerous desperate encounters with press gangs. It was much frequented by privateersmen who spent liberally in numerous taverns and dingy shops. Women in these unsavoury places would first relieve sailors of their prize money and then earn a reward by betraying them to a press gang. But they could expect no mercy from the townspeople if such treachery became known. There is an account of one woman who had disclosed a sailor's hiding place to a press gang being dragged from her house, stripped and then ducked several times in the foul water of Old Dock.

The net of the press gangs was widely cast. Many a slave ship from Liverpool was boarded by the navy within an hour or two of reaching the West Indies and a number of the hands impressed. Crews of the privateers holding the official Letters of Marque were supposed to be exempt from impressment, but there were frequent occasions when gangs failed to honour such authority and captains of men-o'-war often boarded both privateers and slavers in the Mersey or at sea to seize members of the crew.

One of the worst disorders in which press gangs were concerned in Liverpool occurred in 1759. At that time there were a number of whalers running profitably from the Mersey to the Greenland fisheries. One of them, the *Golden Lyon*, returned from the Arctic a few days after the man-o'-war *Vengeance* (a former French privateer) had taken station in the river. The lieutenant commanding the *Vengeance* hailed the whaler as she entered the Mersey and declared that he would impress the entire ship's company apart from officers, whereupon the whalermen brandished their long knives and harpoons vowing to use them if any man from the *Vengeance* dare try to take them; and this so terrified the warship's crew that they took to the boats.

But the lieutenant of the *Vengeance* managed to get on the poop of the *Golden Lyon* and from there ordered both the man-o'-war and her tenders to open fire. Shots from nine pounders carried away the rigging, sails and mizzen-stay of the *Golden Lyon* and others struck parts of the waterfront where hundreds were watching the encounter.

Despite the damage, the *Golden Lyon* reached dock. Next morning her ship's company marched to the Customs House to renew the protection an Act of Parliament was supposed to give whaler crews from impressment. No sooner had they arrived than a large press gang burst into the Customs House firing pistols. They seized the captain of the *Golden Lyon* and six of the crew, but the remaining whalermen escaping by leaping from windows. Some climbed on to housetops and reached freedom after a clamber over the tiles. The six who had been seized were borne away to the catcalls of a large crowd. One woman who shrieked abuse at the press gang was shot in both her legs. Outraged by this incident, magistrates and merchants of the port announced their determination to prosecute the press gang; but if anything came of this intention it was not chronicled.

A safe refuge against the press gangs (and against customs men, too) was Mother Redcap's inn at Seacombe on the Wirral side of the river, a somewhat hazardous sail or row from Liverpool in darkness. There was a mooring place known as Red Bet's from which sailors could either make for the inn's front door (of oak, 5 inches thick and studded with nails) or reach its drinking rooms through caves known as the Red Noses. These were connected to the inn by a tunnel that wound inland from the caverns and ended in steps leading up to a trapdoor in the inn floor.

Mother Redcap was Poll Jones and we know little about her other than that she was the confidante of privateersmen, smugglers and wreckers. Her inn was walled with timber from wrecked ships and decorated with curios brought to her from West Africa and the Caribbean by those she befriended. It must often have been the scene of wild disorders as lawless crews from privateers drank, sang and quarrelled there until daybreak or hid, below that trapdoor, in the damp recesses of the Red Noses which water entered on spring tides. But Mother Redcap had their trust, and it was quite usual for them to leave substantial sums of money in her care, collecting the money when they returned a year or two years later from forays on the Spanish Main or from the delivery of slaves to Caribbean islands.

As many of these depositors did not return, presumably Poll Jones amassed a tidy fortune, but what happened to it we do not know. There are, of course, stories of hoarded guineas hidden somewhere in the labyrinths of the Red Noses. However, these caves have been thoroughly explored without any treasure trove being discovered.

In the 1770s Liverpool suffered a grave decline in trade, and a number of the merchants (including Manesty, John Newton's benefactor) became bankrupt. The outcome of the Boston Tea Party was a catastrophe for Mersey shipping since it seriously reduced trade with Africa as well as with the Caribbean and America. The War of Independence also brought a new tribe of freebooters into the Atlantic and eventually into the Irish Sea, former colonists who had the dash and enterprise of their English ancestors and against whom Liverpool privateer captains were reluctant to match gunpower and courage, being more than half in sympathy with the rebel cause.

The port's councillors made loyal noises to George III, but there were many in Liverpool who considered government action to have been stupidly repressive and who were appalled at the blight which settled on once busy quays. The *Liverpool General Advertiser* lamented: 'Our once extensive trade to Africa is at a stand: all commerce with America is at an end. . . . Survey our docks; count there the gallant ships laid up and useless. When will they again be refitted? What becomes of the sailor, the tradesman, the poor labourer during the approaching winter?'

Well before that winter began, sailors rioted in the town. The insurrection began when men engaged on refitting the slave ship *Derby* demanded 30s. a month in wages, claiming that these had been contracted. The owners refused to pay more than 20s., whereupon the men slashed down the *Derby*'s rigging. Constables seized nine of the men who were committed by the magistrates to the Tower of Liverpool.

At news of this a mob of angry sailors collected and eventually grew to 2,000 strong, armed with pistols, cutlasses, handspikes and clubs. They attacked the Tower and freed the nine men. Then they made for the docks where they remained until midnight tearing down the rigging of every ship.

The next day was Saturday and it was a comparatively quiet

weekend; but on the Monday a large body of sailors marched to a meeting with magistrates who heard their grievances. The following morning the owners of the *Derby* agreed to meet the men's demands; but during the afternoon word got round that about 300 able-bodied unemployed had been hired at 10s. a day to seize the leaders of the Friday's riot.

In the evening an enraged crowd surrounded the Exchange (Liverpool's third town hall). A single pane in a window was broken, either by a flying stone or by the press of the mob; and at this a guard of special constables, merchants among them, opened fire on the sailors, killing seven and wounding about forty. The crowd at once launched an attack on the Exchange and smashed every window.

Early next day 1,000 sailors gathered under the leadership of a man they called 'General Gage', and each wore a red ribbon in his hat. They plundered a gunsmith's and made off with some 300 muskets. More sailors dragged cannon from ships to the main streets. Then once again they surrounded the Exchange and hoisted a red flag. But, this being Liverpool, the affair had its moments of comedy. Here is another passage from James Stonehouse's memoirs:

> A cannon was obtained from Old Dock by a part of rioters. One of the fellows took a horse out of Mr. Blackburne's stables at the saltworks and attempted to harness it to a truck on which the cannon had been placed. The leader of the gang, in stooping down to fasten a rope to the truck, offered so fair a mark for a bite, that the horse, evidently having notions of law and order, availed himself of the opportunity of making his mark upon Jack's beam-end which sent him off roaring, leaving the gun in the possession of the saline Bucephalus.

There was even an instance of chivalry. A body of rioters hammered on the door of a merchant's home in Water Street. Only his daughter was in and she calmly opened the door and asked the leader of the gang what he wanted. The leader, doffing his hat, bowed and solicited, rather than demanded, a contribution. Having received it, he thanked the donor profusely and marched his gang away.

Other householders were less fortunate. A number of homes were plundered and the rioters became drunk on stolen wine.

Meanwhile sailors outside the Exchange were firing a cannon from Castle Street at the Exchange and breaking every window in the street. 'Aim for the goose!' someone shouted, meaning the Liver Bird (a cormorant, in fact) high above the Exchange portico. The cry was taken up and as a result the cannon was pointed high so that less damage was done to the building than would otherwise have been the case.

The riot ended abruptly with the arrival of Lord Pembroke's Regiment from Manchester. Ringleaders took refuge in cellars and garrets, but more than sixty of the rioters were hunted out and sent to Lancaster Gaol. Fourteen of the sixty were later 'suffered to go on board one of his Majesty's ships destined for America'. As this could well have been their fate had there been no riot but they had fallen into the hands of press gangs, the punishment seems to have been remarkably light; and indeed there appears to have been a certain amount of sympathy with the men and a view that the disorder arose primarily from the greed of merchants.

The entry of France and Spain into the quarrel between England and her former colonists changed the situation in Liverpool. Now there was a rush to build and refit privateers—more than 120, of a total of nearly 31,000 tons, were equipped in a matter of eight months. They were armed with 1,986 guns and carried 8,750 men.

It was at this time that the most celebrated of the American privateer captains, John Paul Jones, sailed the *Ranger* into the Irish Sea to wreak havoc among merchantmen before boldly entering Whitehaven harbour and setting the ships there on fire. Soon afterwards he landed on Scottish soil and once again William Hutchinson prepared the port of Liverpool to withstand possible invasion. The precautions were, in fact, on a scale larger than those taken in 1759 against Thurot. But the *Ranger* did not appear. Paul Jones, unlike Thurot, survived his freebooting in the Irish Sea and retired on the proceeds from his plunder.

One of the most savage sea battles during the War of Independence was fought between the *Watt* of Liverpool and the American frigate *Trumbull*. A New York newspaper reported:

The rebel ship was crowded with men and fought 19 guns to a side. The *Watt* mounted 32 guns and had only 164 men on board, eleven of whom were killed and several wounded. The action was obstinate and bloody and the carnage on board the rebel frigate amazing as the vessels were for a considerable time yardarm to yardarm and the *Watt*, by the superior skill of her officers and the alertness of her crew, had the opportunity of twice raking her antagonist fore and aft which made her a slaughterhouse. She at last put before the wind and ran from the *Watt* which chased her for eight hours. . . .

Several Irish mariners, fighting with considerable resource, joined in this harrying of English merchantmen as they had done in the earlier conflict begun by the Boston Tea Party. Pat Dowling had a particularly lucrative career, capturing in the Irish Sea the *Olive Branch* (Liverpool to Charleston), which he ransomed for 7,700 guineas, and numerous other ships which were burned at sea if the ransom demanded was not paid. .

One of his contemporaries was Captain Kelly in *The Terror of England* of twenty-two guns. He had a ferocious three-hour engagement with the Liverpool ship *Molly*, homeward bound from Jamaica, capturing her after the master and four of the crew had been killed. But the prize crew he put on board became so bewildered when a gale sprang up that they surrendered the *Molly* to her ship's company, who took her into the Clyde. A few days later the frigate *Stag*, out from Liverpool, captured *The Terror of England* with Kelly on board.

Captain James Wiseman, of the Liverpool privateer *Isabella* carrying a crew of fifty, wrote this report of an encounter with the American brig *General Sullivan* (fourteen guns, 135 men):

We fought her for two hours and a half, yardarm to yardarm. We gave her the first and last broadside and I believe she is sunk. We had killed Mr. Goodwin, a passenger, and John Taylor, seamen; wounded, John Manesty; third mate shot in the hand which is since amputated and he is likely to do well; Rowland Evans, shot in the leg, since amputated and he is dead; John Jones shot twice through the knee, we expect he will recover. . . .

Wiseman was wrong in his belief that he had despatched the *General Sullivan*. She limped into Martinico in sorry state with eleven dead and twenty-three wounded. 'Her captain acknowledged [it was reported] that he was obliged to sheer off and it was the second drubbing he had had from Liverpool men and wished not to meet any more armed vessels belonging to that port.'

During the War of Independence, which ended in 1783, the number of Liverpool ships sailing to Africa fell from 105 to less than a dozen and some 10,000 of the 35,000 townspeople were being supported either by the parish or charities when hostilities ended. But the port's recovery was dramatic. By 1793 the population had increased to 60,000, and a sixth of all tonnage cleared from English ports was from Liverpool, compared with one-twenty-fourth in 1716.

Between 1783 and 1793 ships from the Mersey transported more than 300,000 slaves across the Atlantic, mostly embarked from New Calabar, the island of Bonny and Old Calabar and the entrances to creeks between these settlements.

A high proportion of the slaves were Ibos from an interior territory that had been part of the vast kingdom of Benin but little influenced by the sophistication of the capital (Benin City had strong ties with Portugal in the fifteenth and sixteenth centuries with an ambassador in Lisbon) except in one or two of the larger communities like that of Onitsha on the Niger. The Ibos, who practised circumcision, were a healthy, affable people, the men tall, the women graceful and modest and perfumed with a scent obtained from a native wood. They were, of course, ancestors of the people who suffered such misery in the Biafra affair of the late 1960s.

In the last half of the eighteenth century most of the slaves were bought in batches of up to 2,000 by parties sent in canoes by the Ijo kings of the Delta to fairs held every few weeks at inland villages by the creeks. They were then borne, in leg chains, back to the Ijo settlements to await the arrival of slave ships, and these announced their arrival in a creek estuary by firing a salute to the king who came out by canoe to collect Comey (customs) and receive dash (presents) from the captain before getting down to bargaining and 'shake hands' over gourds of mimbo, a palm wine. This was a typical price paid for a 'prime' Ibo adult:

One piece of chintz 18 yards long and a piece of baft and a piece of chelloe of similar length; several other pieces of material; 52 handkerchieves; one large brass pan and four iron pots; two muskets, 25 kegs of powder, 100 flints, two bags of shot; 20 knives, four cutlasses; four hats, four caps; six bunches of beads; and 14 gallons of brandy.

The total cost of such an assortment was about £25, and a slave bought at this price would realise at least £50 in the West Indies.

Some of the Delta kings wrote, as well as spoke, English of a sort. Grandy King George of the old town sector of Old Calabar wrote to Mr. Ambrose Lace, a Liverpool merchant and owner of slaves:

> Marchant Lace I did as you bob me for Letters when this tender com I no chop for all man for you bob me, No chop to times for bi-on-bi I back too much copper for Coomey so I do all same you bob me who make my father grandy no more white man so now ship and make me grandy again.*

Another correspondent in Old Calabar, Robin John Otto Ephraim, requested Mr. Lace to remember him to his sons Joshua and William and his daughter Polly. Joshua Lace was the founder and first president of the Liverpool Law Society, and William, a dashing captain of privateers as well as master of slave ships, led expeditions up the Niger into the then unexplored interior.

Robin John's affability was surprising because three of his relatives were savagely dealt with by English sailors in the massacre of Old Calabar in 1767, in which one Liverpool ship, the *Edgar*, was involved. There was intense jealousy between two sectors of Old Calabar—the new town and the old town—over sales of slaves, and the captains of the six ships in the river offered to mediate. Accordingly a deputation set out from the old town headed by a canoe carrying three Robin John brothers. They were directed from the *Edgar* to the Bristol-owned *Duke of York* and were no sooner on board than they were set upon by sailors who put them in irons.

Almost immediately the English ships opened fire on the canoes and at least 300 lost their lives. A canoe from the new town then went alongside the *Duke of York* and demanded the person of the eldest Robin John. His brothers watched helplessly as he was

---

* A possible translation is: 'Merchant Lace, you deceived me in letters which came by tender so I would not exchange slaves, and will not do so, for copper as Comey (customs). You who deceived me, acknowledged my father's authority; so now send me word that you similarly acknowledge mine.'

forced into the canoe and beheaded. They were kept in the ship and later sold as slaves in the West Indies.

Two years later, at New Calabar, a number of the 132 slaves taken on board the Liverpool ship *Nancy* turned on the crew, several of whom were ill. The seamen opened fire, killing six of the slaves and wounding others. Upon hearing the guns, a host of Ijo put out in canoes, boarded the *Nancy*, plundered her, split her decks, took off the slaves and then set the vessel adrift. The captain and crew were rescued from the *Nancy*, now a wreck, by another slave ship.

It was sometimes the practice to put the slaves in chains in the crowded, sweating holds immediately they came on board and to keep them there until they were disembarked on the other side of the Atlantic, many weakened from the privations endured in the ocean's dreaded middle passage. Those stricken with fever were usually brought up on deck in an attempt to limit infection; but there were occasions when they were freed and given arms to help fight against a French or American privateer.

Captain Noble, of the slaver *Brooks*, wrote to the Liverpool owners from Montego Bay in 1777, after a desperate encounter with an American freebooter which he destroyed: 'I had fifty of our stoutest slaves armed, who fought with exceedingly great spirit.' Captain Stevenson, of the Liverpool slave ship *Rose*, informed the owners of a victory over a French privateer near Jamaica and went on:

I had about fifty men, black and white, on deck at great guns and small arms, halfpikes, boathooks, boatoars, steering sail yards, firewood and slack ballast which they threw at the Frenchmen in such a manner that their heads rattled against one another like so many empty calabashes. . . . The French hove such a quantity of powder flasks on board us that the ship abaft was all in a blaze of fire three different times; this hurt the blacks much, having no trowsers on them. . . .

When the slave ships arrived at their destinations the male were mustered on the maindeck and the women on the poop. They might then be disposed of by a 'scramble sale'—immediately gangways were lowered a signal gun was fired and buyers were allowed to rush on board and grab all the slaves they could. Males, of course, fetched the higher prices and, indeed, the

Liverpool firm of Thomas Leyland and Company expressly instructed the master of their vessel *Enterprize*, 'buy as few females as in your power, because we look to a Spanish market for the disposal of your cargo, where females are a very tedious sale'.

Yet Leyland's had at least some thought for the human cargoes the *Enterprize* carried. They instructed Captain Caesar Lawson to allow the slaves 'every indulgence consistent with your own safety and do not suffer any of your officers or crew to abuse or insult them in any respect'.

But there were many incidents of unspeakable barbarity, and seamen were often given licence to rape female slaves. Gomer Williams in *The Liverpool Privateers* wrote:

> A certain Liverpool captain, in a large company at Buxton, related how a female slave fretted herself to a great degree on account of the infant she had been obliged to take with her into the slave ship.
>
> 'Apprehensive for her health,' said this monster, 'I snatched the child from her arms, knocked its head against the side of the ship and threw it into the sea.'

Slaves were sold from time to time in Liverpool. Usually they were children and had presumably failed to fetch a satisfactory price in the West Indies so were kept in the ship—which had no doubt taken their parents either to the Caribbean or to death at sea—on her return voyage to the Mersey with sugar. An advertisement in *Williamson's Liverpool Advertiser* in 1765 read: 'To be sold by auction at St. George's Coffee House betwixt the hours of six and eight o'clock a very fine negro girl, about 8 years of age; very healthy and hath been some time from the coast.'

From time to time there were notices posted in the port and in surrounding districts concerning runaway blackamoors.

However, there were always voices raised against the traffic in slaves (the Quakers denounced it in 1727), and the disposition in Liverpool to which I have already referred, to cast privateersmen in a semi-heroic mould but to see the slave ships' crews as despicable creatures, was perhaps evidence of at least a subconscious distaste for the trade. By the 1780s the port's most influential opponent of slavery was William Roscoe, one of the most distinguished names in the history of Liverpool, poet, pamphleteer, politician, banker, lawyer, painter and botanist. Two of his allies

Dockers
The Spinners at Gregson's Well

were William Rathbone, a member of a family to become notable in Liverpool, and Dr. Jonathan Binns.

Roscoe, an innkeeper's son, had a mainly prosperous legal and banking career; and in his leisure he was a leader of the developing cultural life of Liverpool, its theatre, music hall, various musical entertainments (there is a record of an early performance of *Messiah*) and debate. He also busied himself with reformist pamphlets, writing poetry and songs and political articles. In 1787 he published *The Wrongs of Africa* in which he roundly condemned the transport of slaves.

Paradoxically, some of the slave-ship captains and their merchant employers, notwithstanding the agonies endured by Africans lying chained in suffocating holds and coming under whiplash, were God-fearing, just and humane within their narrow philosophy, sometimes philanthropists and men of education and discernment. Indeed, Roscoe numbered certain of them among his close friends; and he explained this in a speech at the dinner which celebrated his election (in 1806) as one of the port's M.P.s. He said:

> It has been the fashion throughout the Kingdom to regard the town of Liverpool and its inhabitants in an unfavourable light on account of the share it has in this trade. But I will venture to say that this idea is founded on ignorance and I will here assert, as I always shall, that men more independent, of greater public virtue and private worth than the merchants of Liverpool do not exist. . . .
>
> The African trade is the trade of the nation, not of any particular place. It is a trade till lately sanctioned by Parliament and long continued under the authority of the Government. I do not make this remark in vindication of the character of any gentleman engaged in the trade, who stand in need of none, but in order to show that if any loss should arise to any individuals who are concerned in it, it is incumbent upon the Government to make them a full compensation for the losses they may sustain.

But in the last twenty years of the eighteenth century Liverpool Corporation resolutely, and at times passionately, defended slavery against the campaign of Roscoe and his fellow abolitionists. A Spanish Jesuit priest, of English ancestry, who settled in the port and spoke in support of slave traders, was presented with £100 as a token of the Corporation's gratitude.

High above Dale Street looking over the Mersey

E

In the 1790s there was a shift in the traffic away from the Niger settlements to Angola. Of 52,500 slaves transported by 150 vessels from the Mersey in 1798, 23,000 were from Angola, 14,000 from Bonny, 3,000 from New Calabar and 2,500 from Old Calabar. William Lace was one of the captains who had turned to Angola and in a letter to him, requesting seeds of African and West Indian plants to be raised in a heated orangery at the new Liverpool Botanic Garden, Roscoe wrote:

> I have observed with pleasure that your natural disposition is kind and liberal and you can never have a fitter opportunity of exerting these qualities than your present situation affords. Coolness, vigilance, compassion, attention to the necessities of all under your charge are essential requisites. Let it never be forgotten and let the poor imprisoned African find that in all his distresses he is not without a friend.

One of the wealthiest of the slave ship owners was for some years a partner of Roscoe in banking. He was Thomas Leyland, known as 'Lucky' Leyland because the foundation of his fortunes was a lottery prize. He was the second biggest subscriber to the fund which enabled Roscoe to stand successfully for Parliament committed to support abolition (which would, of course, mean heavy losses to Leyland).

Roscoe's term as an M.P. was brief but long enough to see Wilberforce's Bill go through. There was another election soon afterwards (in 1807) and Roscoe returned to Liverpool to find a hostile mob awaiting him. In an ensuing affray one of his supporters was murdered and he thereupon vowed he would not stand for re-election. Though prevailed upon to do so, he was at the bottom of the poll in a three-cornered contest.

The death occurred in 1795, when he was Mayor of Liverpool, of Peter Baker, who made a fortune in perhaps the most astonishing of all the adventures of the privateers. He was a former carpenter turned shipbuilder, who built himself an armed vessel which he named the *Mentor*. She was such a parody of a privateer that those who had promised her builder money changed their minds after one look at her. Desperate to avoid being imprisoned in the Tower of Liverpool with other debtors, Baker mustered a crew as unseaworthy as his ship appeared to be; and the *Mentor* then sailed lobsidedly out of Liverpool Bay in search of booty to pay the owner's creditors.

She soon found it—the *Carnatic*, a French East Indiaman, loaded with treasure including diamonds and gold. This prize fell to the ill-found *Mentor* with scarcely a fight; and three weeks after she had sailed from the Mersey to the jeers of sightseers, the privateer was back in the river in November mist, church bells ringing a welcome, with spoils in her wake worth at least £135,000 (one report put the value at £400,000 and claimed that £135,000 was no more than the price fetched by a single box of diamonds in the captured vessel).

The *Mentor* captured two more prizes *en route* for Jamaica, and then, in 1782, foundered in a gale off Newfoundland with thirty-one of her crew. Meanwhile Baker had bought Mossley Hall on a hilltop overlooking the Mersey, and the house was immediately re-named 'Carnatic Hall' by the wags of Liverpool. It was destroyed by fire in 1891, and a new mansion—this time named by its owner Carnatic Hall—was built at great expense by Walter Holland, a senior partner in the shipping firm of Lamport and Holt (you will remember my mentioning a young volunteer named Holt who died of fever in Captain William Hutchinson's privateer the *Liverpool*—well, he was of that family).

Walter Holland was the grandson of Samuel Holland, a kinsman of Nemehiah Holland, the daring captain of the little *Ann Galley*, one of whose exploits I also recalled earlier in this chapter. Nemehiah, as master of the *Sarah Goulburn*, captured a valuable American merchantman in mid-Atlantic, the year before the *Mentor*'s triumph; and in 1778, now commanding the larger *St. Peter*, he took a prize to rival the *Carnatic*—the French East Indiaman *Aquilone* said to have been worth at least £250,000. But the success was short-lived. French frigates captured the *St. Peter*, retook the *Aquilone* and escorted them (with Nemehiah presumably still on board the privateer) into Port L'Orient. Nemehiah's old ship, the *Sarah Goulburn*, was lost in the same storm that destroyed the *Mentor*.

Walter Holland's Carnatic Hall was pulled down in 1964, and I visited it a year or so before demolition men moved in. The pleasure grounds laid out in the 1890s were completely overgrown by breast-high weeds and brambles; and in the domed hall of marble columns, carved oak and unique porcelain panels made by craftsmen of the long defunct Della Robbia pottery of Birkenhead, were the mummified remains of the Egyptian priestess Tai-Ani who died 2,700 years ago.

Also in the vast hall—lit only by one naked 100-watt bulb—were the mummies of a child of Coptic Christians and the relic of another Egyptian priestess who was known in her day—the fourth century B.C.—as Shep Set (The August One). In a neighbouring apartment scowled the masks of Bundu witch doctors.

Carnatic Hall was, in fact, being used at the time as a temporary repository for mummies and ethnographical miscellanea awaiting a permanent place in the Liverpool Museum, then being rebuilt after the ravages of the last war. So visiting Walter Holland's former home was a distinctly weird experience; but I had the opportunity to walk through the massive dome-roofed cellars—sufficient of them to billet a battalion of soldiers—which survived the fire of 1891 and were therefore as Peter Baker of the *Mentor* knew them.

Now university halls of residence stand on the site of the House of Holland and its grounds, where, before the First World War, peacocks strutted and polo ponies stamped in their stables. But the name 'Carnatic' has been preserved in one of the new buildings; and, a short distance away, is another hostel for University students which bears the name of Roscoe.

What, I wonder, were Roscoe's comments upon hearing of the horror that in 1797 overtook the Liverpool slave ship *Thomas*, her captain, Peter McQuee, described at the time as brave, respectable and intelligent. She was on her way to Barbados with 375 Africans in her holds when, while the crew were at breakfast, three of the women slaves discovered that an armoury chest had been left open. They passed weapons through the bulkheads to the men slaves, and about 200 of them immediately rushed up the forescuttles and put to death all those of the crew who stood in their way.

McQuee and a handful of his men fought desperately with such arms as were to hand in the captain's cabin. They were all either butchered to death or driven over the side. Twelve others of the crew escaped in a boat, but only two survived to land in Barbados. Five more seamen were kept alive in the *Thomas* to steer her.

After forty-two days an American brig went alongside the

Liverpool ship. The slaves at once rushed on board her and the crew took to the boats. The brig was laden with rum, and the Africans soon became so drunk that the five sailors of the *Thomas*, despite their weakness from long privation, were able to recapture the ship and kill the slaves' ring-leaders. The *Thomas* eventually reached Long Island.

But the final decade of the Liverpool slave trade had now begun; and in July 1807 the *Kitty's Amelia* sailed from the Mersey to load the last cargo of black ivory to be transported across the Atlantic by a Liverpool ship. She was commanded by Captain Hugh 'Mind Your Eye' Crow, a Manxman who lost his right eye in childhood and was given his nickname by a Liverpool merchant. As a young man he found the slave trade repugnant but after serving for more than ten years in ships transporting Africans, he wrote this retort to Roscoe and his fellow abolitionists:

Instead of saving any of the poor Africans from slavery, these pretended philanthropists have through the abolition been the (I admit indirect) cause of the death of thousands for they have caused the trade to be transferred to other nations who, in defiance of all that our cruisers can do to prevent them, carry it on with a cruelty to the slaves, and a disregard for their comfort and even of their lives, to which Englishmen could never bring themselves to resort.

Crow wrote these notes on his treatment of his human cargo:

One of our first occupations was the construction of a thatched house on the deck for the accommodation and comfort of the slaves. This practically extended from stem to stern and was so contrived that the whole ship was thoroughly aired while, at the same time, the blacks were secured from getting overboard. The temporary building would cost £30 to £40. . . .

How long such a structure survived in a mid-Atlantic tempest Crow did not reveal. He continued that when the slaves came

on deck, about eight o'clock in the morning, water was provided to wash their hands and faces, a mixture of lime juice to cleanse their mouth, towels to wipe with, and chew-sticks to clean their teeth. A dram of brandy bitters was given to each of the men and, clean spoons being served out, they breakfasted about nine o'clock. About eleven, if the day was fine, they washed their bodies all over and, after wiping themselves dry, were allowed to use palm oil, their favourite cosmetic.

Pipes and tobacco were then supplied to the men and beads and other articles were distributed amongst the women to amuse them, after which they were permitted to dance and run about on deck, to keep them in good spirits. A middle mess of bread and cocoa-nuts was given them about midday. The third meal was served out about three o'clock; after everything was cleaned out and arranged below for their accommodation, they were generally sent down about four or five in the evening. . . .

Misadventure sailed with the *Kitty's Amelia* that July day in 1807. In his haste to be off to Bonny, 'Mind Your Eye' Crow had cleaned ship with much less than his customary thoroughness; and in consequence the crew were stricken with a malignant fever soon after clearing the Irish Sea. The slaver was also frequently imperilled by storms which prevented Crow from carrying out at sea hygiene that ought to have been completed in port. When the ship at last arrived at Bonny it was found that old produce had been repacked in still damp water casks in which it had rotted. The casks were flung into the river but the damage had been done.

A number of ships were waiting at Bonny for slaves and Crow had to take his turn; yet such was his reputation with King Pepple of Bonny that he was able to purchase 'as fine a cargo of blacks as has ever been taken from Africa'. The King, incidentally, was much diverted by the three-leg device on the Manx flag that 'Mind Your Eye' flew when he was in African waters.

The *Kitty's Amelia* set sail for Kingston. Within a few days fever returned to the ship, afflicting first the crew and then the Africans shackled in the holds. The chief mate died, so did one of the two doctors on board. Huge waves crashed down on the decks where sick slaves lay. Then came the horror of a fire in mid-ocean. This was how Crow described it in his memoirs:

> I was in the cabin at the time and springing upon deck the first persons I saw were two young men with their flannel shirts blazing on their backs. At the same time I perceived a dense cloud of smoke issuing from below and, looking round me, I found people in the act of cutting away the stern and quarter boats that they might abandon the vessel. At this critical juncture I had the presence of mind to exclaim in an animating tone, 'Is it possible, my lads, that you can desert me at a moment when it is your bounden duty as men to assist me?' And, observing them hesitate, I added, 'Follow me, my brave fellows, and we shall soon save the ship.'

These few words had the desired effect for they immediately rallied and came forward to assist me. To show them a proper example I was the first man to venture below, for I thought of the poor blacks entrusted to my care and who could not be saved in the boats; and I was determined, rather than desert them, to extinguish the fire or perish in the attempt. When we got below we found the fire blazing with great fury on the starboard side and, as it was known to the crew that there were forty-five barrels of gunpowder in the magazine within about three feet only of the fire, it required every possible encouragement on my part to lead them on to endeavour to extinguish the rapidly increasing flames. When I first saw the extent of the conflagration and thought of its proximity to the powder, a thrill of despair ran through my whole frame; but by a strong mental effort I suppressed my disheartening feelings and only thought of active exertion unconnected with the thought of imminent danger.

We paused for a moment, struggling, as it were, to determine how to proceed. Very fortunately for us our spare sails were stowed close at hand. These were dragged out and by extraordinary activity we succeeded in throwing them over the flames which they so far checked that we gained time to obtain a good supply of water down the hatchway and in the course of ten or fifteen minutes, by favour of the Almighty, we extinguished the flames. Had I hesitated only a few minutes on deck, or had I not spoken encouragingly to the people, no exertions whatever could have saved the ship from being blown up.

Crow's narrative shows that modesty was not amongst his virtues. His story continues: 'I shall never forget the scene that followed the suppression of the flames. When I got on deck, the blacks, both men and women, clung round me in tears, some taking hold of my hands, others of my feet, and all with much earnestness and feeling, thanking Providence for our narrow escape. . . .'

It transpired that the fire had been caused by the two men seen by Crow with their shirts in flames. They had taken a lighted candle to draw rum and a spark from it ignited the spirit. So at last the *Kitty's Amelia* sailed into Kingston. Since leaving the Mersey she had lost twenty-eight of her crew and two doctors; and fifty Africans had died between Bonny and Jamaica.

On arrival in Kingston 'Mind Your Eye' found to his chagrin that the rush to deliver slaves before abolition had caused a glut on the market of human bondage. Sixteen slave ships had laid in Kingston roads for more than five months with their cargoes unsold and both the slaves and the crews were diminishing almost daily through death. Crow had a reputation, however, for shipping Africans who were 'as plump as cotton bags' and it stood him in good stead. Friends ashore arranged for a paragraph to be inserted in a Kingston newspaper stating that the Manxman had arrived with the finest cargo of negroes ever brought to the port; and that did the trick. In five days all the slaves had been sold at higher prices than those obtained by any other vessel in the port, and the *Kitty's Amelia* set out for Liverpool where Crow, aged 43, retired from the sea.

In his early days he had been thrown into gaol with captured runaway slaves by ex-shipmates on the orders of the captain who claimed that Crow had deserted (he had, in fact, persuaded a rival master to engage him as second mate). He had another spell in prison—in France this time—when captured by an enemy privateer and forced to march 500 miles. He escaped and hoodwinked a patrol who stopped him with a torrent of sentences in the Manx language which convinced the soldiers that he must be Breton.

In the year before the voyage in the *Kitty's Amelia*, 'Mind Your Eye' had an eventful passage in command of the 500-ton *Mary* with a cargo of slaves for Kingston. He was in the latitude of Tobago when two men-o'-war appeared and hailed the *Mary* in English. This was a frequent French deceit and 'Mind Your Eye' decided that they were enemy ships and opened fire. A bloody battle ensued, lasting through the night. Soon after midnight a shot took off both the boatswain's legs at the thigh and another entered the hold, killing five slaves and wounding others.

Shortly before dawn Crow was struck by a splinter and fell senseless. According to his narrative, the crew lost heart, believing that he was dead, and struck the *Mary's* ensign. When Crow came to his senses it was to find that he had been fighting two British men-o'-war, the *Dart* and the *Wolverine*. 'In my anguish and vexation' ('Mind Your Eye' wrote later) 'I struck my head several times against the cabin floor until the blood started from my mouth and nostrils; but I was consoled by officers from the men-o'-war who were loud in their praise of my spirited action.'

And (again according to Crow) when the battered *Mary*

reached Kingston a number of slaves wearing their Sunday-best boarded the ship and asked to see the 'Massa'.

> They all rushed into my cabin [he wrote] and crowding round me with gestures of respect and with tears in their eyes, exclaimed 'God bless, massa! How poor massa do? Long live massa, for 'im da fight ebery voyage' and similar expressions of goodwill and welcome. I was deeply affected. . . . Poor Scott (the chief mate) shed tears when he saw them clinging round me and observed, 'How proud, sir, you must be to receive this grateful tribute of regard. . . .'

So, with Hugh Crow's last voyage, ended an enterprise in which Liverpudlians have no pride, even if there is courage, and indeed compassion in its chronicles, as well as cruelty. Where the Piazzas called Goree (after an African island) stood on the quayside of George's Dock, from which many of the slave ships sailed, there is now Wilberforce House, an office block built in the 1960s and bearing the name of the arch-apostle of abolition; and at least the port has made some practical recompense to Africa for the agonies that hundreds of thousands, taken in bondage from that continent, endured in the holds of Mersey vessels. It can be argued that the vital role of Merseyside's commerce in the economic development of West Africa—Nigeria in particular—sprang from self-interest; but the foundation, by citizens, of the Liverpool School of Tropical Medicine at the beginning of the present century was an act of pure altruism which has made—and continues to make—a contribution of profound importance in the social progress of the new nations of the continent.

To see Africans joining in the dedicated quest at that school for new ways to remove the malignancies still exacting a terrible toll among their peoples; to see, in modern quarters near the Mersey, young Nigerian cadets who will in this decade be officers of ships sophisticated beyond the imagining not only of men like William Hutchinson but of the captains of the great Cunarders that sailed from Liverpool between the world wars; to see other young people from Africa at the University and colleges in and around the city—this is to be encouraged to believe that an association which brought so much anguish in its beginnings will have helped, before the twentieth century ends, notably towards the enrichment of all mankind.

THREE

PAUPERS AND PHILANTHROPISTS

DESPITE profits from slaving and privateering (made not only by merchants but by crews, in prize money, and by the numerous townspeople who had shares in ships) Liverpool entered the nineteenth century with as high a proportion of paupers as could be found in any town in England. During the century poverty in the port became so extensive, and the squalor it produced so extreme, that it is scarcely possible nowadays to imagine just how appalling the conditions were and how widespread was the suffering.

At the start of the nineteenth century, the population having doubled in under twenty years, Liverpool had 77,000 inhabitants and 2,300 of them lived in cellars, while many more than this number had homes in small and foetid courts. By 1846 there were 40,000 living in 8,000 cellars and the number of court-dwellers had similarly increased. Between 1831 and 1841 the population rose by 43 per cent and in the next ten years by 37 per cent, this despite the dreadful toll from epidemics of cholera and other diseases, the death rate soaring at one stage by 2,000 per cent.

It is difficult to say how early in the century Irish immigration into Liverpool began to reach embarrassing proportions, but there were Orange and Green riots in the town in 1819—and that was well before numbers of Irishmen arrived to work on the Manchester-Liverpool railway line across the treacherous marsh-lands of Chat Moss. The mass influx, however, was in the hungry forties. In 1847 alone no fewer than 300,000 refugees from famine sailed to Liverpool, a great many of them crammed on the decks of so-called coffin ships, paying 6d. to cross the Irish Sea, their only possessions the ragged clothes in which they stood, herded together, drenched by spray. More than a quarter of this half-starved host stayed in the already grossly overcrowded port.

They dare not apply for parish relief because this so often meant being sent back to Ireland. A large number preferred to go to the congested gaol where at least there was food of sorts, clothing and a roof above their heads. In 1849 Mr. Edward Rushton, Liverpool's stipendiary magistrate, reported to the Home Secretary: 'I saw from day to day poor Irish population forced upon us in a state of wretchedness which cannot be described. Within twelve hours after they landed they would be found in one of three classes . . . paupers, vagrants and thieves.' At one period it was estimated that 23,000 children were running wild in the dockland area alone; and yet one of every two children born in Liverpool at that time died before reaching the age of 11.

The nightly spectacle in those years of hundreds, from tiny children to the aged, sleeping in back alleys, in doorways and on pavements was repeated when throngs of emigrants from Europe flocked into Liverpool by railway and on foot from East Coast ports and from London to await ships to transport them, often unfed and unwashed, across the Atlantic to become new Americans. Many were Jewish refugees from oppression in Russia, but there were also large numbers of Poles and others from Scandinavian countries. In this multitude were those who, through exhaustion of body or mind, sometimes because they were robbed of the few pounds they had kept to pay for their ocean passage, got no further than Liverpool. Their descendants were, in a number of instances, to enrich Merseyside life.

Many who left the Mersey for the New World were claimed by the ocean. In 1853 the *Annie Jane* was twice compelled by storms to return to the river with 500 emigrants who had arranged to pay for their passages by instalments from earnings in Canada. When she sailed for the third time the weather was worse than ever but the captain ignored appeals to put back again. While still in sight of Britain, the *Annie Jane* foundered on rocks, her passengers battened below. More than 450 bodies were washed ashore on the lonely Hebridean island of Vatersay where a memorial marks their communal grave.

By 1880, the year Liverpool became a city, the population exceeded 600,000 (little short, in fact, of the present-day figure), and probably a tenth of this number was destitute or in imminent peril of becoming so.

On the evening of the day in 1881 that he arrived to join the Liverpool staff of *The Catholic Times*, Gabriel Ellis attended a concert given by the Catholic total abstinence League of the Cross. He wrote afterwards: 'There was over a foot of snow . . . in spite of the weather, or perhaps because of it, the hall was packed to the doors by the poorest and most unkempt looking mass of people imaginable. Many of the women, girls and boys were barefooted . . . for the most part, the audience was eager and in good spirits in spite of being half-frozen.'

Three years later an observer wrote of 'hordes of ragged and wretched men in the cruellest grip of poverty, little children with shoeless feet, bodies pinched'; and he also noted that 'the superb carriages of the rich, with their freights of refined and elegant ladies, threaded a way among a section of the population so squalid and miserable that one's heart ached at the sight of them'. The workhouse on Brownlow Hill had at one time more than 5,000 inmates and at no period, even in the twentieth century, did it have room to spare.

Close to the Brownlow Hill institution, and perhaps because it was also near Lime Street station, their arrival point in Liverpool, Jewish refugees settled in such numbers as to constitute a ghetto. This, like the workhouse, has long disappeared; but the district of small wholesalers in neighbouring Islington is a product of it, though nowadays their premises, gradually being dispersed by bulldozers in improvement schemes, serve wholly as businesses in most cases, and not homes as well. Those who run the businesses live comfortably in suburban Allerton or Childwall or 'over the water' in Wirral and this is a tribute to the industry of their forbears in great adversity.

As that 1884 reporter pointed out, great wealth was manifest in the streets of Victorian Liverpool as well as privation; and indeed fortunes were made (some were lost, too) in the port through the nineteenth century from shipping, from merchant adventure, from cotton and other imports and from banking. Within a few hundred yards of hovels, where tens of thousands lived in perpetual distress, public and commercial buildings rose which were of a nobility and on a scale rarely matched elsewhere in Britain.

On the slopes and crown of the hill reached from lanes and alleys of mean and overcrowded courts and cellars and from water-front taverns where sailors roistered away their pay, were built terraces of gracious three and four-storey town houses, some in squares, some in wide, straight avenues wherein stood immaculate carriages, horses and attendant grooms awaiting the command of the well-to-do who lived so stylishly in these opulent residences and who were patrons of music, the theatre and other refinements such as literary clubs and debating societies meeting in buildings of distinction.

Hundreds of the once fashionable houses, nearly all of them leasehold, have disappeared in the last thirty years. The departure of the prosperous from them began before the First World War and was accelerated by the changing conditions that followed it. Many of these houses were erased, or damaged beyond repair, by German bombs; but the leases of a greater number were bought by landlords, some of whom turned the properties into multi-occupation with inadequate sanitation and allowed them so to deteriorate that they became classed by the Corporation as slums and were torn down. Some were rescued—the local authority buying the leases—and divided into comfortable apartments that today give their tenants the considerable benefits of downtown living, the daily work and main street shops within walking distance. Some are now offices, others hostels. Some remain well-cared-for, privately-owned homes. As to the rest that still stand there is a large questionmark over their future. The Corporation, housing associations and such organisations as Shelter are anxious that they should be rescued through the system of State improvement grants. It is too early, in 1970, to say with any certainty whether this is wishful or practical thinking.

In Abercromby Square (which is in the University Precinct), in Gambier Terrace (facing the Anglican Cathedral across a gorge wherein lies the city's most interesting burial ground), in Rodney Street (once Liverpool's 'Harley Street', still largely occupied by the professions, including medicine), in Canning and Huskisson Streets and in tree-lined Falkner Square, there is today the ample evidence of how pleasant these nineteenth-century residences can still look; and it is one of the tragedies of Liverpool that so many of them have been lost through sheer neglect. But the city has the public buildings and clubs that were possible only because of the wealth of the families who once lived in these houses and who, as well as money, had discrimination and discernment.

Euphoria in civic architecture began very early in the nineteenth century with the Town Hall, which was completed in 1811 and largely replaced a building (the third town hall) badly damaged by fire in 1795. Nearly a century after its opening, Edward VII described its suite of reception rooms as being still the finest in England. If any of the wretched inhabitants of those cellar slums of the period were permitted to gaze upon these salons when they were new it must have been in wonderment that such elegance in decor and sumptiousness in accoutrements could exist so close to their graceless world. They cannot have been less astonished by the conservatory—one of the biggest in the country at that time— which was erected in a botanic garden of 10 acres on the ridge overlooking the town and but a few hundred yards from the Brownlow Hill poorhouse.

This garden was the daily resort of persons of quality from near-by terraces and squares, and its first curator, John Shepherd, sent collections of plants to the Emperor Alexander of Russia for the newly made Imperial Gardens in St. Petersburg. Beneath the glass roofs of the heated conservatory flourished plants brought back by masters of ships from the West Indies, from America and from Africa (in later years from India and China) at the behest of their employers, some of the species to flower here for the first time outside their native habitat.

Recent times could be said to have provided a near parallel. Since the Second World War the Corporation, while grappling with the staggering task of rehousing the occupants of 100,000 homes declared slums or sub-standard, has laid out a Botanic Garden with glasshouses beside which Shepherd's conservatory would be puny; and in them is the finest municipal collection of orchids in the world. As in the early nineteenth century when, with thousands living in cellars, the citizens built a lavish town hall, so in the 1950s and 1960s, with a much greater number dwelling in slums, the construction of one great cathedral was advanced and another completed. These projects have not, of course, progressed unopposed, and no doubt the clamour for homes first was infinitely louder than any such protests made by cellar-dwellers as they saw the Town Hall rise with all its expensive embellishments.

But this is the Liverpool way. There was harrowing poverty when St. George's Hall was conceived and it was on a more agonising scale through the years that saw the sequence of museum, libraries and art gallery built. These were the heritage of Liverpudlians of the twentieth century, the great grandchildren many of them, of those who survived babyhood in damp, underground rooms and in stinking courts. Similarly, the two cathedrals and the new botanic garden are legacies from the twentieth century to be prized by future descendants of those who spent their early childhood in slums or in the dismal tenements built between the world wars and who began their education in hopelessly antiquated and overcrowded primary schools.

William Roscoe, that passionate opponent of slavery, was one of the zealots who established the botanic garden opened in 1803 (the genus *Roscoea* was named after him by the founder of the Linnean Society in London). At that time he lived in style in Allerton Hall, 7 miles or so from the centre of the town and commanding a view to the highlands of Wales (a vista preserved today for the grounds of the hall are a public park). But Roscoe was himself to be stricken with the endemic Liverpool affliction of penury. The withdrawal of 'Lucky' Leyland and his wealth from Roscoe's bank left it in no condition to stand heavy losses incurred with the ending of the Napoleonic wars. He became bankrupt and was obliged to leave the hall that had been his home for seventeen years and where, it was said, his father had once been a butler.

It seems likely that, in common with many Liverpudlians, he also lost money during the second war with America. In seven months 382 ships were captured by enemy men-o'-war and privateers, some of which came within a few miles of Liverpool Bay. One of the most audacious of these raiders, the *True-Blooded Yankee*, a brig of eighteen guns and 160 men, made several forays in the vicinity of Holyhead and, in a single cruise, seized no fewer than twenty-seven ships and took nearly 300 prisoners.

These misfortunes occurred in the year when the second Earl of Liverpool became Prime Minister as the consequence of Spencer Perceval being assassinated by a Liverpool man, John Bellingham. The Earl, who held the office for seventeen years, a period not equalled since, had the port's coat of arms, which were adopted by his father when the title was created. His successor for a few months was George Canning who had been M.P. for Liverpool from 1812 to 1822 and who died while Premier.

Almost coinciding with the losses suffered by Liverpool merchants in the conflict with America came an event which was greatly to expand the port's foreign trade in another direction. This was the removal of the East India Company's monopoly of commerce with Indian ports. Though it was to be another twenty years before Mersey ships were to be allowed to sail to China, the opening of Indian ports to them was a valuable reward for forty-five years of campaigning by Liverpool merchants. The first Mersey ship bound for India—she sailed the year after the monopoly was broken—was the *Kingsmill*, owned by Sir John Gladstone, a member of the Liverpool family that produced the Prime Minister of 1868-74, 1880-85, part of 1886 and 1892-94. It is noteworthy that this office was held thrice in the nineteenth century by the Earl of Derby of Knowsley and thrice, also, by the Marquess of Salisbury, a substantial landowner in Liverpool (the present Marquess is the Chancellor of Liverpool University).

Three years after the *Kingsmill*'s departure came a development of even greater significance, the appearance of the first steam vessel in the Mersey. True, the *Etna* was only a river ferry—65 feet in length and driven by a wheel in the centre of a 28-foot-wide deck—her passengers charged 3d. each (half the present day fare for crossing to Birkenhead); and true, the first ocean-going steamship to leave the Mersey was twenty-one years away. But here was an omen of the way the river traffic and the docks were to be completely transformed. It was, in fact, a very gradual change—in 1874, for example, 11,548 sailing ships entered the Mersey against 7,638 driven by steam—and today one still meets occasionally ex-mariners who rounded the Horn under a spread of canvas. The word 'sailmaker' can be seen, though the letters become fainter each year, on buildings in the old part of the waterfront around Seabrow and Wapping.

Four years after the appearance of the *Etna*, a meeting was held which was to bring the world's first important railway line to Liverpool (with Edge Hill as the terminal) in 1830, the year before William Roscoe died. His lifetime had spanned a period of remarkable development, in particular of transport. When he

Hackins Hey

was born (in 1753), Liverpool was still relatively a minor port and had only one road fit for a carriage, the turnpike that ran by Knowsley to St. Helens. The nearest point on a stage-coach route was Warrington and most of those who travelled to the Mersey from London rode uncomfortably on one of the horses that left the capital every Friday morning with goods and mail and reached their destination on Monday night. Roscoe was 7 when the first London bound coach left Liverpool's Golden Talbot Inn owned by a Mrs. Rathbone.

This was the year that James Brindley completed the canal commissioned by the Duke of Bridgewater to carry coal from his pits at Worsley to Manchester. There was an earlier canal—the first, in fact, in England—connecting St. Helens with the Mersey and the work of two Liverpool men, John Eyres, a surveyor, and Henry Berry, an engineer, at the docks; but Brindley's project was much the more important because the canal was very soon extended to Runcorn, thus providing a route by boat between the Mersey and Manchester and emphatically reducing transport costs. Because of the high profits being made by the Duke (about £80,000 a year), Liverpool money was quickly found for a canal from the Mersey over the Pennines to Leeds. The first section was in use by 1774, though it was 1819 before the entire length of the waterway—serving Lancashire cotton towns as well as West Riding woollen mills—was completed. In the meantime the Duke's own dock had been made in the port as a terminal for Bridgewater Canal traffic; and by it was constructed a very large warehouse with six floors and a frame of cast-iron, which was opened in 1811. This striking building, in the classical style, which barges entered through handsome arches almost Venetian in their appearance, endured until 1966, having triumphantly survived Hitler's bombs.

Yet, although the Bridgewater Canal was such a success as a commercial tributary of the port, it was because the tolls for its use were considered to have become extortionate that the merchants in Liverpool and Manchester began to cast about for an alternative way of transporting goods overland. At a joint meeting in 1821 they decided to commission George Stephenson to construct what the Duke called 'a damned tramroad', and it was Stephenson himself who drove the locomotive Northumbrian which hauled the first train into Edge Hill. Whether William

Bank of England

F

Roscoe was able, in his advanced years, to be a witness of this historic event is not recorded, but Liverpool's M.P. of that time, William Huskisson, certainly left a sick bed to be present.

He was anxious to end a political breach with the Duke of Wellington which had opened the year before. When the train arrived with the Duke an imposing figure in the first carriage, Huskisson stepped forward in excitement. He slipped and fell in front of another locomotive, the Rocket, which passed over one of his legs and he died a few hours later. Thus he was the first man to be killed by a train.

Another event in Roscoe's lifetime to prove of immense importance in Liverpool's development was the appointment in 1824 of Jesse Hartley, a burly Yorkshireman, as Liverpool's Dock Engineer. At the time the choice was surprising because Hartley, in his mid-forties, had no marine experience (having been bridge-master to the West Riding) and the Mersey presented then—as it still does—manifold complexities including persistent silting, which Thomas Steers, the first Dockmaster, had been unable to prevent a century earlier. Hartley was also slow in speech and rough in manner and dress. But he was to prove not only an engineer of exceptional capability but also the outstanding architect of dock buildings in the first half of the nineteenth century.

His favourite material was granite, and it was shipped down from Scotland by a fleet of vessels for his quays, river wall and some of the fortress-like constructions on them. These were to withstand astonishingly in the next century nightly pounding from German bombers. At about the same time that Hartley was extending the docks on the Lancashire side of the Mersey, C. E. Rendel was building quays on the opposite bank for merchants of Chester anxious to recoup some of the trade they had lost to Liverpool; yet these began to yield to the action of the tides and weather after so comparatively brief a period that it was Hartley's son—his associate in much of his later Liverpool work—who was called upon to reconstruct them.

Two years after Jesse Hartley's arrival, the unsatisfactory Old Dock was closed, leaving Salthouse (1753), George's (1761), Queen's (1796, enlarged 1816), Duke's (1811) and Prince's (1821). Before George Stephenson had completed the railway line from Manchester, Hartley had opened Canning Dock and this was followed, to the south, by Brunswick Dock, and, to the north, by Victoria and Trafalgar Docks which were operating by 1836.

Hartley's supreme achievement was Albert Dock, opened by the Prince Consort in 1845. It cost £722,000 but almost half this sum was spent on the great warehouses enclosing it and which stand today as an eloquent memorial to this master engineer and to his co-architect, Philip Hardwick, who designed the office block's impressive portico, constructed entirely of cast-iron and supported by four Tuscan columns, reminiscent of an Italian lakeside temple rather than a grubby, northern dockside. More columns in cast-iron make a quayside colonnade; and the lower portion of the brickwork of four storeys towering above them has archways of muscular grace.

In 1966 a development company proposed to tear down the great buildings, replacing them with office anthills in which 50,000 would work. This project was opposed in important particulars by those who considered that at least part of Hartley's warehouses ought to be preserved as a memorial to nineteenth-century mercantile dynamism; and that here should be housed the maritime museum for so long mooted in the port but without progress beyond tentative plans.

Four years later, and just as options on the fifty-two-acre site were about to run out, the company produced a fresh scheme. This was for 'Aquarius City', costing £100 million, wherein the basins of Albert, Salthouse and Canning Docks were to be submarine car parks, above them lakes for pleasure craft; and where tower blocks—one of them of forty-four storeys and 450 feet high—would, with other buildings, have provided 5 million square feet of office space, accommodated the maritime museum and also contained shops and restaurants. In the last days of 1970 this project was abandoned but new plans, less grandiose, may follow. The purpose for which Hartley's mighty storehouses were built has largely gone in the new age of containered cargoes; and, in this city of very high unemployment, tens of thousands of new jobs are unquestionably more important than commercial monuments that, in idleness, would be exceedingly expensive to maintain.

Eight more docks had been added to the Liverpool waterfront when, in 1857, the Mersey Docks and Harbour Board was created to control both sides of the river. For some years before this nearly half of all Britain's imports were entering via Liverpool, and the annual quantity of raw cotton landed in the port had multiplied by 200 times in under fifty years, the increase in other cargoes being almost as emphatic.

Yet, in spite of this tremendous expansion, poverty in the town still remained worse than anywhere in the country. Many of the Irish immigrants were living two or three families to a single room with not so much as a ragged curtain to separate them. At least a third of the population now lived in courts without any sanitation—indeed, fewer than half the streets had sewers and most of these were open. Cholera (which had taken grievous toll in the 1830s) and typhoid constantly threatened. The conditions were at their most appalling in the district between Scotland Road and Vauxhall Road, where large numbers of Irish had settled and in 1855 the army were called in to quell hunger riots in this neighbourhood.

The dire effect of the American Civil War on transatlantic shipping further increased distress in the overcrowded downtown areas; and yet—another Liverpool paradox—fortunes were made in the business quarter in speculative dealing in raw cotton. Supplies of cotton by normal means had, of course, practically ceased; but fast clippers from the Mersey from time to time broke through the blockade of Charleston and returned with cargoes which sold at wildly inflated prices. These plunged catastrophically when the Civil War ended, and total losses in a matter of a few months were put at £12,000,000.

Two Liverpool banks failed, a number of hitherto wealthy citizens were brought either to bankruptcy or the brink of it, and clippers, with no blockade to run, lay rotting on the shore at Birkenhead, where the Confederate warship *Alabama* had been built at considerable political risk.

In the same decade as the Civil War the Corporation pioneered municipal housing with a four-storey tenement block named St. Martin's Cottages (they still stand) accommodating 124 families. This was a minute rescue operation in a town ridden with rotting slums; nevertheless it was a beginning and also the bricks-and-mortar evidence of a re-awakened social conscience—re-awakened because there had been a number of examples of initiative in relieving distress before this but which punctuated periods of indifference. Evidently there was one such period in the 1850s for an investigation showed that more than half the money raised for all the charities in the town came out of a mere 700 pockets. Earlier in the century—in fact, until the reform of the Poor Law in 1835—some of the wealthiest families did not even pay the poor rate, being resident outside the few streets then subject to this levy.

The earliest Liverpool philanthropist of consequence was Bryan Blundell, master of the *Mulberry*, one of the first ships to enter the Old Dock on its completion in 1715. He made money out of the shipment of Africans long before this became a significant factor in Liverpool's economy; but he was also concerned in the transport of hundreds of emigrants, not much better than white slaves, who were put in bond, while in this country, to Virginian planters.

The plight of these wretched and illiterate people, settlers by compulsion, distressed him and he resolved to found Liverpool's first charity school. It was completed in 1718, and today, as Bluecoat Chambers, survives in grace and in usefulness, as will be seen when it is visited in a later chapter. Blundell gave up the sea to be the school's treasurer, an office he held for forty-two years, devoting a tenth of his annual income—much of it from the proceeds of slaving and privateering—to the charity.

In Blundell's lifetime an infirmary was built on the site to be occupied, in the next century, by St. George's Hall. Adjoining it was a hospital for seamen and their families, which was maintained by a compulsory contribution of 6d. a month from every seafarer in the port. A public dispensary founded some years later to provide the poor with medicine had to rely, however, on voluntary donations and was from time to time in financial difficulty. The self-elected borough councillors and those who administered church charities alternated acts of generosity with determined efforts to cut the cost of caring for the growing poor.

So, in the remaining period of the eighteenth century and the early part of the nineteenth, the needy had to rely very largely upon the benevolence of a few individuals such as William Roscoe and some of his fellow Unitarians. The Rathbone family, who were wealthy merchants, were notable benefactors, and another was Edward Rushton, a blind poet, who founded a school for blind children.

Rushton lost his sight as a youth of 19 when aboard a slave ship in which a number of the captives were stricken with a particularly malignant form of ophthalmia which was contagious. He insisted on entering the holds to comfort sufferers and caught the disease. When he returned to his Liverpool home incurably blind he was turned out of the house by his stepmother.

The school he established was moved in 1825 to premises which, in recent years, became the city's police headquarters—a circumstance not, of course, neglected by Liverpool wits and particularly when the breathalyser was introduced.

The first of the cholera epidemics (in 1833) produced a heroine whose upbringing had been very different from that of Roscoe, the Rathbones and the Unitarian altruists. Kitty Wilkinson migrated with her parents from Londonderry to Liverpool where her mother became insane. Kitty's first husband, a sailor, left her a penniless widow, and she became the wife of a porter in the Rathbones' warehouse. When the cholera struck she opened her cellar as a wash-house for the clothing and bedding of victims, and she adopted several children who were orphaned as a result of the epidemic. Kitty received practical help, as well as encouragement, from Mrs. William Rathbone, who was prominent in the movement that brought the country's first public baths and wash-houses, the Wilkinsons being appointed superintendents.

Another who worked tirelessly for the sufferers from cholera was the Rev. John Johns, who had charge of a domestic mission founded by the Unitarians. In one of his annual reports he wrote: 'Mothers newly become such without a garment on their persons and, with infants nearly as naked, lying upon straw or shavings under a miserable covering, without fire or food.' The aged, he said, shivered out their last hours of life in absolute want, and children were made to beg.

No doubt such accounts from those giving dedicated service helped to generate some civic sense of responsibility. Having established the country's first public wash-houses, the Corporation in 1846 appointed the country's first public health officer, the position going to Dr. William Duncan, who had for some years been working in the town's public dispensaries and had spoken passionately about the misery in which so many lived through no fault of their own.

But Duncan's powers were severely limited, and within a few months he was overwhelmed by plagues resulting from the tidal wave of Irish immigration. There were nearly 6,000 deaths from fever and 2,500 from dysentery. In the fearfully congested Vauxhall Road area alone death claimed a seventh of the population, and Duncan estimated that, in the town as a whole, nearly 60,000 caught the fever and 40,000 contracted dysentery. Twenty-four Catholic priests tried valiantly to attend to the spiritual and other needs of these legions of desperately sick in cellars and courts. In so doing, ten of them died and they have been revered ever since in the churches of the Catholic diocese as 'the Liverpool martyrs'.

Then came another notable step forward—the introduction for the first time in this country of district nursing. The system was initiated by William Rathbone as a consequence of the skill and devotion of the woman who nursed his wife. When Mrs. Rathbone died, he engaged the nurse to attend to the needs of sick paupers for an experimental period of three months. After a month she told him that she could no longer endure seeing the wretchedness in which her patients lived; but Rathbone prevailed upon her to continue and then, having sought the counsel of Florence Nightingale, established a training school for nurses which still exists. The founder of district nursing was the grandfather of Eleanor Rathbone, great social reformer of the present century. The family name is borne by a Liverpool hospital and a Liverpool University hall of residence occupying the family's former home.

Almost coinciding with the start of William Rathbone's nursing enterprise, an inspired humanitarian in priestly clothing came to the forefront of the comparatively small band engaged in the relief of poverty and squalor. This was Father (later Monsignor) James Nugent, Liverpool born, his father an Irish immigrant. When he returned to his native town after training for the priesthood he was shocked, particularly, by the plight of thousands of small children trying to make enough money for a meal by selling matches, shining shoes and singing in the street until late at night.

To take a few of them off the streets he opened a Ragged School in a tumbledown building which was reputed to have been haunted. There were some thirty such schools at that time in Liverpool, providing shelter rather than education but this only by day, the children being turned out to fend for themselves as best they could at night. Father Nugent pressed for much more to be done, and soon found allies in William Rathbone and Edward Rushton, the stipendiary magistrate, related to the blind poet who had earlier founded the school for the blind. Their efforts culminated in a town's meeting in 1854 with 'Save the Child' as its slogan.

A significant aspect of this meeting was that the platform was shared by a prominent Orange clergyman, the Catholic Bishop and the leader of the Unitarians. It was perhaps the first time in England that there had been such unity between churchmen of differing creeds, and it dramatically emphasised the gravity of the position.

One of Father Nugent's partners in the cause of rescuing children was an Anglican, Canon Major Lester, Vicar of St. Mary's, Kirkdale, from 1855 to 1903. They became devoted friends and were often to be seen walking arm and arm in the street as they planned new measures to relieve the burden of poverty suffered by the young. But there were Catholics who resented this bond between the two men, and Major Lester encountered similar hostility in his Church. Such bigotry did not affect their friendship, but it did from time to time hamper their untiring efforts to raise money. They also met with some antagonism from well-to-do people, living in the fine hilltop avenues around Falkner Square, who were both anti-Catholic and anti-Irish and considered that the poor were mainly victims of their own fecklessness, if not villainy.

Vice, crime and drunkenness were certainly rampant, and there were two large sectors into which the respectable would not venture by day in a carriage, let alone after dark on foot. One of these was the area around Scotland and Vauxhall Roads and the other along the waterfront, the two neighbourhoods sharing some 2,000 public houses and grog shops—'drunk for a penny, blind for twopence'—many of these the scene of nightly disorder comparable with the riotous behaviour of privateersmen a century before.

In his later years Father Nugent laboured hard in the cause of total abstinence. Before and during this period he found homes in the United States and Canada for numbers of Liverpool orphans, many of whom later prospered and whose descendants must now be numerous in the two countries, both of which the good Father toured on errands of mercy.

He had the fire of a noncomformist evangelist but had inherited from his father a strong Irish sense of humour. He cared little for his appearance, and for years wore a top hat that was green with age. When he died in 1905 the *Liverpool Daily Post and Courier* devoted nine columns to his obituary, and the newspaper's leader that day read: 'Monsignor Nugent was as much trusted and as freely afforded money resources by Protestants as by his co-religionists. No one thought of differences under Nugent's gracious glamour except the differences between good and evil, light and darkness, hope and despair.'

An appealing statue in St. John's Gardens, close to St. George's Hall, depicts him with an arm round the shoulders of a barefooted waif. There is another monument in the Gardens to Canon Lester, who died in 1903. They are as symbolic as those two Cathedrals, one at each end of the street called Hope.

Another philanthropist in the second half of the nineteenth century was Josephine Butler, a great aunt of the present Lord Butler. She was the wife of the then headmaster of Liverpool College and provided a home for the sick and incurable poor and also industrial trainng for healthy waifs and strays. Care for young sufferers from poverty was increased with the introduction of a Liverpool Society for the Prevention of Cruelty to Children (formed a year earlier than the national body) which opened a shelter where children found wandering the streets by night could be fed and clothed. There is an emotional novel about two of the waifs of those times that is still read by Liverpool children in 1970—*Her Benny*, written by the Rev. Silas K. Hocking. More than 200,000 copies of the book have been sold.

One of Liverpool's outstanding benefactors was a Jew, David Lewis, who came from London at the age of 16 and in 1856 established the modest outfitter's shop that was to develop into a great store—the one that now has Epstein's striding man on a ship's bows above its main entrance. From the fortune Lewis left to Liverpool and Manchester came funds to build a hospital and also an hotel and club for working-class men, where in later years

Frederick Marquis, who was to become the first Lord Woolton, served as warden. Louis Cohen, a bearded patriarchal figure who took over control of Lewis's in 1886, was also prominent in philanthropy, and his eldest son presented Liverpool University with a £100,000 library.

Throughout the nineteenth century and the early years of the twentieth, the waterfront district around the Customs House, Canning Place, Park Lane and Cleveland Square was perpetually the resort of hundreds of sailors eager to spend their pay and end months of celibacy. It was accordingly the hunting ground of harlots, thieves, confidence tricksters and also of the crimps who had taken the place of the old press gangs.

The attractions were sin deep. This was the territory of Maggie May—'dressed in a gown so fine, like a frigate of the line, cruisin' up and down old Canning Place'—and others in the sisterhood of shame like Harriet Lane, Jumping Jenny, Cast-Iron Kitty and a tart who was known as 'The Dreadnought'.

Every seafarer with a money belt ran the gauntlet of their blandishments as he lurched along Paradise Street bound for the wheels of fortune and all the other devices to reduce the weight of that belt. These catchpennies abounded in dives along one part of Lime Street and under naphtha flares in its sordid byways; and when the sailor and his escort—as highly painted as any voluptuous figurehead that adorned a prow—had had their fill of these delights they made their unsteady passage back to the dockside area, first visiting the crowded saloons, then going on to some seedy brothel or a boarding house run by a retired prostitute who was often in the pay of the arch-crimps like Shanghai Davies and Da Costa the Yank.

Many, many a spree ashore ended with the sailor dragged from his bed and hustled along cellar passages, or down the dark alleys cleft in tall, brooding warehouses, to the quayside and so aboard a ship ready to sail on the next tide, perhaps bound, round the Horn, for Californ-i-a, perhaps for the China Sea. There was a landlady of seamen's lodgings in Pitt Street—she was known as Ma Smyrden—who bamboozled crimps into shanghai-ing a corpse.

To provide sailors with a sanctuary from harridan landladies, harlots and crimps, the Seamen's Friend Society, founded in the

1820s, acquired the battleship *Tees*, a veteran of Trafalgar and the Nile and known grimly as 'the flogging *Tees*'. She was moored in one of the Liverpool docks to provide quarters for mariners in port; but there was space for only a small fraction of the hundreds ashore every night.

In 1845 shipowners and merchants commissioned John Cunningham to design the Sailors' Home. It was opened three years later and did not close until February 1969, when the Corporation refused to renew a fire certificate for the building until nearly £30,000 had been spent on reconstruction. At the time of writing, this astonishing building still stands in Canning Place, one of its neighbours a brand new block (named after Thomas Steers) with a midnight-blue face, and another the stream-lined School of Nautical Catering, which has an outsize anchor in its forecourt and is, in my view, one of the most handsome of the additions made to the city in the sixties. By the time this book is published the Sailors' Home may have disappeared.

The home was built with little regard for expense and the architect was allowed prodigally to waste space. In designing its exterior Cunningham must have had Derbyshire's Hardwick Hall, built by Bess of Hardwick, Countess of Shrewsbury, in mind because the mullion windows of Victorian home and Elizabethan hall are practically identical, and the two share other character-istics. But inside his pseudo-Elizabethan shell Cunningham built five tiers of cabins, entered from galleries in the shape of a *V*, which he supported with decorative cast-iron pillars and fenced with elaborately moulded iron balustrades, some taking the form of ropes and knots, others decorated with mermaids and sportive dolphins. The home must have seemed palatial to the first occupiers of its 140 individual cabins after months of sleeping, close as corpses, in damp hammocks or on paillasses in crowded fo'c'sles; though looking giddily down from the highest of the five galleries to the court far below will have reminded them of the view, amongst the royals, of a heaving deck.

Despite damage from Second World War bombs, it did not close its doors on a sailor, sober or drunk, between 1848 and 1969 (when it was charging only 15s. a day for a cabin, three hot meals, TV and billiards). But it could no longer meet the requirements of the modern mariner, as much a technician as a seaman, and the refusal to renew its fire certificate was its death sentence. Crews are smaller than they were, and there is no shortage of good accommodation for Jack temporarily ashore in Liverpool; but a need does exist for quarters suitable for retired seafarers and more than half the cabins in the replacement home which is to be built will be reserved for them.

Close to the Sailors' Home is the Gordon Smith Institute for Seamen, run by the Seamen's Friend Society which so long ago acquired the old *Tees*. The Institute was opened in 1898, the gift of an M.P. and named in memory of his son, and it continues in useful service particularly to sailors from Africa and Asia. Atlantic House, the Stella Maris, Plimsoll House (in one of those former homes of the wealthy in Gambier Terrace) and the Mersey Mission to Seamen also provide bed, board and relaxation.

The old-style sailor is fast disappearing, yet there are still men who, when they go ashore in Liverpool, hand over their pay to a publican for safe keeping. This was the customary practice until after the First World War, despite the fact that safes specifically for this purpose were available at the Sailors' Home, the Gordon Smith Institute and other hostels. It must be said that this trust in Liverpool licensees was rarely abused. In the early years of this century seamen had a particular friend in the landlady of the 'Duke's Crown' in Wapping, a widow known through the Seven Seas as 'Fat Annie'—she was Mrs. Cunningham to her face—who was a former schoolma'am; and the likes of Maggie May got no change out of her.

The 'Duke's Crown' still stands (though it is in a block due for redevelopment), and so does the 'Baltic Fleet', the height of respectability nowadays but the scene of many a nineteenth-century fracas. Other famous waterfront pubs of the past were the 'Homeward Bound', the 'Lighthouse', the 'Man at the Wheel' and the 'Baltimore Clipper', this last kept for many years by 'Handsome Mary' (who was anything but).

In the time when they were in their heyday, youths with romantic notions—and others, more desperate, seeking a way to get out of the country—were often to be found in the grog shops asking how they could get to sea. They were undeterred by the tales of hard-lying and bad food which resulted in a seamen's strike in 1889. Sir James Sexton, recalling his own experiences at the time, wrote that the rations 'consisted entirely of weevily biscuit, salt horse—meant to be consumed on its first voyage but now being on its third or fourth—"coffee" made of burned beans, sweetened with filthy molasses, and cracker hash made nice and tasty by dead weevils and ships' cockroaches added indiscriminately and freely. . . .'

Crimps were not interested in recruiting greenhorns; but for the landlubber longing for a taste of the sea there was Paddy West's.

> As I was a 'rollin' down Great Howard Street
> I strolled into Paddy West's house.
> He gave me a plate of American hash
> And swore it was Liverpool scouse.
> Said he, 'Now young feller you're here just in time,
> For aboard a big clipper you'll very soon sign.'

In that house in Great Howard Street (on the opposite side of Pier Head from the Sailors' Home) the Paddy West course produced instant seamen. The candidate was taken to the attic to be taught to furl a main royal (it was an ordinary window blind) and, this lesson over, his hands were placed on a ship's wheel. As he turned it, his feet firmly apart, a bucket of cold water was thrown over him to help him appreciate how it would be when he was helmsman on watch in the teeth of a gale.

In the parlour the aspiring shellback walked several times round a table on which was a cow's horn and in an adjoining passage he stepped over a length of codline. Thus he had rounded 'the Horn' more than once and also crossed 'the Line'. He was then given the papers of a deceased seamen (no doubt one who had come to a violent end in a dockland fight), a wellworn sea chest containing old gear, and salt-stained cast-off clothing; and there he was, quite the Hellfire Jack, until the ship luckless enough to have him in her crew ran into the first Irish Sea roller. His first two months' pay was mortgaged to pay for his tuition in Paddy West's 'nautical school'.

Thus 'Paddy Wester' came to mean any greenhorn, whether he had been to the house in Great Howard Street or not. I wonder how many of Paddy's wretched dupes, later to learn seamanship the hard way, and how many victims of crimps, watched the Liverpool waterfront disappear in the mist from aboard a ship as she passed Perch Rock bound for a far distant shore and who then shared the melancholy of the anonymous writer of the shanty that runs:

> Well, I've shipped on a Yankee clipper ship,
> *Davy Crockett* is her name;
> And Burgess is her captain
> And they say she's a floating shame.
>
> So fare thee well, my own true love,
> When I return united we will be.
> It's not the leaving of Liverpool that grieves me
> But me darlin' when I think of thee.
>
> Farewell to Lower Frederick Street,
> Anson Terrace and Park Lane,
> For I know it's going to be some little time
> Before I see you again.

The tune of that old song is in a suite composed in 1970 by Professor Raymond Warren for the Liverpool Schools' Junior Orchestra. When I hear it sung by the Spinners with its haunting mouth organ obbligato it always moves me—perhaps because there were occasions when I too have sailed out into Liverpool Bay on an evening flood not knowing when I would once more set eyes upon those dirty waters that leave their daily tidemark on the Mersey wall.

In the first decade of the twentieth century began the Mersey's era of regal Cunard and White Star liners, providing a new concept in transatlantic travel, though with no revolutionary improvements, I have been told by those with first-hand experience, in the crews' quarters. These were cramped and sharply in contrast with the opulent accommodation for first-class passengers; but Merseysiders found pride in serving in these great ships bearing the name of Liverpool on their stern.

Every vantage point by the river was crowded on the day in 1907 that the four-funnelled *Lusitania* sailed on her maiden voyage to New York and there was still greater excitement when news came that she had made a record crossing in four days, nineteen hours and fifty-two minutes. Many are still alive, of course, who recall the old 'Morrie' (the *Mauretania*) reducing this time by nine hours eleven minutes in 1911. Those were the years when boat trains arrived regularly at the Riverside Station, distinguished personages among the thousands of passengers who, from the crowded platform, made their way to the gangways of splendid ships bound for the United States, Canada, South America, the Cape, India, the Far East and Australia. Today that station is a forlorn and grubby shell.

Numbers of Merseyside families lost a breadwinner in the *Titanic* (though she did not sail from Liverpool) and when the *Lusitania* met her end there was anti-German rioting in the port. Shopkeepers with German or indeed foreign-sounding names (some of them were in fact the children of Jewish refugees from Russia) had their premises looted.

The years of the First World War brought a period of relative prosperity to most Merseysiders who were not in uniform, the docks always full and the shipyards on the Birkenhead side of the river at maximum production. For many thousands of Americans on their way to France, Liverpool was the first European landfall, and the people of the city gladly played host. But with the peace came the return of poverty; and the August Bank Holiday weekend of 1919 brought the worst riots in Liverpool since the sailors' uprising of 1775.

Primarily they were the result of a strike for higher pay by 930 of the city's police force of 2,270, but there is no doubt that the reappearance of unemployment and destitution was a significant contributory factor. Mobs at first roamed the Scotland Road area then broke into bottling stores and stole a vast quantity of beer. This was distributed among the rioters, who moved into London Road, a shopping thoroughfare near Lime Street Station, where, brandishing empty bottles, they smashed windows and pillaged goods on display. The road and pavements were soon strewn with discarded loot.

Police who had remained on duty charged with batons drawn but could not contain the rioters. The navy and the army therefore became involved, the dreadnought *Valiant* and two destroyers sailing at all speed to the Mersey, while troops moved into Lime Street and were quartered in St. George's Hall. Tanks assembled on the plateau by the Hall ready for action.

On the worst day of the weekend shots were fired, a man was killed and several were wounded. Yet even this grim affair had a typically Liverpudlian streak of comedy for one of the worst hold-ups of traffic was caused by a mass game of housey-housey, the participants squatting in the roadway and on tramlines, refusing, but amicably, to budge. When peace was at last restored more than 400 were charged with looting and other offences. The strikers were dismissed from the force and it was not until 1927 that they (or their relatives) received money they had contributed, during their service, towards pensions.

The end of free trade and the acute depression on both sides of the Atlantic brought more suffering and mainly to those areas where there had been such desperate privation less than half a century before. By 1930 one man in four was out of work. So, beneath the Mersey, another tunnel was dug, as much to provide employment as to speed communication between the two sides of the river. Tall, austere buildings containing ventilating equipment became new landmarks in both Liverpool and Birkenhead, one of these towers joining the trinity of buildings near the Pier Head.

In 1934 the longest underwater highway in the world was royally opened and proclaimed a marvel of engineering—as indeed it was and is still, notwithstanding all the harsh epithets used by thousands of motorists in times of frustration during the past twenty years. The blame for their costly inconvenience is not, as was explained in chapter one, with the designers of the Tunnel who could not possibly have foreseen the developments the next thirty years were to bring.

There are numerous inhabitants of the Liverpool of the 1970s who remember going barefoot to school; and though that was a long time ago it will be a longer time before the city is without a host of children in need. Resources of the city's branch of the N.S.P.C.C., the movement that began in the Liverpool slums; of the Catholic Children's Protection Society, founded through the compassion of Monsignor Nugent in 1881, and of the Child Welfare Association, remain fully committed. Family Service Units, an organisation which has now reached other large cities and extricates parents who are incapable of caring either for their children or themselves, is still at full stretch in the port where it originated. The Liverpool Vigilance Association's staff continues to protect from the moral hazards of the waterfront the girls who arrive in the port from Ireland and elsewhere with little money and no experience of big city life (it must be added here that,

The Town Hall
The Town Hall's smaller ballroom

without the annual influx of girls from the other side of the Irish Sea, Liverpool hospitals would be critically short of nurses under training and domestic staff).

The nineteenth-century hovels have nearly all gone; but there are still many in Liverpool who live in houses which have become slums in the last quarter of a century and where conditions are deplorable. In one street in the Toxteth area of the city in 1970 there were 118 people (sixty-three families) living in 11 homes where they shared 14 baths and 16 w.c.s. In some instances they were sleeping three to a room. As much as £3 a week was being charged in rent for a single room in some of the houses where the backyard was let to a haulage contractor; and the gross weekly income to the landlord was £28. Is it any wonder that vice and vandalism are rampant in this district of Liverpool?

In the dreary, dusty Corporation flats that replaced slums on the slope of Brownlow Hill, off Scotland Road and in the vicinity of Park Lane there are the obvious symptoms of social malaise. Offices of the Personal Service Society, which runs citizens' advice bureaux and provides other welfare facilities, and those of the Women's Royal Voluntary Service are still busy every day of the week. The League of Welldoers (formed in 1893) continues to look after as many who are in want, of all ages, as ever it did.

Neighbourhood units and community groups are a comparatively recent development in the districts of Corporation flats and a number of them have made heartening progress under the persuasive and unwavering leadership of men like the bearded Terry Gold. His sphere of operation, off Brownlow Hill, is the 'Bull Ring' (so called because the galleried flats are in a circle and because there was once some sort of cattle market and also an abattoir here). In the Brontë Centre, which is part of the 'Bull Ring's' community set-up, hitherto wayward youth now sits in council devising means to combat hooliganism and to repair the ravages of vandals. One of the several encouraging consequences of this type of social work has been a lessening of the ingrained antagonism among tenants against officers of the 'Corpy'; but, even so, the authority withdrew many of its rent collectors from rounds of flats because cases of assault upon them had become so frequent.

Young Volunteers of Merseyside, a body that co-ordinates the voluntary service of hundreds of youngsters, the University's

The Albany
G

strong corps of social workers and a large number of societies caring for the old, the lonely and the handicapped are all operating to the limit of their means. Much of the philantrophic work is financed by the United Voluntary Organisation, to which go contributions deducted every week from tens of thousands of Merseyside pay packets. All this is, of course, additional to the work of State Social Security and Corporation welfare, both of these also under pressure.

'What shall we do with the drunken sailor?' no longer poses a significant problem, though Liverpool has a bad record for insobriety particularly among young people. Some of the sea-farers of the 1970s are involved in a worse vice than drunkenness. From time to time the rings of dope smugglers, distributors and pedlars are broken only for others to be formed. The forces ranged against drug-trafficking in marijuana, heroin and the once-lawful opium (there was a period when some Liverpool merchants made fat profits from it) are dedicated but depleted; and this evil commerce will continue, with high earnings for those who evade the law, for as long as there are addicts desperate for supplies.

This chapter, and the one that preceded it, have shown how the mould of the Liverpudlian was filled from a crucible wherein fused privation, squalor, inhumanity and violence but also adventure, courage, farsightedness and intellectual vitality.

The surprise is that the dominant characteristic produced from such an extraordinary alchemy is an inimitable sense of humour. This is resilient to changing fortunes, is pungent yet peaty and has composed a vocabulary that, even when he has lost his adenoidal accent, will distinguish the Liverpudlian in whatever company he keeps.

FOUR

LIVERPUDLIANS

Rob Wilton, Tommy Handley, Arthur Askey, Ted Ray, Ken Dodd and Jimmy Tarbuck are six names from generations of famous funny men who were cradled in a city where, for as long as anyone can remember, it has been claimed with a perverse pride that 'you have to be a ruddy comedian to stick the place'. Merseyside-born comics have not, in fact, been more numerous than their compatriots in other echelons of entertainment (using this word in the widest sense) and have been fewer than the musicians produced by the region in the twentieth century; but, through them, the Liverpool lingo has been dinned into the ears of an ever-widening audience since the early days of 'the wireless'; and nowadays, through TV, Knotty Ash (the Liverpool suburb wherein lie Ken Dodd's 'jam butty mines') is as nationally well-known as once were 'Frisby Dyke' and 'Poppy Poupart', characters in the late Tommy Handley's 'ITMA'.

Tommy used names that were familiar to him in boyhood. Frisby Dyke—played in 'ITMA' by Liverpool-born Deryck Guyler—appeared over the windows of a drapery store in Lord Street for many years before the last war; and Poupart is the name of a firm of wholesale fruit salesmen (still in business) and, until demolition work in the last weeks of 1969, was on a sign a few yards from the stage door of the city's Royal Court Theatre—where, of course, Tommy appeared. I have been told that, before 'ITMA', very few people referred to Liverpudlians as 'Scousers' or to their language as 'scouse'. This word then meant, generally speaking, only the stew made from cheap cuts of mutton, potatoes and onions and originally favoured by Scandinavian (and perhaps

some German) sailors who called it 'lobscouse' and, from neces-
sity, substituted ship's biscuits for the vegetables after the first few
days at sea.

It seems most likely that the dish was familiar in Liverpool
before the arrival of Scandinavian crews in the port brought it a
specific name, for it was obviously suited to the impoverished
families of the nineteenth century. Very often they had to forego
the mutton to flavour their potatoes and onions and the result was
then 'blind scouse'. Even in its most refined form—that is with
pickled cabbage—it is (anyway to me) still undistinguished, and I
doubt if there are many families in present-day Liverpool who
eat it once a year. Coal fire ovens have largely disappeared, and
the cost of electricity and gas being what it is, fish and chips
cooked in a shop are probably as cheap as scouse. Proprietors of
some restaurants in the city who put on scouse as a gimmick in
recent years found the demand for it was negligible.

Fritz Spiegl (born in Austria but long established in the city as
musician, wit and collector of Liverpudliana) discovered a
comedy entitled *The Sailor's Farewell*, printed in Liverpool in
1768, in which a character, speaking in dialect, said admiringly
of a virile Guinea chief with many wives, 'he must be a wacker,
ecod'. So perhaps 'wacker' was the first of the sobriquets for a
Liverpudlian. It is still the one used most by Liverpudlians though
these days usually abbreviated to 'wack'.

Fritz suggests in his introduction to *Lern Yerself Scouse* (an
invaluable phrase book by Frank Shaw, who was an enormously
genial retired Customs officer and a leading authority on the
vocabulary and traditions of his native city) that 'wacker' may
also have come from a dish—'pea wack' (pea soup). I dare to
differ with him and think that the root is the word 'wack' as used
in the North and in the Midlands to mean share—'I'll stand my
wack' and 'Give me my wack' are phrases still in common use.
So a mate, and particularly a shipmate, became a 'wacker' whose
friends shared with him and he with them.

'Dicky Sam' was a nickname in vogue from about the mid-
nineteenth century to the First World War, and almost certainly
this came from Richard Samuels, the landlord of a pub much
frequented by seafarers. It stood on Mann Island, then truly an
island and connected to the waterfront by an iron bridge over
which horse trams at one time rattled. The genuine 'Dicky Sam'

was probably born within a mile of the Mersey wall and earned his living at sea or in the docks.

It was once possible, I understand, for a student of the Liverpool dialect to be able accurately to determine the district of birth by inflexions in speech. The mass shift of population due to slum clearance and for other reasons has largely removed such differences, which were quite subtle, anyway; though, as a very rough and ready guide, it can be said that north of Pier Head the speech becomes a throatier and more catarrhal sound whereas to the south it has a more pronounced cadence, the penultimate word in a sentence being at the highest note. The native of the Cheshire side of the river introduces a faint whine, is not so emphatic in pronouncing chair 'churr' and is less likely to drop the 'h' in 'thing' and 'think'.

Until Liverpudlians began to live in large numbers outside boundaries of their native city the accent disappeared short of Widnes, St. Helens, Ormskirk, Formby and mid-Wirral so the 'scouse'-speaking region had, until quite recently, a range of under 10 miles, much smaller than the areas in which 'Geordie' and 'Brummagem' are spoken. On the other hand Liverpool voices are heard in any port between Chicago (ships sail regularly in summer from the Mersey to Lake Michigan) and the Cook Strait.

When I was in a suburb of Marseilles a few hours before the Germans in that city surrendered, I was astonished by a woman's joyous cry of 'Eh thurr, wack!' from across the street. I had been sighted—her first Englishman for years—by the wife of a Chinese who had lived in Marseilles for twenty years or more but still had an accent that could not have been more patent had she stayed all her days in her native Bootle. I am ashamed to say that for some minutes, I suspected her of being an enemy agent. Her children, all born in Marseilles, spoke English with a faint Liverpool twang!

It is impossible to write the Liverpool dialect phonetically. Even the sound of the 'pool' in 'Liverpool', when this is bayed in excitement from the celebrated Kop at Anfield, defies the printed word. 'Pewl' will not do, neither will 'poool'—the true pronunciation is between the two. There is a certain amount of pure Lancashire in the Liverpool speech—the bus conductor (the older generations call him 'the guard') goes upsturrs to collect furrs.

But the sound of 'ck' in 'back' is almost that of the 'ch' in the Welsh 'bach'; and there have, of course, been strong Irish influences so that, for example, the Liverpudlian, like the Dubliner, makes 'film' the two-syllable 'fillum'.

Most strangers find the Merseyside accent less incomprehensible than broad Geordie, Buchan Scots or the speech of a Yorkshire dalesman; and they can usually cope with such deformities of grammar as 'you should have went' and 'whurr is us sustifikit?' But they will be baffled by words in the Liverpudlian vocabulary, unless they arm themselves with Frank Shaw's *Lern Yerself Scouse* and its companion primer, *The ABZ of Scouse*. These aids had not been written when I arrived in Liverpool, and it took me weeks to become conversant with slang in everyday use.

'Abnabs' are sandwiches, so are 'sarneys', and if they are packaged for lunch they are 'me carryin' out'. A 'bevvy' is an alcoholic drink (normally, but not necessarily, beer), and to be 'bevvied' is to be drunk. A 'butty' is bread (which is also 'chuck') when it is buttered or spread with margarine (which is 'Maggie Ann'). 'Conny-onny' is condensed milk, and there was a time when 'conny-onny butties' were as popular with the young as 'jam butties' and 'bacon sarneys'. 'Come 'ead' is hurry up.

A 'cogger' can be either a Catholic or a footballer whose best foot is his left. 'Me da' ' is 'de owd feller' (father), 'diddy' is little, 'earwiggin' ' is eavesdropping, 'fades' are bruised apples and 'fender ale' is beer bought to consume at home. 'De gear' (lately adopted by many young people throughout Britain) is first-rate and 'kecks' are trousers.

A 'jowler' is a rather wider alley than a 'jigger', which is also a 'back entery'; and a 'jigger-rabbit' is a stray cat ('moggie'). A 'judy-scuffer' is a policewoman, a 'liblab' is a library and a 'lolliman' is a school crossing warden. 'Mojo' means methylated spirits, 'macing' is getting goods by fraud, 'mickies' are pigeons and 'ollies' are marbles.

A 'Paddy Kelly' is a dock policeman, 'saggin' ' is playing truant, 'scowin' ' is idling, 'sticky-lice' is liquorice and 'togo' is brown sugar. The ' 'urry-up cart' is the Black Maria (also called 'de battle-taxi'), a 'Wet Nelly' (much used in 'ITMA' scripts) is a Nelson cake and 'wingeing' is the whimpering of a petulant child.

Liverpudlians like to 'diddy-mise' words, thus best clothes are 'bezzies' and a bathing costume is a 'baydin' cozzie'. Biscuits are

'bickies' (so 'chocky bickies'), cigarettes are more frequently
'ciggies' than 'fags' and a 'cuzzie' is a Customs officer. 'Avvy' is
afternoon, 'ozzie' is hospital, 'proey' is programme and 'lanny' is
landing stage (Princes or Georges—and, incidentally, apostrophes
more often than not go by default on street and place nameplates
and on official maps. Queens Drive, the city's principal ring road,
is never given the possessive).

A number of street names have distinctive pronunciations.
Cazneau Street is 'Caz-er-new' Street, Ranelagh Street—a main
shopping thoroughfare—is 'Ranlee' Street and Beaufort Street is
'Bewfort' Street. Park Lane is today less frequently called 'Parkee
Lanee' than it was. This runs near what was the Chinese quarter
and 'Parkee Lanee' is supposed to have been an oriental version;
but I believe it was used long before the Chinese arrived in any
number. Gateacre, a heavily populated outer suburb with much
post-war Corporation housing, is pronounced 'Gatakker'.

Leece Street is invariably 'Leeces' Street and even Department
of Employment officials who work there, and are often non-
Liverpudlians, get into this habit. Seaforth has a number of streets
named after composers, one of them Verdi. It is always 'Vur-die'
Street.

Some Liverpool place and street names seem to have been
devised specially to suit the native's catarrhal accent: Fazakerley
(the 'ak' given a throaty, expectorating sound); Toxteth, Croxteth, Bixteth (the street leading to the city's stadium), Dingle,
Bootle (the 't' barely sounded), Garston (quite impossible to
write the wacker pronunciation of the first syllable; he gets the
same sound in 'car') and Warbreck, Melbreck, Orrell, Aigburth,
Zante, Booker, Cazneau, Fontenoy and (but of course) Knotty
Ash.

When I first came to live in the city I asked where Liverpool
Show (much more than an agricultural-cum-horticultural show)
was held and was informed 'on "The Mizzie" '. This is how the
native knows Wavertree Recreation Ground which was given
to the inhabitants of an area of the town anonymously and so
was called 'the Mystery' until it was 'diddy-mised'. I was also
completely baffled in those early days when, outside 'Markses', I
heard a small boy asking his 'mam' to buy him some 'desert-
wellies'. I knew that 'wellies' were Wellingtons but 'desert-
wellies'? They turned out to be sandals.

Liverpudlians have their own treasury of phrases: 'It's cold, enough for two purrs of bootlaces'; 'his hed's as big as Birkenhead' (meaning 'he is cocky'); 'a cargo of Irish confetti' (a load of stone chippings); 'You say everyt'ink but your prurrs' ('you are loquacious'); 'He's gorra face like a ruptured custard'; and 'He's as randy as a butcher's dog'.

'Chief' and 'boss' are commonly used substitutes for 'sir'. 'Whurr's we goin' boss?' asks the taxi-driver. 'Now then, chief?' inquires the male shop assistant. Waitresses, conductresses, the flower ladies and barrow girls address customers of both sexes as 'luv'. This is of course common throughout Lancashire and Yorkshire; but only in Liverpool have I heard men use 'Mrs. Woman' instead of 'missus'. 'Eh up then, Mrs. Woman' is a commonly employed warning given by workmen carrying ladders or other equipment through a doorway or across a pavement.

Then there are what the late Frank Shaw called 'malapudlianisms', some unconscious, others deliberate like 'it were a good party with a stupor-abundance of bevvies'. On a bus passing Smithdown ('Smivvy') Road Cemetery I heard a woman passenger confide: 'The cemmy's gettin' fulled up but if the Lord spurrs me I want to spend the rest of me days thurr.' As hundreds of twittering birds came in to roost on trees fringing St. John's Gardens near St. George's Hall, a passer-by observed to her companion, 'Just listen to them starvelings.'

Other examples: 'What's this then, parsley-monious sauce?' (irate query to a waitress). 'They wuzz proper demarmalised' (demoralised). 'Didn't you 'ear me ding the buzzer?' (irate protest to driver of a single-operator bus). ''E suffers somet'ink crool from 'ammer-rods' (piles). 'She wuz wurring 'er stimulated mink and lookin' a right scrubber (tart).'

Comment about a poster advertising a revivalist meeting to be addressed by a hot gospeller—'It'll be all about infernal combustion.' ''E wuz Dixie-lated in the first half' (praise for a footballer with reference to the great Dixie Dean of Everton). Jibe at a conscientious checker 'You wouldn't pass the salt.' ... 'D'yer fancy an intricate?' (meaning entrecote steak) ... 'They've 'ad impotent relations together.' ... ''E's gone with 'er on a knee-trembler' ('he has taken her for a little "slap and tickle" ') ....
''E's got so many judies he's punch-drunk.'

Punch and Judy, for most children in Britain an entertainment restricted to seaside holidays, is in Liverpool an everyday spectacle and has been so for more than a century, throughout this period associated with Lime Street. When the search was on for a name for the pedestrian subway under this thoroughfare hundreds of Liverpudlians suggested 'Punch and Judy Way' (or Walk or Weint), this title coming a good second to 'Sub-Lime Way' with 'Maggie May Way' in third place and inspired, of course by the song:

Oh, Maggie, Maggie May,
They have taken her away
And she'll never walk down Lime Street any more. . . .

The Codmans, for so long Liverpool's Punch and Judy men, are from coastal Wales. In 1850 Richard Codman arrived in the port from Llandudno with puppets he had carved from pieces of driftwood picked up on the shore of the resort. He began giving shows regularly on what was then the Lime Street Quadrant, close to St. George's Hall which opened four years later.

He was over 90 when he died, and his son, also a Richard and the first Codman to call himself 'Professor', was by then fully experienced in the craft. The show went on triumphantly through two world wars with men in uniform from many nations joining the children in Lime Street to watch.

The second Richard died in 1951, aged 83, and Richard the Third was there to carry on. Now in his seventies he has a son, Ronald, in a business which includes shows in most of the clubs in and around Liverpool and at children's parties by the score. Richard and Ronald are rather grave, soberly-dressed quietly-spoken men with the look of small shopkeepers. Ronald has a little son, Robert, already becoming adept at manipulating the puppets, some of which belonged to his great-great-grandfather. There is another branch of the family at Llandudno who put on Punch and Judy shows there in the holiday season; so the Codman tradition seems secure well into the next century, assuming the children then still want Punch and Judy. The youngsters of the seventies certainly do.

The dogs Toby in this show have from time to time been as much-loved by audiences as the puppets. The present canine partner in the Lime Street enterprise, a veteran of 12, came from the R.S.P.C.A.'s home for strays and is 'Judy' off the stage. All the Codmans become greatly attached to their dogs (usually bitches, always mongrels with terrier in them, and either strays or bought cheaply). In 1969, Richard the Third's younger brother, Albert Codman—he was Punch and Judy man at Colwyn Bay—died a few days after his Toby (also a 'Judy' and aged 19) had been killed while crossing the road.

If ever there is an attempt to forbid the gaily painted Codman Theatre its customary off-duty resting place against the south wall of St. George's Hall, the first voice that will be raised in protesting wrath will almost certainly be that of Arthur Dooley, briefly mentioned in my first chapter. He figures as well in the Chapter, 'Arts Nearly All Alive', as he must, because he is a sculptor in metal of immense talent; but he also has his place in this chapter as one of the most colourful of all the present-day Liverpudlians, an amiable but forthright personality, in a sense still to Liverpool what Brendan Behan used to be to Dublin, but with his feet much more firmly on the ground and with a warmer, more expansive sense of humour. He is a wacker to his extraordinarily sensitive finger tips, using the Liverpool vernacular—'bevvy', 'diddy', 'mickies' and so on—but insisting that this is a spoken, never a written language; indeed, he objected strongly to a publication called *Gospels in Scouse*, which was illustrated with photographs of his sculptures of religious subjects.

He is a relentless opponent of any move to 'sterilise' the city, for example by banishing barrow boys from the streets and flower ladies from Clayton Square in the heart of the main shopping area. It is typical of Arthur that, for a 1969 'demo' he organised against the John Moores exhibition of contemporary paintings in Liverpool's Walker Art Gallery being taken over by 'that bunch of Hampstead creeps' ('a lower middle class group who have invented their own peculiar culture which has so little humanity it amounts to artistic fascism', he argued), he and his brother sculptor (and painter) Brian Burgess, both arrived on horseback. Their protest outside the Gallery turned into a riot, in the happiest sense of that word, with attendant policemen and the Director of the Art Gallery joining in the laughter. Nevertheless, Arthur made his point.

He is a political animal who has reconciled Catholicism with Communism, and he has been at loggerheads with both Conservative and Labour councillors over the future of the city. He believes passionately in Liverpool's native virility and flair for colour, its individuality in outlook; and he is devoted to the Liverpudlians with whom he worked when he was a deckhand and then a docker and who have remained his friends, some of them amateur painters and fellow members of the Worker Artists' Association. He warned years ago that plans for the new Liverpool were for 'a chromium-plated, automated, jackpot city with a Las Vegas look ... like the new Birmingham and the new Manchester.'

'This,' thundered Arthur, 'is democracy falling into the ravine. ... the new mentality is out to destroy not just individuality in design and in buildings but in people, too. Not only is every city in the world to look like a yard of upturned Coco-Cola crates but we, the people in them, are to be drilled with the same organisation worship as the Americans. ...

'Is Liverpool going to be a city tailored for the people or a city of chrome juggernauts which disintegrates the community, mangling its culture?' My quotation powerfully underlines his often repeated statement, 'I speak scouse but I don't write it'. I hope his words have also served to show why, as a lover of Liverpool and aspects of the Liverpudlian way of life, I am an admirer of Arthur Dooley, the doughty champion of a number of Merseyside causes which I hold dear.

Mrs. Bessie Braddock was as Liverpudlian as the Mersey and as dearly loved by fellow citizens who resented every unkind jibe made at her from the stage (though never by Liverpudlian comedians) and in print for nearly a quarter of a century. Many of those who disagreed profoundly with her politics and with her views on religion were in all other respects her warm admirers. She was an untiring crusader in defence of rights and against innumerable wrongs (some of them nothing to do with party politics) in her native city. She was acknowledged to be an expert on the hospital care and rehabilitation of the mentally sick; and she did as much as anyone to prevent a conflict between races in Liverpool (not necessarily white against black). Early in 1970 the City Council made her a Freeman of her city, a distinction many years overdue.

She was born Elizabeth Margaret Bamber. Her father, an easy-going and genial man, kept the family in comparative comfort, though every penny that could be spared (and many a penny that could not) went to help those in the distress of poverty. Her mother was one of the seven children of an Edinburgh lawyer who took to drink when he failed to achieve an ambition to be Lord Provost. To feed their family, his wife had to go out charring. 'Ma' Bamber is remembered as a woman of immense resolution, revolutionary principles and apparently inexhaustible energy, who addressed political meetings passionately but also made soup to serve to hungry queues.

Bessie attended her first political meeting when three weeks old, carried by her mother in a shawl. She was also with her mother— an official of the Warehouse Workers' Union—when, on the 'bloody Sunday' of August 1911, police charged thousands who had gathered to hear Tom Mann speak about a railway strike.

As a child she never went barefoot, but she saw daily many who did. She knew all about the suits given by the police to boys of destitute families, suits made of corduroy that stank to high heaven when they were wet and were distinctively marked so that no pawnbroker would accept them.

She was not called Bessie as a schoolgirl, but acquired this name when she joined a Socialist cycling group in which there were already two Elizabeths. To avoid confusion it was decided to put three names into a hat—Betty, Bessie and Elizabeth. The youthful Miss Bamber drew the abbreviation that has stayed with her ever since. She and her fellow cyclists, when on rural outings, used to stick Socialist slogans on the flanks of grazing cows.

She met John Braddock, a Communist and—save to his friends —an apparently somewhat dour man. Their courtship lasted seven years, and when they married the wedding party rode to the register office in a Corporation bus. Both were of too independent a spirit to stay devout Communists for long. They became Labour councillors, then aldermen. When Labour gained control of the Corporation, John became Leader of the City Council and proved a shrewd administrator.

When I first met her—and she was then in her early fifties—it was to be astonished that Mrs. Braddock should photograph so badly that almost every picture I had seen of her had been virtually a caricature. I was most surprised, I think, by her complexion, which almost any teenage beauty would have envied and was particularly unexpected in a woman who had spent all her years in an intensely urban atmosphere. During my first year in Liverpool I saw her frequently, for at the time I was nearing the office she was often on her way from the municipal offices to the post box, an arm full of mail. She walked briskly in those days, purposefulness in every stride, most of the men she passed raising their hats, most of the women giving her a smile. At one period she was receiving letters at the rate of 250 a week. One she treasures came from the crew of the submarine *Scythian* and ran:

> Dear Scouse, we would like it very much if you would be our heart-throb for 1955. Please send us a picture, but not a big one for this is a small submarine. . . .

She had beaten Marilyn Monroe to first place in that heart-throb poll!

Bessie and John were married forty-two years. The partnership ended with cruel abruptness when John collapsed at a civic dinner and died within a few minutes. A fighter all her life, Mrs. Braddock tried valiantly to overcome the consequences of this shock upon her health. But in 1969 she announced that she would not defend the Parliamentary seat she had held since 1945, and in November 1970 she died in the hospital which bears the name of Rathbone. Though brought up in circumstances very different from those of the founder of district nursing, one feels that if they had been contemporaries they would have been both allies and friends in the alleviation of poverty.

Mr. John Moores, a septuagenarian, was given the Freedom of Liverpool on the same day as Mrs. Braddock. While she achieved fame as a Labour M.P., he was twice unsuccessful as a Conservative Parliamentary candidate, though he did win election to the City Council. He was a member of the British Board of Boxing Control and she was president of the Professional Boxers' Association.

He is a former chairman of Everton F.C., loves to paint and finds much pleasure in the theatre. I have mentioned the art exhibition bearing his name—he is also president of the Merseyside Arts Association with which more than 100 organisations are affiliated, many of them musical; so it doubtless delights him that the wife of Gordon West (the international goalkeeper he brought from Blackpool to Everton) has achieved prominence in the North-West as a concert pianist and has, indeed, been a soloist with the Royal Liverpool Philharmonic Orchestra.

Mr. Moores, slight in build and quiet in manner, has a will which matches Mrs. Braddock's. He was born in a pub near Manchester and his first job was a Post Office messenger boy. He trained as a telegraphist and was posted to a cable station at Waterville in The Ring of Kerry. It was in this unlikely place that he went into business. And so, like a great many before him, he sailed to Liverpool from Ireland to seek a fortune. He found it in football pools and mail order.

Colonel Charles John Cocks looks every inch a retired officer, his bearing and his manner military. He holds a unique office, being Registrar of the only extant Court of Passage. This sits five times a year in St. George's Hall.

Its age and origins are uncertain because all early records were destroyed in the fire that badly damaged Liverpool Town Hall in 1795. It probably got its name from 'Passagium', the term used for the destination of ships sailing in convoy (as a protection against piracy) in the Middle Ages; but was earlier than this the Mayor's Court, a 'piepowder court' or 'court of the dusty feet' dealing with claims by people visiting the port. Several ports had courts of passage, but only Liverpool's has survived into the twentieth century and is as busy now as ever it was, the modest and old-fashioned office frequently crowded and mostly by very ordinary people, with little knowledge of the law, who are dealt with patiently and understandingly as well as efficiently by the small staff. Yet 1970 brought its sentence of death.

Broadly speaking, its business is that of the County Court, though there are important differences. There is no limit on the damages that the Presiding Judge can award; and it is the only inferior court in which proceedings can be taken against the Crown. It has kept up with the times—for example, it reduced the age at which it surrenders funds held in trust for minors (an important part of its work) before the Act changing the age of majority actually came into force.

After the Presiding Judge and the Registrar, the Court's most important officer is the Sergeant-at-Mace and Marshal. Through the centuries he has had the authority to arrest a ship, nailing a writ to the mast (in these days of steel masts he ties the writ with string!). He also has the power to arrest aircraft and has done so. Normally such action is taken when the owner is allegedly in debt. The emblem of the Sergeant-at-Mace has, for as long as is known, been a silver oar; and it seems that, strictly he should still carry it when arresting a ship. In the early nineteenth century there was an occasion when, having crossed the Mersey to make an arrest on the Birkenhead shore, the Sergeant was obliged to return to his office to fetch the oar because the sight of it was insisted upon.

The present oar is in the city's regalia (for which, technically, the Sergeant-at-Mace is responsible) displayed to the public occasionally in the Town Hall. The oar was bought in 1785 to replace one stolen by Charles Cooney, who was executed for the crime though his booty was not recovered.

By virtue of being Registrar of the Court of Passage, Colonel Cocks might hold the following offices, were he to lay legal claim, because they have lapsed by default rather than decree; Moss Reever and Burliman, Register of Leather Sealers, Scavenger, Alefounder or Taster, and Fryer of Seized Shoes.

As Moss Reever and Burliman he would protect the Queen's Liege People from being aggrieved by any 'Ffishing' and Digging of Holes. As Scavenger he would save them from the annoyance of wayners' carts 'without fear or dread, profitt or disprofitt'. As Alefounder he would have to be satisfied that both the products of Liverpool brewers and Liverpool bakers were good and wholesome; and as Fryer of Seized Leather he would indifferently and straitly examine that Shoes seized were sufficient and serviceable, according to the best of his Skill and Judgment, so help him God.

The man who might hold these unusual offices is himself unusual, maintaining a compleat bachelor's establishment close to the Mersey, without television and without a car. He is an accomplished cook and a gifted pianist, so that he prepares dinner for his guests and entertains them after it (he is particularly fond of the works of Edwin York Bowen, reckoned by the pundits to be a minor composer but the pundits haven't had a word with Colonel Cocks).

He is an expert on military medals and had a large collection of them but preferred to dispose of it rather than have to visit it in a bank's strongroom. He is also an authority on Turkish and Japanese pre-war artillery; and he cultivates orchids.

Kwok Fong spent his boyhood in a village among paddy fields some miles from Canton when the corrupt rule of the Manchus was paramount. As a pigtailed youth he made his way to Hong Kong and from there went to sea in a Liverpool ship. He made two or three voyages to the Mersey before deciding to settle near the river. There were then no more than eighty of his countrymen living in the port, most of them from his own part of China and including several from a particular quarter of Canton who had set up as laundrymen in various parts of Merseyside, specialising in starching Victorian collars.

There was animosity against them at that time because of the Boxer atrocities. Kwok Fong visited ships with Chinese crews and sold various necessities to seamen who did not wish to venture ashore in the alien city. But his main work, and it was to continue for more than half a century was with the welfare of Asian crews who sailed under the flag of a Liverpool firm.

He met and wooed a Manchester girl of Galway parentage. When they married they opened a boarding house for Chinese seafarers. In due course they moved to a larger house in Pitt Street, which was then in the heart of a considerable Chinese quarter.

As the number of Asian seamen sailing into Liverpool grew, Kwok Fong opened other boarding houses in the neighbourhood, and then, when the family was bombed out of Pitt Street in the 1941 blitz, he established 'The Far East' restaurant in a house in Great George Square that had balconied Georgian windows. It quickly became a rendezvous for servicemen from the far west as well as from the Orient. Friendships were made then, and in the years after the war, that endured. The man who was Mr. Kwok to many Liverpudlians, Americans and Europeans, was 'Uncle Fong of Liverpool' to scores of Chinese he had befriended and helped over the years.

When he died, aged 87, in the autumn of 1969, tributes came from several parts of the world; and in the cortege that wound round the palisaded green of Great George Square were a number of Chinese from overseas.

Museum, Picton Library and Wellington Monument
Noble background for a race down the Museum steps

Many Chinese restaurants have been established in Liverpool since 'The Far East' opened behind balconied, Georgian windows, but this establishment—though not the first of its kind in the city—has always held an especial place. Number of Merseysiders who look at night across Great George Square from the remnant of Chinatown and see the letters and Chinese characters spelling out 'The Far East' in glowing neon, remember Mr. Kwok and Uncle Fong.

Death removed in 1969 another notable character from the Liverpool stage, 'Sir' Frederick Bowman (and woe betide a journalist who dared to call him plain 'Mr.'). He was knighted by the self-styled 'King Wladislav V of Poland, Bohemia and Hungary'; and he was also a member of the 'sovereign, knightly and religious order of the Crown of Thorns', which originated in the days of the French monarchy and was revived in 1880 by a bishop who broke away from the Roman Catholic Church.

He was imprisoned at Brixton for a period during the last war for refusing to work on the land as an alternative to military service and made an unsuccessful attempt at escape from the gaol by masquerading as a clergyman. He described himself as an author and actor, but he was also the editor of the *Liverpool Examiner* and *Talking Picture News* (both apparently of very restricted circulation, for I did not see either of them) and as such was present at various civic functions to which the Press were invited. If these occasions were in the day he wore a frock coat and a buttonhole. If they were at night he appeared in formal evening dress wearing the insignia of his 'orders'. Newspapermen were scared stiff of him—I was solemnly warned soon after my arrival in Liverpool: 'Be very careful, he'll sue for libel at the drop of an aitch.'

He had friends, even if journalists steered clear of him; but they became fewer as the years passed, and he died a lonely man, still Sir Frederick (and without the quotes he so detested) in the telephone book which gave his address as 15 Sandown Lane, Wavertree, though he always called his home 'Humanimal House' and in it fed numerous stray cats on a strong-smelling food of his own concoction.

He provoked laughter in court on several occasions, once

The Phil, Charles Groves conducting

H

when he answered counsel, 'I am a man of substance when things are prosperous with me. At the moment I am not as prosperous as I should be.'

At the 'Youth Makes Music' concert held annually in the Philharmonic Hall, Liverpool, I listened to a dozen or more youths play with evident enjoyment a tune on Melodicas (simple wind instruments with piano-like keys). Every one of those youths was so mentally retarded as to be incapable of learning to write his name; and some in the group could not even dress themselves.

Their performance crowned months of endeavour by Mr. Philip Bailey, small in build but prodigious in patience and a man of great compassion and infinite invention. He had employed colours to teach music to the unteachable, covering each key of each Melodica with paper of a basic shade—blue, red, black, white, yellow, green, brown and orange. When a yellow disc (or ball) was held up, the players pressed a yellow note, when a red disc was shown they pressed a red note and so on. Eventually they learned to associated a sound with a colour.

Mr. Bailey uses colours to teach music to the mentally handi-capped in a number of ways, sometimes by the boys wearing sashes and the girls dressed in various hues. He discovered very early in this work that the colours had to be precise—rose pink would not serve, for example, as a substitute for scarlet, this baffled the child. He enlisted the expert assistance of the British Colour Council and won the co-operation of manufacturers.

He was then music adviser to the city's Youth Music Com-mittee and had a devoted assistant in Mrs. E. G. Beddows, whose husband made a number of gadgets at home in his spare time to Mr. Bailey's designs. Their work ran on a shoestring budget, and part of their time was devoted to the physically handicapped as well as the mentally backward. Another part was given to normal children and teenagers, for Mr. Bailey was a founder of the Music Boxes, a Merseyside innovation which was taken up in some other areas. The Boxes are groups for anyone between the ages of 13 and 23 who thinks he or she would like to play an instrument, and they are run on the lines of the musical evenings held in parlours before the gramophone and radio came. The kind of music played in the Boxes does not matter—

what does is that everyone who makes the music should enjoy it and give all that they are capable of in its performance.

I got to know Mr. Bailey some months after the first thalido-mide babies had been born. He was at that time devising various instruments and musical gadgets that could be manipulated with the feet because he felt it was important that these cruelly mal-formed little children should find dexterity in their toes as quickly as possible; and making musical sounds seemed the best way to encourage them. He perfected a stand which holds music in braille and also grips a woodwind instrument so that a blind child can play with one hand and read with the other. Thus it is no longer necessary for the player, in the elementary stages of tuition, to commit tunes to memory from the braille before they can perform them.

Eventually Mr. Bailey was able to work from Liverpool University, devote the whole of his energies to the handicapped and train teachers in various parts of the country in his methods. His inventions include a record player operated by the mouth and a tape recorder which can be worked by a child with only a little finger on each of its hands.

He is a man who does not care for personal publicity, which is why so few of the general public, even on Merseyside, know of his extraordinary achievements and his dedication. Fortunately the Carnegie Trust and the Gulbenkian Foundation are aware of both and have supported Mr. Bailey with grants. I have seen him strumming away on a piano surrounded by youngsters playing recorders, mouth organs and tambourines as well as more sophis-ticated instruments. And I have seen his face when a crippled child, using one of his devices, has succeeded, to its intense joy, in playing a simple melody. I looked at a supremely happy man.

The diverse bedrock stratas of the Liverpudlian character are exposed in the pubs, in the markets and in the clubs which range from the Athenaeum and the Lyceum, established to serve litera-ture and the arts when the slave trade was at its height, to the survivors from the boom in beat, the Mersey Sound that echoed round the world in the mid-sixties.

Many of the pubs in the downtown area are Victorian or Edwardian, some tarted up since the Second World War, a few rebuilt. There are still dozens of them in which the most significant changes in half a century have been the switch from gas to electric light and from barrel to keg beer. The bow front of 'The Baltic Fleet' still looks on to a part of Wapping, by the docks, that has changed little physically since the days of crimping and promenading Maggie Mays. A re-incarnated 'Fat Annie' would have no difficulty in recognising the 'Duke's Crown', the pub she kept in the early days of this century; and the ghost of Shanghai Davis would be in familiar surroundings if it appeared in the 'Red Lion' on Seabrow.

The most remarkable pubs are the 'Vines', in Lime Street, and the Philharmonic Hotel at Hope Street's corner with Hardman Street (a continuation of 'Leeces' Street). These were truly palaces in the gin palace era and must have appeared as unbelievably sumptuous to the paupers of Edwardian times as the Town Hall did to the cellar-dwellers of a hundred years before. The architect responsible for them both was Walter Thomas, a large and jocund dandy who married into the family then owning Lewis's. The brewers apparently allowed him to spend their money with the utmost lavishness.

The Philharmonic Hotel is partly a Caledonian castle from the outside, and in its baronial entrance are wrought-iron gates with female heads, mythical beasts, rosettes and much baroque ornamentation. They were designed by a German-American and executed in a workshop at the then comparatively new University College's School of Art. Inside, the large and ornate rooms are embellished with stone carvings, copper panels and much elaborate plasterwork, a deal of it representing the female form and said to be that of a Mrs. Ryan, who, it seems, graciously consented to pose in the semi-nude for the sculptor, Charles Allen. The 'shooting gallery' (Liverpudlian for the 'gents') is even today about the ultimate in pulchritude for a urinal with its slabs of matching marble.

There is a wealth of beautifully turned and carved mahogany in panelling and lintels, the work of the highly accomplished carpenters and craftsmen who furnished the luxurious interiors of the liners that crossed the Atlantic from the Mersey in the first decade of the present century. From time to time they were laid off by shipbuilders and were then employed on similar work in the city. Rooms in the 'Vines' contain much evidence of their skills in the elaborately carved mahogany panelling. Here the female form, breasts bared, is in wood (whether Mrs. Ryan also obliged in this case I do not know). In the cocktail bar the highly ornamental ceiling has a glass dome for its crown and the walls are graced by oil paintings. Elsewhere there are glass screens cut with intricate patterns.

More mahogany panelling carved by carpenters in spells between working on the early luxury liners, is to be found lining walls in the 'Lisbon' (which also has ceilings to rival those of the 'Vines' in their plasterwork) and in the 'Beaconsfield', two pubs in Victoria Street with bars below street level, a Liverpool idiosyncracy. These pubs are used by men whose business is in the nearby exchange, where imported fruit and vegetables are auctioned, and in the warehouses of neighbouring alleys where such produce is stored. In one of these warehouses is the 'Cavern', shrine of the Mersey Sound.

In complete contrast to the former gin palaces is the pub known as 'The Slaughterhouse' in Fenwick Street, almost opposite the modern Corn exchange building. This tavern was denied, as a deliberate policy, any ornamentation for perhaps 150 years, the only concession to the twentieth century being the installation of electric lights and these unshaded. In a line behind the bar are giant-sized casks from which wines and spirits were sold by the draught. The appearance of this pub's rooms is presumably that of the early nineteenth-century grog shops, their old furniture of the plainest and the floorboards bare; but the character of the place has, in my view, been to some extent impaired by the installation of a jukebox, presumably intended to lure pop addicts into the place, though surely they are the least likely to find such surroundings to their taste.

'The Slaughterhouse' is the pub's correct name and not a colloquialism like 'The Muck Midden', the title Liverpudlians have, for reasons obscure, long given the Poste House in narrow Cumberland Street. Beasts bought at a market close by were apparently slaughtered more or less on the spot where 'The Slaughterhouse' was built (in the reign of George III) by wine merchants who chartered their own vessels to sail in supplies from France, Spain and Portugal. For many years the tavern has been a lunch-hour meeting place for businessmen from the surrounding citadels of commerce, and in 1968, with offices above, it changed hands for £53,000.

Another pub of character that came under new ownership at about the same time, but retains its old name of 'Ma Boyle's', is the oyster saloon founded in 1880 at one of Old Hall Street's corners with Chapel Street and in premises previously occupied by a hatter. For many years it was kept by a notable personality, Mrs. Catherine Boyle, who put up a notice 'Gentlemen are not to smoke before 2 p.m.', this because connoisseurs had complained that the heavy fumes from (presumably) plug tobacco, so much more popular then than today, affected the flavour of the oysters. Mrs. Boyle died in the sixties and is remembered with affection.

Two throws of a stone downhill from 'Ma Boyle's' is the 'Pig and Whistle' at the entrance to another narrow street, Covent Garden (nothing to do with fruit and vegetables). In the porch of this pub is a brass plate, polished daily, bearing the words 'Emigrants supplied', a relic from the period in the nineteenth century when the port was swarming with Europeans waiting for ships to the United States, their new world.

In the opposite direction from 'Ma Boyle's', on the other side of Exchange, is a minor open space, Pownall Square, with three pubs, one of them called 'The Wedding House'. The downtown district also has a 'Why Not?' and an 'Old Stile House' (another of Walter Thomas's creations) and a 'Ye Hole-in-Ye-Wall'. A number of pubs both in and around Liverpool are called 'The Coffee House', perhaps the oldest of them at Woolton, now well within the city boundaries and with towering flats yet still keeping—around 'The Coffee House', anyway—the semblance of a village despite supermarket frontages. In this particular 'Coffee House', as in a number of other pubs, there is a 'news room' that used to be a place where you could have a free look at the daily papers.

'Ye Crack', in Rice Street, a street leaning steeply towards the Anglican Cathedral, goes one better and has a room labelled 'the war office'. The name is said to date back to the Boer War and to have originated because amateur military strategists monopolised the conversation with their opinions on the way campaigns were being misconducted. This pub has, for as long as anyone can remember, been favoured by members of the Royal Liverpool Philharmonic Orchestra and also the male members of the Philharmonic Choir (for some years, indeed, 'Ye Crack' was better known as 'The Songsters').

Seafarers the world over know the Nook Hotel in the centre of what remains of Chinatown, and many of them have sent odds and ends of curios to decorate it. Hanging from the ceiling in the lounge, which has oriental-style muted lighting, are two stuffed flying fish, a present from an Asian seaman and known as Scobie Breasley and Lester Piggot by the proprietress, Mrs. Eileen Jones, who greets her customers each evening with 'Hello children' in a soft Irish brogue and who likes to wear very large picture hats (she is said to have forty or more of them). Mrs. Jones has been lending her personality to the 'Nook' a long time but if you dare ungallantly to ask her how old she is, she will reply firmly: 'I am thirty-nine. I was thirty-nine last year and the year before that and this year I am thirty-nine again.' She walks like a queen among customers from three Continents in rooms where the decor includes both hunting prints and willow pattern plates. She speaks a little Chinese, and it is the custom in the 'Nook' to call 'Time, Gentlemen please' in that language.

One of the strangest looking establishments from the outside is in Park Lane and used to be called the Mayfair Hotel (though Liverpool's Park Lane is as different from its London namesake as a street could be). It seems a brewery firm was under the impression that, when a railway tunnel was made, more than a mile long, from the then newly-opened Edge Hill station to Park Lane, it was the intention to build a passenger station there. But, instead, a goods depot was constructed, and from this waggons were hauled by stationary engine up the steep incline through the tunnel to the main line at Edge Hill. However the hotel was completed before the brewers discovered their error. It was given an extraordinary rooftop and upper-storey collection of urns, balustrades, dolphins, mermen, liver birds, ships, shells, anchors and shields together with a jolly King Neptune. Despite all the bombs that fell in the vicinity during the last war none of the items contributing to this example of Liverpool baroque was disturbed. Appropriately, the little pub opposite the collection is called 'Curiosity Vaults'.

Incidentally, the erstwhile 'Mayfair'—it is now a private hotel—has outlived the goods depot. This, in 1970, stood disused and decaying, another of the eysore sites of Liverpool.

As I have said, as well as running up against bedrock Liverpudlians in the pubs you meet them in the markets—and, in particular, Paddy's Market and the Tatters' Market, which, these days, are near neighbours off Great Homer Street.

Paddy's—its official name is St. Martin's Market—was established in 1826 off Scotland Road and stayed there for 131 years, despite its home being blown up in the 1941 blitz. Almost throughout that period it was a market mainly of used garments, and these clothed families by the hundred; and it also had among its customers many foreign sailors. For some years after the last war it was uncomfortably accommodated off 'Caz-er-new' Street, but when its site was required for approaches to the second Mersey tunnel it was moved to its present premises, opened by a Lord Mayor who so aptly remarked, 'This is not so much a market as a way of life.'

Numbers of sailors from Asian and African ports still make a beeline for Paddy's to buy secondhand togs, though the market's stallholders, more than a hundred of them, nowadays display many other articles, including antiques and crockery. Mrs. Polly Birchall, aged 93 and a stallholder for seventy-seven years, was still going strong at the beginning of 1970, and the mother of Cilla Black, the pop singer, also had a stall there.

The Tatters' Market—officially the North General Market—is held on Saturday afternoons, when hardware is sold in its widest variety—cycle accessories, chamber pots, electrical equipment, horse brasses, lawn mowers, cutlery—to a motley clientele. There are Liverpudlians to whom Saturday is not Saturday without a visit to the Tatters'.

Another Saturday market is held in the fork of London Road and Pembroke Place, and this is a relic of one which used to occupy a narrow street outside the old Market Hall and was always jam-packed in the afternoon. I remember that for most of the afternoon a large horse stood equably in the middle of the elbowing crowd, unperturbed by the cries of hucksters, while rubbish from the Market Hall was shovelled into its cart. A brown horse and a black one did this duty on alternate Saturdays and were great favourites with the shoppers who provided them with a continuous supply of carrots, biscuits, apples, chocolates, boiled sweets and potato crisps so that they must have had iron constitutions as well as unshakeable *sang froid*.

I sometimes used to ponder, when small boys passed beneath

the duty horse's nose with balloons or squeaking toys, upon the
carnage there would be if the animal took it into its head to bolt.
The two horses vanished when demolition men moved into the
street, which now lies beneath the St. John's Precinct containing
a market hall opened in 1970.

It was almost a daily experience in the sixties to be stopped in one
of the main streets of the city by visiting Beatle-worshippers,
many of them from overseas, who wanted to know how to get
to the 'Cavern'. As I have said, it is in the area of fruit importers'
warehouses, along an alley called Mathew Street and is nowadays
the Cavern (Liverpool) Ltd., keeping company with Cavern
Enterprises Ltd. Its character has changed since the steamy,
primitive period of the early-to-mid sixties when it was a teenage
temple. These days it has a top coat of sophistication (as, of course,
have those who patronised it as youngsters and went through the
rituals of those times); and, alas, nobody pays heed now when I
remember aloud how I used to stand most mornings at the same
bus stop as John Lennon who then seemed to me to be a very
ordinary-looking schoolboy save that his hair seemed a thought
too long.

It was not so much the Beatles, Gerry Marsden and Co. who set
the Mersey Sound spinning on records the world over as it was
Brian Epstein, the young, extraordinarily dynamic Liverpudlian,
who promoted, projected and jet-propelled entertainers of his own
generation from the city into global reputations. His influence was
seismic but the period of it was short, ended by death at the age of 32.

Years before Epstein, the Beatles, Cilla and the rest ran into
a show business bonanza, two schoolteachers fresh from training
college appeared at the 'Cavern' in a resident skiffle group called
the Gin Mill. They were Tony Davis, 6 feet 7 inches tall from
Wallasey, and Mick Groves, of Irish-Jewish-Lancashire parentage,
from Salford, who left the 'Cavern' in May 1958, fugitives from
the then enveloping Mersey Beat. They turned to folk songs,
modern as well as traditional, and before 1958 had progressed
from a basement in a Liverpool restaurant to the Royal Festival
Hall. Tony and Mick, Cliff Hall from Jamaica, and Hugh Jones,
a wacker who is an authority on sea shanties, are the Spinners.
Though they have now long been established internationally,
they nevertheless continue to perform most weeks in a room at a

Liverpool pub called 'Gregson's Well', uphill from the city, where the Spinners' Club meets. The dimensions of the room limit the audience to 150 and gross receipts are under £30.

It is all very different from the quartet's money-spinning concerts before thousands. They wear jerseys or are in shirt sleeves, never in the smart, yellow, mandarin-collared tunics worn before TV cameras and in the Albert Hall, the Queen Elizabeth Hall and the biggest halls outside London, including the Philharmonic Hall, Liverpool, where the 2,000 seats are always sold days in advance of every Spinners' appearance. But the four see their Club Night as a point of contact with the folk in Folk, a combination of refresher course, sabbatical and family party.

They sing under two orange, barrel-shaped lampshades and a naked orange-coloured bulb. There is a platform but the audience use that, it is part of the half-moon round the pinchbeck clearing the Spinners occupy. The audience at the 'Well' are on Christian name terms with themselves and with the quartet. More of them are over 30 than are under 20, and a nucleus have been followers of the group from the late fifties and remember the year when Jackie McDonald, another former schoolteacher, was a Spinner, driving over the Pennines to and from Bradford in a bubble car to take part in Club Nights when they were held in a Liverpool restaurant, later in the ornate concert room of St. George's Hall (then she teamed up with Bridie McDonnell and in a short time they were filling the Philharmonic Hall, too; and they also have a weekly Folk Night at the Coach House Club).

It is a participant audience at the 'Well', not only joining in the Spinners' choruses—uproarious, nostalgic, salty, sad—but also moving singly, in pairs and trios, into the clearing to sing or to read verse of their own composing. There are usually as many men as women in the audience and numerous mums and dads. Pint glasses crowd side-tables and balance on chair arms.

Regulars at Club Nights include two writers of modern songs in the Folk idiom about Liverpool, Tony Murphy—he composed 'The Orange and the Green'—and Stan Kelly, the chorus of whose anthem for exiled wackers runs:

> I wish I was back in Liverpool,
> Liverpool town where I was born
> There isn't no trees, no scented breeze,
> No fields of waving corn;

> But there's lots of girls with peroxide curls
> And the black and tan flows free.
> With six in a bed by the old Pier 'Ead,
> And it's Liverpool town for me.*

Tony Murphy often wears a polo-collared sweater in bright blue, as befits a dedicated Evertonian. Stan Kelly, as uncompromisingly of the Anfield Kop, habitually wears something red.

Stan Francis, quietly middle-aged, once a Spinner, a former ship's engineer who now makes and repairs six and twelve-string guitars and banjos, is often at the Club Nights and joins the Liverpool Fishermen ('wakes, weddings, ceilidhs and Irish fights' says their card) when they squeeze their quart into the pint-pot space of a clearing when the Spinners vacate it. The Fishermen consist of the Jaques Brothers (Tony, Jimmy and Brian), ex-dockers with quayside shoulders and much hair on their cheeks, Bernie Davis, Bob Dyson and Alan Fitzgerald; and they specialise in masculine folk songs and pungent yarns. A highly picturesque character seen around on Club Nights is Tony Wilson, enormously ginger-bearded, who likes to wear an old-style railwayman's peaked cap (he is a steam era addict) pulled down over one eye, and a reefer jacket with nautical buttons so that the general effect is of a shellback who has come ashore from a windjammer without bothering to change out of seagoing gear.

Liverpool songsmiths like Hughie Jones, Tony Murphy, Stan Kelly, Pete McGovern, Glyn Hughes and Molly Armstrong, all represented in the Spinners' repertoire, are the heirs and successors to numerous anonymous composers of skipping, counting and street game songs and rhymes which are still heard in playgrounds of Merseyside schools. Many of them have been collected by the indefatigable Frank Shaw and published in a paperback which takes its title from the first line of

> Y'know me Anty Nelly,
> She has a wooden belly,
> An' ev'ry time you knock her down,
> Three shies a penny.

Some of the old rhymes are of Irish rather than Liverpool-Irish origin such as:

* Stan Kelly/Leon Rosselson, Heathside Music Ltd., 1964.

> Dearly beloved brethren,
> Don't yiz t'ink it is a sin
> T'peel the good potatoes
> Then t'row away the skin?
> The skin feeds the pig,
> The pig feeds you
> Dearly beloved brethren
> Isn't this true?

Orange and Green is the basis of

> Catty, Catty, go to Mass,
> Ridin' on the divil's ass.
> Proddy, Proddy, on the wall,
> A penny bun to feed yiz all.

The phrase 'Liverpool gentleman, Manchester man', used often at one time, is heard much less frequently these days; but when it does occur it brings to my mind Teddy Behrend, and this because of an affectionate profile of him by his nephew that appeared in *Portrait of a Family Firm*,* a book published in 1970 for the entertainment of customers and staff of Bahr, Behrend and Co., shipping agents, founded in Liverpool in 1793 by a native of the island of Bornholm. Teddy, who became senior partner of the firm and was also Swedish Consul (he was awarded the Order of Vasa for his services), died in 1954 and is still remembered by many Merseysiders. He collected books, mainly in de luxe and limited editions, knew a great deal about port and was devoted to music, playing host to Kreisler and other eminent performers when they visited the city. 'For many years,' wrote his nephew, Mr. Arthur Behrend, 'the review of Philharmonic concerts by the *Daily Post* critic, A. K. Holland, rarely failed to arouse his indignation. . . .' And this was his day at business:

His first daily task on arrival in his room was *The Times* crossword, and if he hit upon or was stumped by a difficult clue he would telephone in jubilation or distress to my mother or to a stockbroker friend, both of whom were similar addicts. . . . For many years he lunched in the dingy cafe in the basement of 5 Chapel Street. But when we moved to India Buildings he preferred the Exchange Club in Fenwick Street, and after lunch he invariably disappeared into the room upstairs for a rubber or two of bridge. . . . He then returned to the office for a short while before going home early. . . .

*©Arthur Behrend.

He gave his nephew three months off to write a novel. Mr. Arthur Behrend, who became senior partner and continued to write books in his leisure time, has this to say about another uncle who was in the firm:

> Harry was a monocled man-about-town. I still wear his morning trousers at weddings; of superb cloth they were made in 1910 by Samuelson of Maddox Street and Paris, and his panama hat of superfine straw came from Andre of Piccadilly and is now at rest in my summer house. . . . I do not think he was as extravagant as his half-brother Charlie, who drove a tandem and pair and who, distrusting Liverpool laundries, sent his shirts by sea to Sweden to be decently washed.

Mr. Arthur Behrend's grandfather smoked 20 cigars a day, bought claret for 25s a dozen, had judges to dinner and was a friend of Carl Rosa who then owned the Royal Court Theatre. Grandfather Behrend lived up to the last shilling and soon after he died, at 77, 'the side-whiskered butler was the first to go, next the bay horse which drew the brougham. The brougham itself remained, the owner of the livery stables where it was kept providing a horse and coachman . . . but in the end he bought the brougham too.'

For years the firm had a cashier named Mr. Wealthy. Tom Ashcroft, who looked after the horses, was killed by a hurtling crate while trying to entice a tiger off the roof of Princes Dock shed (the firm imported wild animals). And a pipe of port mysteriously found its way from the docks to a Peak District cave, there to be broached and sold illicitly.

There is a story (retold at the 1970 Methodist Conference) of a boy who, in a school essay, wrote, 'Liverpool police is bastards.' His teacher passed the comment on to the police who, as a public relations exercise, gave the children a party. Days later the teacher again asked for an essay on the city force. This time the boy wrote, 'Liverpool police is cunning bastards'.

What an agglomeration this chapter is! Yet, when wackers are its subject, could it be otherwise?

FIVE

UPRIVER

LET us suppose we are inward bound on a calm, clear, sunlit early evening in midsummer; that we are approaching the Bar Light Vessel, 19 miles out from Pier Head and at the vestibule of the Port of Liverpool; and that we are on the upper deck of a tall ship so that we can see a smudge that is the Isle of Man as well as the tinted shore of Anglesey and the blue-grey peaks of the Snowdon range. On our port bow is Formby Point, at which the sea has been nibbling all this century, edging nearer each year to the flat lands which lie beyond the barrier dunes and below the level of the highest spring tides.

This is a trip I have made so often: in time of war with some anxiety about what might have happened to Liverpool since last I saw those giant Liver Birds, wings spread but anchored to their perches; and in time of peace, if the sun was out and the sea subdued, with deep content, and this in spite of some melancholy memories of this part of the bay. Early on a bright summer's evening is much the best time to be at the Bar, for the air then is curiously limpid and the sky has the colour of newly laundered, long faded jeans.

So many ships passed the Bar Light between 1939 and 1943 on their way to destruction by U-Boat and Focke Wulf Condor. So many more limped past the lightship, heading for home, gaping holes in their flanks, superstructures mangled. And since the war so many stately liners dropped their pilots at this point for the last time, outward bound never to return to the Mersey— *Britannic, Parthia, Cilicia, Apapa, Accra, Reina del Pacifico, Reina del Mar, Empress of Scotland, Empress of France, Empress of Britain* and, in 1970, the *Empress of England*—queens of the Liverpool river, much loved, much missed, yet their leaving inevitable in the age which has brought the jumbo jet and Concorde to cross the oceans in a few hours.

But, as we will almost certainly see on our chosen summer evening, there are still many, many ships in and out of the port—more than 30,000 a year in fact; and as we pass no doubt some of them will be keeping the lightship company for a while, awaiting pilots. If the big liners have nearly all gone for good, many thousands of passengers in a year sail past the Bar and into the Crosby Channel aboard car ferries from Dublin and Belfast and in the daily packets from Douglas, Isle of Man (there are hundreds of Merseysiders so in love with the sea that they make regular day excursions to the island just for the pleasure of the sail).

We are likely to see at the Bar the *Arnet Robinson* or the *Edmund Gardner* or the *Sir Thomas Brocklebank*, each with 'Liverpool Pilot' in large letters on their sides. We are within sight of the high dunes of Ainsdale where watchers stood helpless as another pilot boat, the *Charles F. Livingston*, lay fast in the sand and local boatmen, in frail pleasure craft strove vainly to reach her over a wall of sea, built by a south-westerly gale. That was in November 1939, and only ten of the thirty-three on board (eleven pilots, two examining officers and a crew of twenty) survived. Yet the vessel was salvaged, returned to the pilot service and in later years, as the *Aura*, sailed to and from Newfoundland with freight.

Worse calamity befell the pilot boat *Alfred H. Read* at the Bar in 1917. It was not established whether she was torpedoed (though a warhead was recovered from one of the lifeboats which were, of course, on their davits when disaster came) or whether she was mined (the cradle of a mine was also found); but in the early morning, an explosion forward where the pilots were sleeping, ripped the vessel open almost from stem to stern and she sank within a few minutes. Nineteen pilots, eight apprentice pilots and twelve others, including soldiers (she was on patrol duty) went down with the *Alfred H. Read*. There were only two survivors.

The first Liverpool Pilotage Act was passed in 1766, but there were 'pilots' long before that, some of them fishermen who dredged for oysters off the Wirral shore and regarded piloting in the same light as smuggling—a hazardous but lucrative sideline. Some ventured as far out as the Skerries Light (a fire in a basket), off the north-west tip of Anglesey and 70 miles from the Mersey entrance, to offer their services to inward-bound ships. Several who boarded outward vessels in the river were carried to Africa and from there to the West Indies because it had been too rough in the bay to put them off.

Eighteen ships were stranded in the Mersey approaches in 1764, and there were unofficial pilots among the seventy-five men who perished. It is unlikely that the loss of life disturbed Parliament as much as the forfeiture of more than £18,000 in duties (mainly on tobacco) but two years later the Pilotage Act was passed without difficulty, and about fifty pilots were officially appointed, it being stipulated that they must be able seamen and able to write. There were nine boats in the service and within four years one of them, the *Two Brothers*, had been lost with eleven pilots on board. The *Prudence* and the *Betty* also foundered.

William Hutchinson (to whom I referred in my second chapter) was largely instrumental in introducing the pilotage service, and it was he who, in 1779, chose Point Lynas, near Amlwch, in Anglesey, and 50 miles from the Mersey gate, as the westerly station. This is still used today though there have been moves from time to time to dispense with it. Indeed, there have been attempts through the years to dispose of the pilots, largely because of resentment at the way their charges cut into merchants' profits. In 1826, Fawdingham Theakstone, a Liverpool merchant, told a meeting of the Pilotage Commission: 'As to the respectability of the business of a pilot, it never will be respectable and he who looks forward to the respectability of his son will never place him in a pilot boat.'

But the truth is that there has always been a strong family tradition in the Liverpool service. One of the present pilots represents the fourth generation of his family in this profession, and there are several fathers and sons, uncles and nephews. The Port of Liverpool has 182 pilots, a rather special breed of men whose hours of duty play ducks and drakes with home and social life and who have to keep in tiptop physical condition as well as being exceptionally alert mentally. They are good company to be in when they are ashore—and, incidentally, a number of them spend a fair slice of their leisure sailing their own craft. Until the last war they were, by tradition, bowler-hatted, but now all wear peaked caps. The craft which take them between ship and pilot

South front of St. George's Hall from Concourse House
St. George's Hall. The Great Hall and the rarely seen tiled floor

boat are still called 'punts' though they have, of course, long been powered.

The pilots are required to know every hazard of the sea and every aid to navigation from St. Bees Head, Cumberland, south to Anglesey and from the Point of Ayre, northerly tip of the Isle of Man, to Eastham locks, where vessels enter the Manchester Ship Canal. There are more than a hundred lighted buoys and boat beacon lights in the Port and its approaches, numbers of them to be selected with absolute certainty from the constellations which at night festoon the banks of the river. Pilots are on an almost continuous refresher course because the shoals, bars and banks in the river and the bay are ever changing, the charts constantly being revised. At no major port overseas, and in Britain only in the Bristol Channel, is there so sharp a rise and fall in the tide. A Mersey spring tide will rise as much as 9 feet in an hour.

So a Liverpool pilot undergoes a long and exacting period of training before he is entrusted with a ship and cargo worth millions. When his responsibility is a 200,000 ton tanker he must think in inches not feet—sometimes there is not the width of a motor car wing to spare between jetty wall and the side of the ship. His is a task more demanding than steering a vehicle through a narrow gateway because the pilot has to take wind, tide and current into account.

The service has been under the regulation of the Mersey Docks and Harbour Board since 1859. There have been several attempts to abolish compulsory pilotage, but a statement made in 1870 (when one abolition proposal was submitted), declaring that the Mersey was too dangerous a river and estuary to be left to unaided ships' masters, still holds good today, despite modern aids such as radar and radio compasses. Perhaps the time will come when computers take over, but there seems small likelihood that the seventies will bring any significant extension of pilotage exemption certificates. These number about 300 and are held by masters of the Isle of Man, Dublin and Belfast passenger vessels and a number of coasters regularly using the port.

A memorable painting by Samuel Walters in the Dock Board's possession records a memorable incident on a wild day in 1866. A vessel was sighted in Liverpool Bay with her foremast carried away and running before a storm-force nor'-westerly under her

St. George's Hall. Concert Room
Rodney Street
I

maintops'ls. The pilot schooner *Duke* signalled her to follow, the seas being much too high for a pilot to board her, and led her into the Mersey. Meanwhile, the pilot schooner *Pride of Liverpool* had signalled a dozen other ships, carrying cargoes worth a total of £500,000, to heave to. She then hoisted a signal 'Will you follow me?' and led this fleet up the Crosby Channel to safety, a remarkable feat.

The *Pride of Liverpool* sank in a collision 6 miles from Point Lynas in 1890, one of the scores of pilot boats lost in the long history of the Liverpool service.

A few months before the *Charles F. Livingston* calamity off Ainsdale there occurred the tragedy of the submarine *Thetis* between the Bar Light and the Anglesey beaches.

Built by Cammell Laird at Birkenhead, she sailed out from the Mersey on 1st June 1939, to carry out a diving trial. There were 103 on board—fifty more than the normal crew—and they included shipyard officials and workmen, nearly all Merseysiders. She cleared the Bar Light about noon with the Liverpool tug *Grebecock* in company, and at 1340 signalled that she was about to dive and to remain submerged for three hours.

There was some uneasiness amongst observers in the tug at the manner in which the submarine dived, and at 1645, when there was no sign of the *Thetis* a naval lieutenant aboard the *Grebecock* sent a message, via Seaforth radio, to Captain Submarines, Gosport, asking what was the duration of the dive, his intention being to convey some degree of anxiety but not to cause alarm. The message arrived at Gosport Post Office at 1738, but because the duty telegraph boy was busy repairing a puncture in his bicycle tyre, it did not reach its destination until 1815. By that time the *Thetis* had been lying for two-and-a-half hours with her bows in mud 160 feet below the surface.

At 0754 next morning the tail of the submarine was sighted, above the water, by the destroyer *Brazen* 14 miles from the Great Orme, Llandudno. By the afternoon the stern had been raised higher, held with wires from the Liverpool Salvage vessel *Vigilant*, and rescue hopes were high. But only four men escaped from the submarine tomb.

The story of the *Thetis* tragedy is long and complicated and has been told graphically in *The Admiralty Regrets* ... by C. E. T.

Warren and James Benson. She was eventually beached in Moelfre Bay, Anglesey, later dry-docked at Holyhead (where the ninety-nine who perished lie buried) and subsequently towed back to Birkenhead. There she was rebuilt and renamed *Thunderbolt*. She left the Mersey in October 1940 and in June 1943 sank off Sicily, depth-charged by an Italian sloop.

Less than a mile from the Bar Light, in a December storm in 1909, a great wave engulfed the mail steamer *Ellen Vannin*, Mersey-bound from the Isle of Man, and she sank in a few moments. Her story is told in a song that is simple yet moving (particularly when the chorus is sung *pianissimo* by an audience of 2,000 in Liverpool Philharmonic Hall at a Spinners' concert). It was written by one of the Spinners, Hugh Jones.

So, even on a bright summer's evening, there is a haunting sadness about the Bar to anyone who knows the history of it; and most of those who sailed regularly out of Liverpool in the last war will have personal memories that are poignant. I have mine— and one, in particular, of the *City of Benares*, a fine modern liner. She passed the Bar Light with eighteen other ships in Convoy O.B. 213 in darkness on Friday 13th September 1940, aboard her ninety children (a number of them from Merseyside families) bound for the safety of Canada. The following morning, making my first voyage in a Liverpool-based destroyer, the *Hurricane*, I also passed the lightship.

At 2205 on 15th September, in a gale and with the full moon heavily veiled by racing storm clouds, the *City of Benares* was struck by a torpedo from U 48. She began to settle and boats were lowered into the turbulent sea, their occupants nearly all in night clothing. Nearly 200 miles away to the north, on watch for the first time without being double-banked by the petty officer telegraphist, I took down this plain language radio message: *City of Benares torpedoed 56 43 North 21 15 West. Sinking. Proceed immediately best possible speed.* I remember praying that I had taken the position correctly.

As daylight was beginning to fade the following afternoon we sighted the first raft—two young women on it and a man with a smashed leg, one of the women lying almost senseless, a hand clutched by the man. Then we saw two schoolgirls and an Indian seaman clinging to a keel; and, soon after that, a crowded lifeboat, very nearly awash, the water bathing the faces of children in pyjamas and nightdresses who lay dead in the stern sheets. A boy of 11, his name Colin Richardson, waved to us from the thwart and began to sing 'Rule Britannia'. We were all in tears.

Seventy-seven of the children in the *City of Benares* perished. One Merseyside survivor who lost her mother that terrible night, wrote regularly to me through the war years and now lives in Australia. The present home of another who was saved is half-an-hour's walk from my own; and I have seen on her right hand the permanent scars left by weals made as she clung for hour after hour in mid-ocean to a rope from an upturned boat. Her brother is married to another of the survivors.

Let it be supposed that I recalled these incidents to you as we sailed towards the Mersey over a sun-gilded sea. By the time the stories were told we would be well up the Crosby Channel, passing, as though in review, along the line of restless buoys. On the starboard bow is New Brighton, a suburb of Wallasey, tall flats (privately owned) with a marine view rising from a promenade, amusement places nearer the entrance to the river and on a brick-clad hill behind them, the verdigris-green dome of the large church of SS. Peter and Paul. Ever since the war Wallasey councillors have been trying to decide whether this coastal strip should be residential or a resort or a playground in the evening and at weekends for all Merseyside. It cannot satisfactorily be all three.

An ample open-air pool ensures that, on warm days at any rate, Merseyside bathers will flock there; but a deal has to be done in New Brighton if it is to stand a chance of competing for day trippers from the inland cities and towns, let alone wooing those who wish to spend a conventional week's holiday. The main shopping street is down-at-heel, and the beach by the river is little better than a mudflat when the tide ebbs. The seaward shore is more pleasant, though inclined to be bleak. Seabirds in the widest variety congregate at various periods of the year on the spits of Mockbeggar Wharf, a sand bar some 4 miles long running parallel with the Wirral coastline.

Up to the mid-eighteenth century ships were from time to time lured on to the quaking sands by wreckers who doused the guiding beacon on Perch Rock (which we will pass shortly) and lit a fire on the dunes in line with Mockbeggar Wharf. An old rhyme runs

> Wallasey for wreckers,
> Poulton for leaves.
> Leasowe for honest folk,
> Seacombe for thieves.

There were probably as many wreckers in Leasowe—which overlooks Mockbeggar Wharf—as in adjoining Wallasey; but William Hutchinson's lighthouse at Bidston, on a wooded bluff inland from Leasowe, put them out of business. From our ship we can see the dome of an observatory among the trees of Bidston Hill, where there is an old windmill and where a sixteenth-century manor house, until recent years in virtual ruin, has been lovingly restored.

But we should now turn our eyes to the Lancashire coast, at Seaforth in the borough of Crosby, where a new port is being built at a cost of more than £40 million. This area was until the late sixties a desolate and muddy foreshore, though on the north side of it stands a line of handsome villas with an esplanade. Naturally enough, their occupants did not welcome the massive development of the foreshore by the Mersey Docks and Harbour Board; yet, upon this extension, which will provide ten deep-sea berths, the commercial future of the river now very largely depends. Even with Seaforth, it is by no means certain that the dock authority will recover from insolvency and that the Mersey will keep its place as the nation's second largest port.

On the starboard side we now draw level with Perch Rock which once had a battery of six guns to protect the river entrance and was built in 1775, covering the site of a perch with the guiding fire basket. The lighthouse on the rock was erected in 1830 by Liverpool Corporation, though this is, of course, Wallasey territory—a causeway leads to the Tuscan-style entrance of the fort from New Brighton.

Once past Perch Rock we are in the Mersey proper and sailing almost due south, a fact which frequently disorientates those conditioned by elementary geography lessons to assume that the river runs from east to west. Soon after passing between Widnes and Runcorn it flows south-west and then describes an arc northwards on its way to the sea. Birkenhead is thus west of Liverpool not south.

Now, on the port side, we pass the 80-foot tower of the port's radar station and come abreast with the cranes and wall of Gladstone Dock, the entrance to it (pointing south-east) at present hidden. Gladstone was opened in 1927.

In the late sixties quays were adapted to handle containered freight and to serve as the main terminal for this type of cargo (its development the most revolutionary in postwar shipping) until the Seaforth complex is complete. Gladstone, the largest of the Mersey Docks, is partly in Crosby but mainly in Bootle. Its upriver neighbours, Hornby, Alexandra (with one of the biggest cold stores in Europe), Langton and Brocklebank Docks are wholly in Bootle. Canada, which adjoins Brocklebank, is the first dock in the city of Liverpool to be reached sailing south.

Langton and Canada docks, built in the second half of the nineteenth century, were very largely reconstructed, the work completed in the early 1960s at a cost of £20 million; and this was the biggest dock improvement programme in the country to be undertaken in the first twenty of the postwar years. It provided a new deep water entrance and seven berths with the most up-to-date handling aids.

On the opposite side of the river Wallasey Town Hall stands on a high, lawned bank. Some distance to the north of this was 'Mother Redcap's', the hiding place for fugitives from the press gangs (as described in the second chapter). Upriver from the Town Hall is the tower of the Seacombe ferry terminal and south of this the entrance to a line of docks biting deep into Cheshire and dividing Wallasey from Birkenhead. In this dock estate are lairages for the scores of thousands of cattle landed annually from Irish ports. In mid-1970 the Dock Board announced that the lairages would close at the end of the year because the number of beasts handled had fallen from 230,000 in 1960 to 94,000 in 1969; and because it was uneconomic to modernise the landing stages. Thus the Mersey is losing another traditional and once important section of its traffic.

The Liver Building and its two neighbours now dominate the view over the bows of our ship, and beyond this Pier Head trinity stand Albert Dock's warehouses in dour bulk. Ferries bustle across the Mersey to and from Pier Head and Seacombe and the more southerly landing stage at Woodside, Birkenhead.

On our port side we pass Huskisson Dock, constructed in 1852. In one of its branches vast quantities of raw sugar are scooped out of holds by grab cranes and spilled on to conveyors that feed a silo with a capacity of 100,000 tons. South of Huskisson come Sandon, Wellington and Bramley-Moore Docks in that order, so terminating the Northern Group. Then follows Nelson Dock, commencing the Central Group, used mainly by coasters. Nelson Dock's southerly neighbour is Salisbury Dock, its entrance dominated by Jesse Hartley's castellated Victoria Tower in begrimed granite. The gruff Hartley must have been possessed by fey influences when he designed it for, particularly in summer evening light, it has the look of some component of a fairy fortress.

Behind it, Salisbury Dock links with Collingwood Dock, which in turn runs into Stanley Dock; and then follow a line of locks to the Leeds and Liverpool Canal. This is dockland's deepest penetration into Liverpool. The locks are little used, and the canal has for many years been the subject of bitter contention because so many children have been drowned in its vile waters. A strong body of opinion wants the canal filled in; but this would be difficult technically because it is a drain into which several watercourses run. There are others who would like to see it as an amenity instead of an eyesore, its banks made ornamental with a tree-lined walk and its bed stepped so that no more children could drown; but that would be an extremely expensive undertaking. At present this once-important waterway, which transported raw cotton to Lancashire looms and brought woollen goods to the Mersey from Yorkshire mills, stays an exceedingly ugly weal through North Liverpool, Bootle and Litherland; yet when it reaches open country it is a pleasant, almost sylvan, route for weekend pleasure craft. Why should it be dirty and dangerous only when it is in town?

One flank of Stanley Dock is occupied by a vast, fourteen-floor bonded tobacco store known as the Stanley New (it was, in fact, erected at the beginning of the century), 750 feet long, 165 feet wide and 125 feet high. It is said to be the world's biggest repository of tobacco, the contents at most times of the year worth more than £300 million (ten times the price of that new Seaforth dock layout) if you count the duty. To inspect every door on every floor (and this is done daily) entails a walk of more than

10 miles. All the main doors have two locks, one the Dock Board's, the other belonging to H.M. Customs. Sixty trucks are employed in the movement of the golden hoard, all of it destined to burn to ash.

But obviously there is a strict no smoking rule in Stanley New and stringent precautions against fire. If this lot went up in flames before it could be distributed to go up in smoke the loss to the nation's revenue would be calamitous. Consider all the wines and spirits (particularly rum) also in bond in Liverpool warehouses and vaults, and you begin to understand just how valuable Mersey dockland is to British taxpayers.

The Victoria Tower is now astern as our ship passes Trafalgar Dock, which is at the feet of three tall chimneys of the Central Electricity Generating Board's Clarence Dock power station. Liverpudlians know the chimneys as the Ugly Sisters, and for years after I came to Liverpool their filthy tresses, flying in the wind, shed dandruff on every sill, doorstep and roof for miles around, making nonsense of the Clean Air Act and talk of a smoke-free city. There is vapour from the chimneys now, not smoke, but what goes up them must surely come down somewhere. A large sector of Liverpool is subject to smoke control regulations, and it would have been much larger at the start of the seventies had it not been for the delaying policies of past governments.

Our ship glides past the entrances to Victoria and Waterloo Docks and the Princes Half-Tide; and then we are looking at the Princes Landing Stage, afloat on the Mersey, behind it the Riverside station, now closed, and then the floating roadway that at ebb tide climbs steeply up to the city. Here once waited the queens of the Atlantic, high piles of baggage and provisions stacked on the stage, scarlet-capped porters hurrying between railway platforms and gangways. This is a Liverpool scene gone forever, and the stage and its setting look forlorn. Even most of the holiday cruise liners have gone from the Mersey. There are more attractive points of departure for a vacation at sea than this shabby back door; but its renewal would cost more than £2,500,000.

Liverpudlians like to see people on ships in their river; and some of them have pointed out emphatically that when Southampton gets £1 18s. port tax on every person sailing out into the Solent, people can be very profitable, too. As matters stand, however, it looks as if the Princes Stage, once the Mersey's pride, has only a few more years to run.

No doubt Dock Board officials would answer this by pointing across the river to the Tranmere Oil Terminal, opened in 1960. In February 1970 the 206,000-ton tanker *Melo* arrived there, the first of the super-leviathans (their coming delayed by eighteen months because a vessel rammed a Terminal jetty and repairing the damage cost a million and a quarter). Thousands lined the banks of the Mersey to greet her.

Against such marine goliaths as the *Melo* the old transatlantic liners would look diminutive indeed. And, of course, it is argued that the future lies not in carting people to the sun and back but in such mighty tankers coming in to feed refineries.

The Mersey is now the third largest of Britain's oil ports, and no doubt this traffic will continue rapidly to grow. There were tentative proposals to construct an island out in Liverpool Bay to receive the half-million-ton oil carriers that will be afloat before the end of the seventies and to pipeline their contents from the island to the Wirral's refineries, now being extended. Obviously the resorts of North Wales were relieved when, in 1970, the plan was dropped. Damage to Cornish beaches from the 1967 disaster would be infinitesimal in comparison with the catastrophe there could be if a tanker so much larger than the *Torrey Canyon* came to grief in Liverpool Bay. Onlookers who, gasping, measured the length of the *Melo* as she passed Perch Rock, then talked of the possible consequences of such a giant running into trouble in the river. They scarcely bear contemplating.

South of the Princes Stage is Georges Landing Stage used by the ferries; and it has to be said that in 1970 this looks tatty too. Since the ferries lose a great deal of money every year, and those belonging to Birkenhead are heavily subsidised by Tunnel receipts, the future of this floating platform is also uncertain. The ferries are now under the control of the Merseyside Passenger Transport Authority, and this body is required to make the various forms of public transport pay their way. It remains to be seen how long the authority can allow river boats to sink deeper and deeper into debt. Higher fares would inevitably mean fewer passengers and a minimal increase in revenue. Hovercraft may link Liverpool with New Brighton, however, instead of summertime ferry boats.

You will have noticed the river drawing in its breadth as our ship approached the Pier Head. Now that we are past the landing stages and nearing the massive wall on which Jesse Hartley's Albert Dock warehouses sit, the Mersey broadens and continues to do so for several miles.

On the Birkenhead side tall cranes compose a web above the Cammell Laird shipyards. Polaris submarines were built here, but that work went from Birkenhead to Barrow-in-Furness and this began the chain of disasters that brought this famous firm to the brink of total collapse in May, 1970. The Government came to the rescue with a £6 million credit but insisted on unprofitable shipbuilding orders being cancelled so that redundancies seemed inevitable. It was painfully ironic when, less than a month after the yards' desperate hours, one of the most famous vessels built there, the carrier *Ark Royal*, visited the Mersey.

Beyond the shipyards and well out into the river are the T-shaped stages of the Tranmere Oil Terminal, extremities of concrete jetties extending like long arms from a trunk which thrusts out of land reclaimed from the Mersey. Each of the stages is 366 feet long and moored by four booms to steel pillars set in the river bed. Because of the sharp rise and fall of the tide—often exceeding 30 feet—pontoons, encircling fixed pillars, were provided ahead and astern of each tanker berth to act as mooring dolphins and so minimise the necessary attention to the mooring wires of tankers while they are discharging. On the reclaimed land there are storage tanks for more than 150,000 tons of fuel, and from here the oil is pumped through pipelines several miles long to the great refineries at Stanlow, close to Ellesmere Port.

Further upriver on the Wirral side, and with its own esplanade, is Rock Park, an enclave of Victorian houses of considerable character, a tiny, private world into which, after a drawn-out battle, by-pass builders have leave to intrude. One of the houses was the home of Nathaniel Hawthorne when he was American Consul on the opposite bank of the Mersey.

The view of the Liverpool shore is now entirely dominated by the Anglican Cathedral, high above its own hill, magnificent in all degrees of daylight, but in a summer evening's last hour of sun spectacularly beautiful for it is then that the sandstone blushes pink. Nearly all that can be seen from river vantage points of the foreground and surroundings of the vast church is sombre—like the congregation of blind warehouses—or shoddy or woebegone; and yet the anthem in twentieth-century gothic soars above these undefiled, supremely majestic. England has very few wholly urban landscapes as stirring as this; but subtract the Cathedral and there is only dross. Suppose that there were lawns or woodlands from the river's edge up to the Cathedral's mount—as might have been done in Norway or in New Zealand—would the effect be as magical? I think not.

We have been sailing past the now doomed Southern docks— Canning, Albert, Kings, Wapping, Queens, Coburg, Brunswick and Harrington and so reach Herculaneum, the upriver extremity of the 7-mile line behind which lie nearly 40 miles of quays, locks and basins known to the port's pilots as 'The Rockery'. Ships carrying passengers sail to the Canaries from Kings (notice, by the way, this absence of apostrophes as mentioned in my last chapter), and there are big grain silos at Brunswick and Coburg.

The name of Herculaneum Dock is a reminder that Liverpool once had potteries of note. The ware they produced became popular towards the end of the seventeenth century, and by 1760 there were more than a hundred potters in the town. Thereafter the industry sharply declined against Dutch competition, but there was a temporary revival as the result of a discovery by John Sadler, who was a printer.

He gave his children some unwanted printed material and they stuck pieces of it on fragments of crockery which they used to furnish a doll's house. Sadler noted that the print had adhered to the crocks and so he began experimenting with transfers on to pottery from copper plates. His enterprise soon attracted attention, and even Wedgwood products were sent to Liverpool from Stoke-on-Trent to be printed. He specialised in printing rhymes about sailors and pictures of ships and battles at sea (particularly those of Nelson's fleet). Jugs and plates so decorated were in demand for a number of years but then went out of fashion. The Herculaneum Pottery, at the riverside, was the last to close, and fifteen years later (in 1866) the dock bearing its name was opened.

The prospect across the water from here used to be made more engaging by the presence of two training ships anchored with the Cheshire bank their nearest. The splendid frigate *Conway* arrived in the Mersey in 1859 to stay more than a hundred years. She lay down river from the *Indefatigable*, a veteran of steam. Both suffered some damage during the last war. The *Conway* then moved to Anglesey and came to grief in the Menai Straits. Both 'training' ships are now shore establishments by the Straits. Succeeding generations of sailors continue to add lustre to the annals of both institutions.

John Masefield was a cadet in the *Conway* and wrote these impressions:

> At all seasons, at all states, the River was beautiful. At dead low water, when great sandbanks were laid bare to draw multitudes of gulls; in calm, when the ships stood still above their shadows; in storm, when the ferries beat by, shipping sprays; and at full flood, when shipping put out and came in, the River was a wonder to me. Sometimes, as I sat aloft in the cross-trees in those early days, I thought how marvellous it was, to have this ever-changing miracle about me with mountains, smoky, glittering cities, the clang of hammers, the roar or hoot of sirens; the miles of docks, the ships and attendant ships, all there for me, seemingly only noticed by me; everybody else seemed to be used to it by this time, or to have other things to do.*

Next door to Herculaneum Dock is another estate of large oil tanks, more than seventy of them, their capacity nearly 350,000 tons. Clustered round them, like clutches of their eggs, are smaller tanks. These receptacles empty into barges at a jetty and are replenished by pipelines from a quay in one of Herculaneum Dock's branches, the final elements of 'The Rockery'.

South of this, well within living memory, was the 'Cassy' Shore, at ebbtide a stretch of muddy beach leading to a nest of shallow caves much loved by the children who then lived in the nearby Dingle, many of them in houses which have been demolished since the Second World War as slums. 'Cassy' was short for cast-iron, and the shore got this name from its proximity to the Mersey Foundry. Thomas Cragg, its proprietor in the early part of the nineteenth century, had a forceful personality and believed passionately in the use of the products of his foundry for building. To prove his theories he constructed, immediately to the south of Dingle, a hamlet of cottages with cast-iron windows, frames, sills, fireplaces and doorposts.

* Quoted by permission of the Society of Authors as the literary representatives of the Estate of John Masefield.

He joined forces with Thomas Rickman, born in Kent and the son of a Quaker pharmacist. Rickman was himself a chemist and then a clerk before coming to Liverpool, where he worked as an accountant, in his spare time studying gas lighting, geology, steamship construction and meteorology and also constantly adding to a fantastic toy army of several thousands, the uniform and arms of each soldier modelled and painted in meticulous detail. He then turned his attention to architecture and became as fanatically interested in gothic as he had been in his toy troops, spending every moment he could spare in visiting churches built in this style and recording all details. By the time he became friendly with Cragg he had been elected Professor of Architecture at Liverpool Academy.

Together they conceived a gothic church in cast iron and found for its site that of an old lighthouse on the hillside at Everton. This church is St. George's, completed in 1813, its shell constructed of stone—in deference to the donor of £12,000 towards the cost of its erection—but its interior, including a gallery, is wholly in iron. The decorated columns, moulded panels of the gallery and astonishingly delicate window traceries were all cast at the Mersey Foundry and then transported to Everton to be bolted together. The result was, at the time, the most remarkable parish church in the kingdom; but it was very soon to have a parallel in Cragg's hamlet.

This second iron church is St. Michael's-in-the-Hamlet, its exterior of brick instead of stone but with metal parapets and finials. Much of the ironwork inside the church was cast in the moulds used for St. George's but the components were differently arranged. They have elegance, even daintiness, in their slender lines; and here—as in the Vines Hotel's woodwork and the Cathedral's carved stone—is an example of the highly accomplished craftsman who seems to have been inside so many Liverpudlians—indeed, probably still is but awaiting a chance to show himself.

There was naturally great interest in the Cragg-Rickman churches, one of the earliest essays in prefabrication. It was seen that if churches could be built from moulded components there would be a notable financial saving. Parts for churches to be assembled in what were then our colonies were manufactured at Cragg's foundry and shipped from the Mersey.

His hamlet still stands and, in ways difficult to define, has the
air of a country village which, when built, it virtually was. It
was even given a countrified railway station, the last stop before
the line from Manchester Central curved round to the riverside
and then burrowed its way to Liverpool Central.

The ship taking us up the Mersey is now abreast with another
private residential park built in the last century; and between it
and the river is an enormous rubbish tip, which in fact covers the
'Cassy' Shore. A stranger to the river would be pardoned for
supposing that the residents of the big houses in Fulwood Park
were resentful about this; but, on the contrary, they are delighted.
The tip is essential to the last stage of an enterprise as inspired, in
its way, as that of Cragg and Rickman.

Between the wars Liverpool, ever short of vacant land, was
having difficulty with refuse disposal. For a time the city's discard
was taken out in barges and dumped in the sea, but this was an
extremely costly way of getting rid of it. When excavations began
for the Mersey Tunnel the problem of what to do with the spoil
obviously became acute. Then it was decided to build a wall
alongside the river south of where a stream known as Little
Jordan meanders through a wooded glen; to pile Tunnel spoil
and other refuse on marshy ground behind the wall; and then to
construct a promenade on top of heaped discard amounting to
millions of tons.

The result is an outstanding amenity. Shrubberies of species
selected to withstand the salt-laden winds which sweep in from
Liverpool Bay now cloak banks of varying heights into which
steps have been cut to lead to winding paths and a parkland motor
road. There are ample shelters for the protection of the species
homo sapiens on a windy day; and inland from the promenade and
its gardens are playing fields and parkland incorporating the glen
watered by the Little Jordan. The entrance to this glen is almost
directly opposite an entrance to the expanse of Sefton Park which
adjoins Princes Park, this only 2 miles from the city centre.

The riverside promenade is called Otterspool, a free adaptation
of 'Oskelbrooke', the older name for the Little Jordan. Whenever
I fulminate about shortcomings of the Corporation I remember
Otterspool and then my temperature drops. The final phase of
the promenade, bringing the total length to more than 2 miles,

will be planted up and on its way to maturity during the seventies. What to do with the city's rubbish need not then again be a problem; for there are plans to construct a similar promenade some miles up the river towards Widnes.

Continuing our voyage upriver we pass the southern extremity of Otterspool Promenade and then reach another group of docks, those at Garston, run not by the Mersey Docks and Harbour Board but by the British Transport Docks Board and this authority's principal port in the North-west. Powers to build docks at this elbow of the Mersey were granted to the St. Helens Canal and Railway Company in 1847.

Curiously, Garston Docks rarely get a mention in Liverpool Corporation's publications showing off the city, yet millions have been spent on their modernisation since the last war, the tonnage handled has increased year by year and hundreds of dockers are employed. Coal and coke shipments to Ireland and the Isle of Man and imports of timber (including cargoes from Scandinavian and Russian ports) are the main traffic, but substantial quantities of fruit and other food, iron and steel also pass through the port and there are containered cargo services to Belfast and Lisbon.

Almost directly across the river from Garston is the entrance, at Eastham, to the Manchester Ship Canal, opened in 1894 in the teeth of determined opposition from Liverpool. Such a waterway was, in fact, mooted some seventy years earlier, the proposal then being to link Manchester with the Dee estuary near Parkgate, cutting out the Mersey altogether. Parkgate was once a port of some consequence (Handel sailed from there to Dublin for the first performance of *Messiah*), but for many years its wall has been reached by the sea only at the highest of the spring tides and then barely at a depth sufficient to float a dinghy.

Our ship cannot take us farther up the Mersey than Garston because, although the river is at its widest a mile or so nearer Widnes, it presents a great many navigational hazards. We can see a lighthouse on a promontory near Hale, a short distance beyond the Liverpool city boundary, but this has become part of an unusual private house. Beyond the bluff the river narrows abruptly to divide Widnes in Lancashire from Runcorn in Cheshire. Here it is crossed by an old bridge of several arches carrying the main railway line Londonwards; and by a new road bridge which spans it in a single, dramatic, latticed arc. The road crossing replaced a transporter bridge, a somewhat Heath Robinsonish contraption that motorists found it almost an adventure to use.

Occupying 800 acres on the Lancashire bank of the Mersey between Garston and Hale is Liverpool Airport—at Speke—with a comparatively new runway more than a mile and half long that cost £3 million, and up-to-date instrument landing systems; yet it is almost absurdly under-used and losing money at the rate of more than £600,000 a year. Dreams of Speke becoming an international terminal to rival Manchester have faded. Before such ambitions could have even a remote hope of realisation there would have to be new and highly expensive passenger accommodation, and early in 1970 it was made clear that no help towards the cost would come from the Government of that time. It would be the height of folly to spend yet more millions of Liverpool ratepayers' money on a Merseyside amenity to which the other authorities of the region make no contribution.

During the drawn-out arguments over the siting of a third airport for London, sources in Liverpool urged that Speke be considered as a means of at least temporarily relieving congestion to Heathrow. With a train journey of little over two-and-a-half hours to Euston, landing transatlantic passengers at Speke would not be a harsh inconvenience to those among them bound for the capital; while, as a staging post or a place for changing planes for those bound for other European countries, Speke could be just as convenient as London. It was also pointed out that main objections to supersonic airliners would be removed if they departed and arrived at Speke because they could penetrate (or re-enter) the sound barrier over the Irish Sea.

Such notions had no interest for the Government. It appears that the only international airport in the provinces is to be at Manchester—yet what will happen when Ringway too is congested? By that time it will almost certainly be too late to look to Liverpool; for the Corporation's policy, it now appears inevitable, must be one of contraction, parcelling off part of the land lying fallow at Speke into sites for factories (the area around the airport is already largely occupied by industry, including the great Ford plant and the factory of Standard-Triumph).

When Ringway is shrouded by fog then Speke (less prone to

this hazard) is used to a limited degree as an alternative landing place; but B.E.A. and B.O.A.C. are much more disposed to take their Manchester-bound passengers on to London or to decant them at Prestwick in Scotland. The truth is that the only State-run airline to have evinced genuine interest in Liverpool Airport is Aer Lingus.

The Corporation resumed control at Speke (taken over by the Government at the outbreak of war) in 1961, whereupon B.E.A. withdrew. Prospects brightened with the advent of British Eagle, but the sudden demise of this airline—obliged by the licensing authority to charge the same fares from Liverpool to destinations as B.E.A. charged from Manchester—and disinterest in Whitehall virtually destroyed hopes of any spectacular increase in traffic. Even the holiday flights to Europe have been below expectation, Manchester getting the lion's share of the North of England charter business.

Speke can show an increase in freight, but otherwise the airport has been expensively disappointing. Moreover, even when it is accepted that its future can only be modest, it will still have to be given new passenger reception buildings, though not, of course, on international airport scale. Thus, until reorganisation of local government distributes the cost of it over the whole of Merseyside, it will remain a millstone round Liverpool ratepayers' necks. At the time this book was revised the Corporation was making an earnest appraisal of the airport's potential.

Immediately beyond the airport and, indeed, close enough to it for the noise of jet aircraft to be earsplitting, stands Speke Hall, the partly fifteenth-century home of the Norris family, half-timbered in the traditional Cheshire style and with a Great Hall, its panels said to have come from Holyrood House. Liverpool Corporation, its caretakers for the National Trust, maintain lawns, floral beds and leafy walks.

The old house, once moated, is reached by a bridge which leads through an arched entrance to a gracious inner courtyard. A guide is available to conduct parties round the hall and point out the priest's hole (the Norris family were Catholics) and remnants of the manor house which originally occupied the site. The hall is appropriately furnished and contains numerous antiquities. Its southern windows contemplate, across wide water, the marshlands of Ince, where large numbers of seabirds, duck

Bluecoat Chambers
The old and the new in the University Precinct

K

and geese at present collect though they may cease to do so when considerable industrial developments in the vicinity are completed.

From the Bar Light Vessel to Speke Hall it is a little over 25 miles. The purpose of this chapter has been to show that in so comparatively short a distance, from the open sea through the bustling port to the almost sylvan surround of a venerable mansion, there is a vast amount to interest, much to admire—and a deal to ponder upon, for the Mersey of the early seventies has nearly as many question marks as it has buoys.

SIX

DOWNTOWN

COME for a walk in the city. Let us set out from the riverside, the part of the Pier Head piazza where orators expend their Sunday passion. This is close to the often defaced memorial to Merchant Navy crews of many nationalities who were lost between 1939 and 1945, a simple column which has a beacon head and is mounted on an arc of panels inscribed with the names of scores of ships, the list beginning with *Anking* and ending with *Wokang* and including numerous other names that came from east of Suez. Nearby is the statue of Sir Alfred Lewis Jones, the founder of the Liverpool School of Tropical Medicine which is described in Chapter Eight.

Opposite us is the southerly constituent of the Pier Head trinity of buildings. It contains the offices of the Mersey Docks and Harbour Board and has three domes, that in the centre, which is much the larger, having been taken from the design entered by Professor Sir Charles Reilly, of Liverpool University, in the Anglican Cathedral competition in 1902, five years before work on the Dock Board headquarters began. The architect of this mock palace was Arnold Thornley.

If we look across Mann Island—for many years merely an appendage to the Pier Head plateau—we see a building that may remind a Londoner of the original home of New Scotland Yard and, indeed, it was by the same architect, R. Norman Shaw. Cupola-capped turrets suggest a chateau, balconied windows a Venetian façade. Once the headquarters of the White Star Line, it now contains the offices of the Pacific Steam Navigation Company and has several new and large neighbours.

The Mann Island extremity of Pier Head is scruffy, and there is an appalling building—under suspended sentence of death—serving as a rest-room for old-age pensioners. This is on the tentative site for a maritime museum, but, as has been explained in an earlier chapter, there is a counter scheme to adapt a section of the Albert Dock warehouses for this purpose.

A street divides the triple-domed headquarters of the Dock Board from the Italianate architecture of the Cunard Building (still called this, although purchased by the Prudential in 1969 for £2,750,000). The Portland stone facing is deeply tooled and the 1971 removal of soot unveiled the elaborate carvings on each cornice. It was built during the 1914–18 war and was the last of the Pier Head trinity to be completed. Within it are the offices of H.M. Customs and of the American Consulate General, oldest of the thirty-four consulates in the city.

The Royal Liver Building (and photographs of it would be immediately identified by any sailor in any port) was one of the first multi-storey constructions in reinforced concrete, though its walls are faced in Jesse Hartley's favourite material, granite. Two domed towers, each with giant clocks, are the perches for the verdigris-coloured Liver Birds, their wings outstretched. The architect was W. Aubrey Thomas and the building was completed in 1911, its present occupants being numerous and varied and including the navy (they took over the greater part of it for the period of the last war), Inland Revenue and local taxation and licensing staffs and the consuls for Greece and Uruguay.

The Royal Liver Friendly Society had a humble beginning as a burial insurance co-operative during the nineteenth-century period of epidemics in the port, eventually developing side by side with the insurance companies founded in Liverpool because quotations from London for both fire and marine risks were considered extortionate. The oldest of the companies was the Liverpool Fire and Life, founded in 1836, the Royal following nine years later. In 1860 the Thames and Mersey was established as the first marine insurance company outside the capital. Liverpool remains one of the major insurance centres of the Commonwealth, and there is ample evidence of this in the commercial quarter we are about to explore.

We take the street between the Cunard and Liver Building to reach the Strand, now a double-carriageway section of the busy road which runs the length of the docks but destined to be part of the Inner Motorway designed by Graeme Shankland to ring the central area of the city. We can now see that, behind the Dock Board's headquarters stands one of the six (three on each side of the river) ventilating stations of the Mersey Tunnel, its tall shaft austere in countenance despite mural ornamentation. Almost opposite this is the turreted Pacific Building already described; and between this and where we cross the Strand are new blocks, Mersey House and Wilberforce House, which are of limited appeal.

On our opposite hand—that is, looking north—we see another of Aubrey Thomas's contributions to the waterfront area, the Tower Building, one of the first steel-framed constructions in the country and clad in white glazed tiles which shed the dirt of dockland. It is a handsome erection, considerably decorated; and one of its attractions is a tunnel leading to steps that ascend to Tower Gardens, which turns into Old Churchyard, a small remnant from the beginning of the nineteenth century bordering the cool lawns of St. Nicholas's, the city's parish church.

This was devastated in the last war but was restored with immense care. Its unusual tower, looking out towards Pier Head and the river, was spared grave war damage. It was built in 1815, replacing a spire (erected in 1746) that fell during a service and killed twenty-four children, all girls. There are some relics remaining of the church built in 1356 on the site of the chapel of St. Mary del Quay.

Close to the church is the dock entrance to the Mersey Tunnel and beyond this a large open space that will eventually be occupied by high buildings containing the *Liverpool Daily Post* and *Echo* offices and plant and commercial firms, neighbours of the towering Littlewood giant which brings Arthur Dooley's 'upturned Coca-Cola crates' to my mind.

Having crossed New Strand we are in Water Street, a canyon between the offices of insurance, banking and shipping; and here the Liverpool characteristic of shop floors below the level of the pavements will be observed. On our left, as we walk uphill, is the refined building known as Oriel Chambers, built in 1864 to the designs of Peter Ellis, a local architect. It has spiky yet gracious oriel windows, twenty of them overlooking Water Street so that there is as much glass in this frontage as in any modern office block. The building is at Water Street's corner with the narrow

Covent Garden and the architects who repaired the extensive war damage to the Covent Garden flank deserve the city's gratitude for so faithfully keeping to the spirit of Ellis's intentions. In Covent Garden the lower ground floor, beloved by Liverpool's mid-Victorian architects, can be seen in modern dress and I think it is completely appealing, though doubtless expensive.

On the opposite side of Water Street, but a few yards down the hill, is the entrance to Drury Lane, where, appropriately enough, Liverpool's first theatre was built in 1759. It is today an undistinguished gap in tall buildings, and it leads to what many Liverpudlians call 'The Contraption' or 'The Clanger', a grotesque affair of metal scoops which, having baled water noisily from a reservoir, make even more din emptying it in a wholly idiotic, if not maniacal, manner. This was the gift of the Civic Society to the city, and to my mind a single tree, if it could have been persuaded to grow in this courtyard of Wilberforce House, would have been infinitely more ornamental.

Beyond the so-called fountain are steps leading to the first length of the elevated walkway invented by Graeme Shankland; and there are more steps, at the end of Old Ropery, a tributary of Drury Lane, that climb up to a jigger off Fenwick Street near the postwar bulk of the Corn Exchange. Old Ropery is a reminder of the era when rope-making was an important local industry.

If we return now to Water Street and turn right, still on the opposite side to Oriel Chambers, we reach India Buildings erected between the wars and heavily damaged in the 1941 blitz. Its architects were Herbert Rowse (the local man who also designed the six tunnel ventilating stations) and Arnold Thornley, the creator of the Dock Board headquarters; and the edifice was described by Professor Sir Charles Reilly—Rowse's tutor—as the leading office block of its type in Britain. It cost rather more than £1 million and a huge part of it crumbled in a single night of high explosive bombs. Rowse had the unusual experience of having largely to reconstruct his pre-war handiwork, and the resurrection, begun in 1947, cost more than £500,000. Its facades were cleaned in 1971.

A prolonged passage runs underneath the building to the James Street underground station of the Mersey Railway. Thousands of office and shop workers scamper down it every weekday evening to catch trains to their homes across the water, but far fewer use

it in the mornings for the toiling slope from the station to Water
Street is a searching examination of lung power.

The principal appeal of the block is the lofty and elaborately
decorated arcade, with shops, which runs the width of it. It is well
worth a walk through the arcade, ornamented in keeping with the
title of India Buildings, to Brunswick Street and from there to
look left for the best view there is of the majestic frontage of the
Bank of England branch in Castle Street. This appropriately im-
pregnable-looking building was designed by Charles R. Cockerell
who gave it Roman nobility in four mighty pillars but also a
touch of the baroque in a quaint balustrade immediately below a
triangular pediment. There are protective iron palisades, and
some of the windows have grills of heavy steel bars.

We can use Brunswick Street to get to Castle Street, one of the
most handsome thoroughfares in England, despite an undistinguished new block (fortunately there is another, even newer, to
compensate it, the architect having contrived to simulate the
elegance of Oriel Chambers without slavishly copying).

Castle Street is dominated by the Town Hall at the Water
Street end. The look of this splendid building would be even
more spectacular if the twentieth-century office blocks at its rear
had been three storeys shorter in their height. The gilded statue
of Minerva, by the Italian sculptor Felix Rossi, sits regally in
Britannia-like pose on the dome; and below her the warm and
variable shades of the stonework, restored by face-cleaning
operations during the sixties, have added notably to the elegance
of the frontage.

The Town Hall is opened to the general public for only a few
days each summer; but let us assume that we have been invited
by the Lord and Lady Mayoress to one of the numerous receptions held during the year and that we therefore enter beneath a
scarlet awning, erected beneath the columns above the porch, as
is customary on these occasions.

The entrance hall, we find, is decorated with frescoes (painted
in 1909) depicting events in the history of the city from the
granting of the Charter by King John. There will be banks of
flowers from the conservatories of the Botanic Garden; and
either the Police or the City Transport band will be playing at the
foot of the great staircase because this is nearly always the case
when receptions take place. At the head of the first flight of the

sumptuous staircase and in an alcove with a floral surround—
poinsettias and azaleas in the winter months, begonias and
gloxinias in the summer—is Francis Chantrey's statue of George
Canning, so briefly the Prime Minister in 1827. Above this hangs
a coronet-surmounted portrait of Queen Elizabeth II by Edward
Halliday, and flags are hung from brackets at either side of it.

As we ascend the second flight of stairs we look up into the
high dome, magnificently embellished in blue and gold, and with
A.D. 1749 and *Deus nobis haec otia fecit* encircling it. The words
('God has provided for us this leisure') are the city's motto, which
incidentally has been answered by the motto of the University,
Haec otia studia fovent ('This leisure fosters our studies').

From the head of the staircase we turn into a series of salons
with lofty, elaborately ornamental ceilings and graced with
Empire furniture in mahogany, rosewood and amboyna inlaid
with brass. The fireplaces are replicas of those ordered for Carlton
House when it was a royal palace.

Depending upon the size of the reception we are attending, we
will be directed to either the large or the small ballroom, both
of great elegance. The large ballroom has a musicians' gallery and
there are three chandeliers, each 28 feet tall, weighing more than
a ton and containing some 20,000 pieces of crystal. The chandeliers
in the other ballroom are smaller but still spectacular and are of
Georgian cut glass.

We will assume that this is a reception important enough for
the city's treasures to be on view—including the Sword of
State, which was the sword of Sir William Norris of Speke Hall,
who died while Ambassador to the Great Mogul. We will also
see the silver oar of the Sergeant at Mace of the Court of Passage
(mentioned in Chapter Four) and three maces, two carried by
bailiffs and the other that which precedes Lord Mayors. There are
some exquisite pieces in the Civic Plate, among them candelabras
and epergnes and an eighteenth-century galleon in silver.

The Town Hall's treasures, including the great chandeliers,
were safely crated when a bomb blasted the east side of the building in 1941, shattering all the windows and seriously weakening
the fabric and the dome. Extensive repairs were carried out with
the utmost attention to detail after the war.

One of the most enjoyable receptions I have attended in the
Town Hall was in the smaller ballroom and was for the Welsh

National Opera company on their first visit to the city where so many of Welsh ancestry live. Members of the company sang impromptu choruses from *Nabucco* and *La Traviata*, the sound soaring to the chandeliers and echoing through the suite of reception rooms. I wished then that there could be concerts periodically in one of the salons and that they could be televised in colour so that millions could see the glories of this building. But Liverpool is uncommonly well off for concert halls, large and small, so it is perhaps unlikely that this particular desire of mine will be satisfied, unless, of course, the initiative comes from either the BBC or Granada.

The Town Hall's next-door neighbour, in Water Street, is the former head office of Martins Bank, now joined with Barclays, and is the work of Herbert Rowse, more compelling than his India Building. An acquaintance of mine calls it 'the Taj Mahal of the North' and has a slight basis for this apparently outrageous claim because there is a suggestion of a Mogul emperor's mahal in both the interior design and decor, also in the air of opulence. It was erected in 1932 when the city was still in the depths of industrial depression with many thousands out of work; so the luxury of the style and the trappings accord with the Liverpool tradition of building palatially at times when the populace is poverty-stricken. Rowse, it certainly seems, was able to spend the bank's money liberally.

The roof of the main banking hall is nearly 40 feet high, and ceilings and arches above the columns forming arcades are richly embossed and embroidered. The walls are lined with travertine marble and columns supporting a balustraded gallery are of the same material. The Liver Bird and the grasshopper (the one the emblem of the Bank of Liverpool, the other that of Martins Bank in London long before it came North) are used repeatedly in the decorative friezes and panels. It surprises me that so few Liverpudlians tarry, when on workaday errands into Water Street, to look inside the banking hall just a few yards from the pavement; for this is, in my opinion, one of the sights of their city.

The external friezes of the building are decorated with Neptune heads, stars, tridents, crabs, lobsters and, of course, Liver Birds and grasshoppers; and they were the work of H. Tyson Smith, a

Liverpool sculptor of considerable skills who has for many years had studios in the Bluecoat Chambers, the doyen of the colony of artists who work there.

Facing the Town Hall from the junction of Water Street and Castle Street is the former main office of the District Bank, different in character from the edifice of Herbert Rowse. It has a Georgian bearing, modest but dignified. Opposite this building, and between the former headquarters of Martins Bank and the Town Hall, is an entrance to Exchange Flags, for long a pedestrian concourse and in past centuries a centre of commercial trading. It has been said that slaves were regularly sold here but there appears to be little truth in the story which may have had its origin in chained figures, a striking feature of the monument to Nelson that adorns the Flags.

William Roscoe, the abolitionist, played a leading part in the raising of funds for this memorial to celebrate Trafalgar, so it is just conceivable that he had something to do with the men in chains, although the monument was, in fact, put out to competition. It was completed in 1813—eight years after the battle it commemorates—with the familiar 'England expects . . .' message prominently displayed. Statues of Columbus, Cook, Drake, Galileo, Mercator and Raleigh stood on Exchange Flags until despatched to the less congested surroundings in Newsham Park.

The nineteenth-century buildings looking out across the Flags were colonnaded, but the modern flanks (Derby House and Exchange Buildings) have nothing much to show off apart from height and bulk and a war memorial. Derby House has a large basement fortified against fire, and this was used for the direction of the Battle of the Atlantic by the Royal Navy's Western Approaches Command, the officers passing the Trafalgar monument as they went on duty, perhaps obtaining some inspiration from it. Presumably they suffered aerial attack, as civilians do today, from the pigeons that haunt the Flags. There used to be a rule forbidding anyone to feed the birds in the square but, like the regulation against smoking, it has gone by default.

There is a way out from the Flags through Derby House into Chapel Street, which, with Tithebarn Street (its continuation) has become a corridor between great office blocks, some of them constructed in the late sixties, domineering yet expressionless. One wonders how long all those who work in them, at desks in open-plan offices sowing and reaping fodder for computers, can escape being depersonalised.

We are on our way to an example of speculative office building in a wholly different era; and perhaps passing Ma Boyle's oyster house at the corner of Old Hall Street is a good preparation for it. The Albany is a few yards above 'Ma Boyle's' and reached, mercifully, before the new frontage given to the Cotton Exchange, a bland face without character substituted for a façade that had the look of a palace in Rome (its removal surely one of the worst offences committed in Liverpool this century in the guise of 'improvement').

The Albany, completed in 1856, interrupts its eloquence in the classical style with exclamation marks in gothic. It was built by Richard Naylor, an immensely rich banker and sportsman who won the Derby in 1863 with Macaroni, a stumpy colt that cost him £100 and which he backed at 50 to 1 to win £100,000 (in celebration he gave £1,000 to the poor of Liverpool). The Albany's architect was James Colling, a Londoner and an enthusiast of the gothic. Naylor, who had travelled extensively in the Mediterranean countries, insisted on the classical style and Colling drew inspiration from the Palazzo Farnese in Rome. He slipped in bits and pieces of gothic where he could, however, using medieval floral motifs and carvings on the capitals.

The building was a shrewd investment to serve King Cotton before the reign had reached its full importance. The North Lights (or wing) contained cotton sample rooms, and there were complementary offices in the South Lights. They were still being used for this purpose long after the Cotton Exchange was opened next door in 1896.

Wrought-iron gates, embellished with Naylor's coat-of-arms, stand at the entrance, and from this steps lead down to a courtyard between high, white-painted walls. The yard is spanned by a bridge patterned in wrought iron with a spiral staircase in the centre. Set high in a wall opposite the main entrance to the courtyard is a gilt-framed clock set between two columns of words in black on a gilt ground

TIME	TARRY
AND	FOR
TIDE	NOMAN

The painter, pinched for space, was obliged to make 'Noman' one word (someone ought to have told him to substitute 'none').

Until the late sixties the Albany had surroundings to suit it in George Street and Ormond Street, for these were so wholly Victorian that Dickens, who knew Liverpool well, would have found little changed in this locality. The streets remain but much of them have been procured by subjects of the Brobdingnag that this part of the city has become.

We return to traffic-packed Chapel Street and its continuation Tithebarn Street, look at the curving arcade of Exchange Station and the hotel frontage still clad in Liverpool soot, then cross the road to Hackins Hey, a bustling lane just wide enough to take a beer lorry but which cannot be closed to vehicles because of the difficulty there would be in servicing its pubs, cafes and shops. Hundreds of Liverpool office workers lunch daily in the Hey, which has modern skyscrapers peering down both ends of it.

Quakers' Alley, so narrow that two cyclists could not pass without great care, joins Hackins Hey (where the Quakers had a meeting place until 1790) with Leather Lane (free from traffic) and is also a link with Tempest Hey and with Eberle Street which was once called Blackberry Lane because a Mr. Black lived on one side and a Mr. Berry on the other. Once there was a cockpit here, and it was used as a theatre on at least one occasion before the playhouse opened in Drury Lane.

These quaintways have something of the character of an oriental bazaar, refuges for small shopkeepers who have been priced out of the high streets. They are Victorian in visage but much older in origin and belonged to the Moor family, one of whom had this to say of the Liverpudlians of 400 years ago: 'They are the most perfidious knaves to their landlords in all England. . . . there is no such thing as truth or honesty in such mercenary fellows. . . . such a nest of rogues were never educated in one town of that bigness.'

He also described the wife of one of his tenants as 'a notorious whore and wicked woman. . . . she hath been once at the bride-well, twice carted and once ducked.'

Hackins Hey takes us into Dale Street, and we see the Town Hall on our right, though the view of it from this point is offensively obscured by a giant gantry, containing traffic directions, spread above the street. Next to the Town Hall, on the

Dale Street side, is another example of Charles Cockerell's work, the offices he handsomely designed for the Liverpool and London and Globe Insurance Company. Facing this are the entrances of two almost untouched remnants of Victoriana, Sweeting Street and Queen's Avenue, alleys elbowing round into Castle Street. Opposite us, from the entrance to Hackins Hey, is a tall and powerful office block—one of the better new buildings in the city—occupying the site of the Angel Hotel referred to in Chapter One; and to the right of this is the glassy countenance of a 1971 bank which, in my opinion, has a quirky modernity wholly unsuitable to be opposite the Town Hall.

We are also facing North John Street, walled in one side by another of Rowse's ventilating shafts, exceedingly sombre; though a building of the seventies close to it, housing a firm of outfitters, is another commendable addition to Liverpool. Running along the other side of North John Street and turning the corner into Dale Street is the virile head office of the Royal Insurance Group, another of Norman Shaw's buildings and with something of the look of a Venetian town hall. Gracious windows have wrought iron balconies and there are sculptured groups between pillars on the upper storeys. The dome is gilded.

Our route is to the left along Dale Street with a peep down a narrow, warehouse-lined lane, to a sign reading 'Banco Espanol en Londres' adding a slightly exotic touch. The bank is in Victoria Street, in the part of it occupied by fruit importers and the Fruit Exchange and auction rooms. Other streets on the same side of Dale Street give us blinkered views of the Head Post Office, also in Victoria Street, built in the style of a chateau but denuded of its top storey by 1941 bombs and its good looks ruined thereby.

But we pass, in Dale Street, a notable building that escaped war ravages, the offices of the Prudential built in the 1880s to the designs of Alfred Waterhouse, more of whose work we will be seeing later. Waterhouse—who built Manchester's Town Hall— excelled himself in this Dale Street office block, and because it is clad in brick impervious to grime it looks young for its age. We also pass the municipal offices and, on the opposite side, another new high building close to where one of twin flyovers, designed to relieve congestion in the approaches to the Mersey Tunnel, flows into Dale Street.

Now we have before us the splendid bulk of St. George's Hall beyond the flower beds and lawns of St. John's Gardens. This is the first view of Liverpool motorists get as they emerge from the Tunnel after driving from Birkenhead—the gardens, the Hall and, on the left, the noble uphill procession of college, museum, roundel library, art gallery and sessions house, colonnaded and making a Roman forum of the triangle, with its fountain, at the base of the high Doric column on which the figure of Wellington stands, bombarded daily by pigeons.

We cross Byrom Street, portal of Scotland Road and criss-crossed by flyovers, into William Brown Street and, from the pavement at the foot of the many steps leading up to the six columns at the entrance of the Museum, look into the Tunnel's mouth.

From this main entrance the Tunnel's roadway descends a 1-in-30 gradient to a point beneath the river, continues on the level for a little over 550 yards and then ascends to Birkenhead, the gradient again 1-in-30. The distance from end to end for through traffic (that is vehicles not using one of the dock branches) is 2.13 miles. It was opened in 1934 and cost more than £7 million. It is, in fact, an enormous metal pipe with concrete flesh and the roadway is a bridge across its diameter. From Rowse's ventilating stations air is blown under the roadway and then through openings at the kerbs.

The Museum was founded when the thirteenth Earl of Derby bequeathed to the citizens his natural history collection and Joseph Mayer, a Liverpool goldsmith, gave his archaelogical collection. The building was designed by John Weightman and presented by one of the local M.P.s, William Brown. All but the handsome frontage was devastated by bombs, and reconstruction has been a protracted process because of the other heavy claims upon the city's finances; but the first phase, which cost nearly £300,000 was completed in 1966 and admirably embraces modern display techniques. In 1970 a public planetarium—the only one in the country outside London—was opened and so was a transport museum containing one of the sedate coaches from the old Overhead and wagons drawn by beautifully modelled horses, life-size.

One of the treasures that cannot be put on public show is a herbarium containing 100,000 specimens which dates back to the period of William Roscoe's interest in botany and John Shepherd's term as curator of the garden on Mount Pleasant described in Chapter Three. In recent years eminent professors of botany from the United States have spent holidays here studying the specimens of American plants, the gift of the botanical explorer, Thomas Nuttall, which are unparalleled on the other side of the Atlantic.

Uphill from the Museum are the Central Libraries, also heavily damaged in the war but now restored. In the beginning they were the first specially built public library of any size in the kingdom and for many years after were the largest in the country. The Brown Library, largely rebuilt, occupies six floors and contains numerous departments including a particularly notable technical and scientific section. Corridors lead to the International Library of some 100,000 volumes, and there is a separate American Library of 10,000 books.

But the circular Picton Library is the gem of the group. It was designed by Cornelius Sherlock, who took the Pantheon in Rome as his model. It is named after Sir James Allanson Picton, historian and architect, and is a vast storehouse of 92,000 books with reading desks for more than 200 students. Opening out of it is the Hornby Library with an outstanding collection of first editions, prints and fine bindings; and in the adjoining Oak Room is the Edward Lear collection (Lear was for a number of years a tutor to the Stanley children at Knowsley where he wrote the Nonsense Rhymes and painted animals and birds in the estate's zoo).

The Picton's easterly neighbour in the Forum, to which the north, semi-circular front of St. George's Hall belongs, is the Walker Art Gallery, at its entrance statues of Raphael and Michaelangelo. The gallery, also designed by Sherlock, is named after its donor, the mayor in 1873. It was opened in 1877, much improved in 1933 and today houses a collection as notable as any outside London. During the war the Ministry of Food occupied it and was in no great hurry to leave when the peace came.

In 1960 *Virgin and Child with St. Elizabeth and the Child Baptist* by Rubens was purchased with Treasury help, and there have been a number of important acquisitions since then with the aid of a fund to which Merseyside firms and individuals subscribe. The gallery possesses one of Rembrandt's earliest self-portraits, and George Stubbs, who lived for some years in Liverpool, is represented by *Horse Frightened by a Lion* and *Molly Longlegs*.

Henry Holiday's *Meeting of Dante and Beatrice* and *Lorenzo and Isabella* by Millais are two other well-known pictures in the gallery and here, too, is the Yeames *When Did You Last See Your Father?*

There are works by the fourteenth-century Simone Martini, Gainsborough, Hogarth, Constable, Turner, Murillo, Van Dyck, Sickert, Augustus John (who worked for some years in Liverpool), Lowry and Paul Nash. Another of its prizes is the collection of William Roscoe, who had to dispose of his paintings when he became bankrupt. They reached the Walker via the Royal Institution which we will be visiting in this chapter.

The Walker is the venue of the John Moores International Exhibition, introduced in 1957. I have to confess that at least 95 per cent of the entries received for it have absolutely no meaning to me. Doubtless this is because I am stupid—but should not art communicate something even to ignoramuses like me? When I leave the John Moores I glance at the statues of Michaelangelo and Raphael and wonder what on earth they would have made of it.

It always depresses me, when I look from the art gallery entrance over the fountain at the foot of the Wellington memorial to the Plateau between St. George's Hall and Lime Street, that city councillors could have brought themselves to allow the William Brown Street end of the great open space to become cluttered with cars and spindly parking meters, thus diminishing the grandeur of the curved north front of the hall and the drama of the line of noble columns when these are viewed from the Walker. Perhaps future councillors will recognise that it is essential to the grand scheme of the Liverpool forum to keep the whole of the Plateau free from impediments; and that they will then make provision elsewhere in the vicinity for vehicle parking. Doubtless there would be an outcry if cars were allowed to drive up to the lawns of St. John's Gardens, on the west side of the hall and park there; yet the use of part of the Plateau for this purpose is hardly less heinous (the fact that it has a hard surface is irrelevant). Councillors have destroyed the view of St. George's Hall from northern Lime Street by blanking it out with monster traffic sign gantries to aid motorists. They should at least rid the Plateau of vehicular invasion.

Surely the most astonishing fact about St. George's Hall is not

The University's Victoria Building (foreground) and the two Cathedrals
Liverpool Cathedral

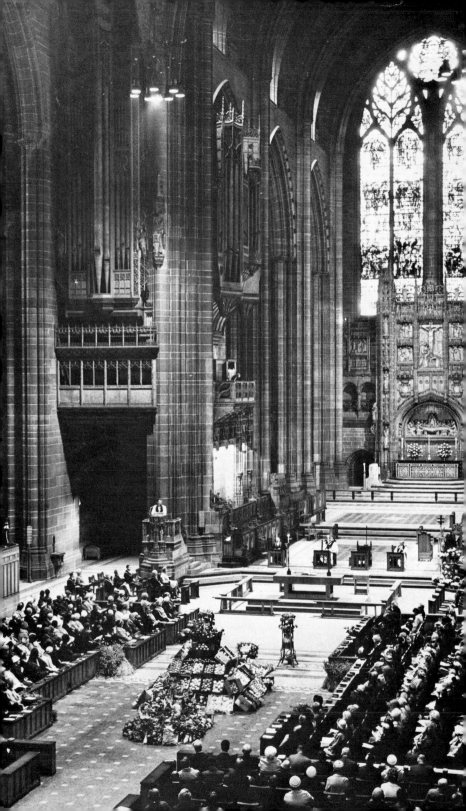

that it was the inspiration of an architect only 24 years old, but that there was a time when leading citizens had the mettle to give a commission of such magnitude to one so young. More than sixty years later the same audacious enterprise was found in those who accepted the even more youthful Gilbert Giles Scott as the architect of the Anglican Cathedral. It is repeatedly claimed nowadays that we are in an era unequalled in its opportunities for gifted youth; and yet is there a civic authority or a commercial company that in the seventies would entrust an undertaking equally immense to someone scarcely out of his pupilage?

Harvey Lonsdale Elmes won an open competition for a Liverpool concert hall held in 1836 by a committee that had collected £23,000 for the project. The following year he was first in another competition for an assize court. He was allowed to put both designs in a new plan for a single edifice and the result has been described as the greatest Greco-Roman building in Europe.

The Corporation are, of course, fond of quoting this description in their guide books and publicity. Yet they were apparently quite content to allow one of the great treasures of the Hall, the encaustic tiled floor, to stay hidden under protective wood, unseen by the citizens between 1965 and a few days in August, 1971.

Work on the hall began in 1838. Seven years later Elmes was dead, months in the West Indies having failed to arrest tuberculosis brought on by the damage done to a frail constitution by long periods of overwork. Charles Cockerell, whose Bank of England building and insurance office block we have already inspected, was given the responsibility of completing the great building, and it was fully in use from 1854.

The elevation facing Lime Street across the Plateau has sixteen Corinthian columns, 60 feet high, supporting the massive entablature. On either side of the row of columns are seven square piers with sculptured panels between them. At the south end—that is, the extremity farthest from the art gallery—a portico supported by twelve columns has an inscription that, translated, reads: 'Freemen have established a place for arts, laws and councils.' The west side, by comparison with the east, is almost severe; but it has to be borne in mind that there was a church here in Elmes's day, and he, of course, took this into account in his designs.

Liverpool Cathedral's Central Space—photographed during a harvest festival service

On the Plateau are many standards, supported by entwined dolphins, holding handsome globes of light. Between the equestrian statues of Queen Victoria and Prince Albert stands the city's cenotaph, a monument that does not much impress but does not disfigure. Behind this, and set into the second flight of steps running the length of the sixteen columns, is a pedestrian statue of the Earl of Beaconsfield. The steps climb to the bases of the columns and to a loggia showing signs of wear and tear. The wooden doors to the hall from the loggia are disappointing, and their dark-blue paint has been disfigured with felt pen and chalk graffitti from the idiotic to the obscene. There is more scribble on the stone walls from which more than a century of soot and grime was removed at enormous expense during the sixties. Such defacement, like that of the Merchant Navy memorial at Pier Head, is a saddening sight; but, as I said in the opening chapter, it is the Liverpool way to scuff new shoes.

The doors are entrances to a wide corridor running the length of the hall and connecting with a similar passage on the west side, each serving a considerable number of rooms used by counsel, solicitors, juries, witnesses and others attending the courts. Ornate doors in filigreed and patterned bronze are the entrances from the corridors to the balconied Great Hall, 151 feet long and 73 feet wide, where magnificent pillars in polished, pink and mottled granite support the barrel vault, so badly damaged in the last war but beautifully restored and decorated. The many panels in the elegant ceiling curving to a height of more than 70 feet above the floor present a bewildering range of intricate designs, in some of them the coloured coats of arms of the city and County Palatine. Exquisitely veined marble and alabaster add to the splendour.

In alcoves beneath the balustrades of the balcony are the statues of M.P.s and civic dignitaries and, from the arched spandrels between the arcading, winged females and cherubs, representing the graces and virtues, look down as if in the hope of one day again seeing that wonderful encaustic floor, its design a complexity of inlaid circles. What a great pity it is that it cannot be exposed to view for at least a few weeks every year.

At both extremities of the Great Hall there are richly panelled archivolts and huge semi-circular windows, one of these depicting St. George slaying the dragon and the other bearing the city's coat of arms. Below the coat of arms window is the organ with ornately decorated pipes and on a rotunda which has a strikingly decorative ceiling and is supported by pillars. Elmes was against installing an organ, intending that the judge in the court at the south end should be able to see, looking down the length of the Great Hall, into the courtroom at the north end. However, his wishes were not respected after his death.

At six o'clock in the morning in the main hall at the 1851 Great Exhibition in London, six aldermen of Liverpool stood with the great Henry Willis ('Father' Willis) before the organ he had built and asked to hear it. 'There is a young organist from Liverpool here,' said Willis, 'so why not ask him to play it?' The musician's reply to their invitation was, 'How much will you pay me?' The aldermen handed over five guineas—a fat fee in 1851—and the organist, W. T. Best, obliged. As a result, Willis was commissioned to build the organ in the St. George's Hall, and when the work was completed Best was appointed the first Borough (later City) Organist.

The four-manual instrument with 124 stops has 6,701 pipes varying in length from a few inches to 32 feet, the largest having a diameter of 2 feet. Restored between the wars it was wrecked by bombs in 1940 and rebuilt in 1956 at a cost of £26,000. Now, alas, it is urgently in need of further expensive restoration, much harm having been done by the central heating, installed in 1968, making the atmosphere too dry. Humidifiers were put in but they proved inadequate and part of the woodwork warped badly. What is to become of this superb instrument is, at the time I write, uncertain; but at least a thoroughly dismal proposal made in 1969 that it be preserved as a mute museum piece appears to have been dropped. Incidentally, there were no problems about humidity when the organ was built because air entering the great hall from beneath the southern portico passed over water jets which could be controlled to give anything from a fine mist to a drenching spray, an early essay in air conditioning.

It is high time the balconies in the Great Hall lost their extremely ugly form seats. People rarely sit in the balconies anyway; and it would be better to discard the forms altogether and turn the balconies into elevated promenades from which to view the marvellous ceiling.

South of the Great Hall is the nobly pillared Crown Court. In

1970 work was put in hand making a second court (because of the ever-increasing rise in crime), and it was interesting to see how well the surroundings were matched.

A walk along either of the main corridors running from south to north, our footsteps echoing on the stone flags, brings us to the Civil Court. Hereabouts there is a curiosity—a passage leading from east to west which is so narrow that two broad-shouldered men could not stand side by side in it; and anyone over 5 feet 8 inches in height has to duck his head.

From the northern entrance hall, with more pillars and statues, staircases lead to the Concert Hall, a truly resplendent rotunda with a semi-circular balcony which has a series of curving, delicately latticed panels and is supported by voluptuous caryatids. The platform has a front of delicately filigreed grills, and at the rear of it four Corinthian columns support an archivolt, lavishly carved and decorated. The Concert Hall is lit by large chandeliers of glittering crystal glass and is altogether sumptuous. Remember that all this magnificence, on the most lavish scale, was conceived and constructed in years when thousands of Liverpool people were living in destitution.

On the side of Lime Street opposite the Plateau stand a rebuilt pub (with a face that repels me), the considerable neo-Greco façade of the Empire Theatre, which I rather like (though some authorities on architecture do not share my view) and—still in the deep mourning of soot that until the late sixties was worn by St. George's Hall—the six-storey, turreted building once the North Western Hotel. This was erected to the designs of Alfred Waterhouse, but is perhaps the least impressive of his contributions to the city (though it contains a staircase grand enough for the most stately of mansions). Part of it was used as offices and much of the first floor, which is on a level with the concourse of Lime Street Station, serves as cafeteria and bar for passengers, comeliness having been turned into coarseness by British Railways furnishings and plastic bric-a-brac.

The building is marked for demolition and, indeed, it is impossible to conceive any future purpose it might serve; but it is of prime importance to the city that what takes its place should be wholly appropriate to the magnificence on the other side of Lime Street—as, by all accounts, the frontage of the original station was.

The first Lime Street terminus was opened in 1836, six years after Stephenson's station at Edge Hill. Tunnels were bored (at great cost and much engineering skill) steeply downhill through the sandstone rib that runs across Liverpool from Everton Heights to St. James Mount. No locomotives used the tunnels for thirty-four years, the coaches being hauled from Lime Street to Edge Hill by endless rope attached to a stationary engine.

The original station, and the one that replaced it in 1851, had a frontage in the classical style two storeys high. Both stations could boast the largest single span roof in the world at the time; and this was also the case with the third station, opened in 1886, when the original frontage was demolished to make way for Waterhouse's hotel.

Before the end of the nineteenth century some of the tunnels between Lime Street and Edge Hill had been turned into cuttings and the long, deep ravine with walls of lichen-clad, virgin sandstone continues to make a dramatic entrance to the city.

As I explained in the first chapter, a great arc of station roof has been opened to view from Lime Street instead of being largely hidden by inconsequential buildings. This roof was given to an extension of the station brought into use in 1886. The demolished buildings have been replaced by a ribbon of single-storey shops terminating in the towering glass box called Concourse House, which has an elevated forecourt looking across to the new St. John's Precinct. Downhill from the Precinct and towards the mouth of the Mersey Tunnel, mean buildings which overlooked St. John's Gardens have been removed to make room for a traffic artery that should noticeable ease congestion.

As a result of this clean sweep, what was Queen Square—for a great many years one of the city's two wholesale fruit and vegetable markets—is a true square no longer; but when the redevelopment of these acres is complete there will be far more attractive views of the Royal Court Theatre (which has been welded into the St. John's Precinct) and the Stork Hotel, a former mansion, at what was the opposite end of the old square. The only other building of any architectural consequence in this area (all of it due to disappear in the next decade or so to make way for a new civic centre) is the much-decorated Victorian office block at the fork of Whitechapel and Victoria Street and overlooking the Mersey Tunnel entrance.

We continue our walk along Lime Street with the Anglican Cathedral now an imposing horizon. We pass cinemas, shops and amusement arcades and then the 'Vines', that pulchritudinous pub described in Chapter Four, to reach the meeting of six roads presided over by the massive bulk of the Adelphi Hotel. This began 1970 with a clean face. It looks down Ranelagh Street to Central Station (the main buildings of this scheduled for demolition) and windows also stare at the 'exceedingly bare' statue by Epstein, his striding man intended to represent the city's triumphant emergence from the war ruins of 1941, when, in fact, this store was seriously damaged.

It is worth our while to turn for a few yards up Mount Pleasant so that we may look at the circular memorial in a small, green square, whereon the name of William Roscoe appears with those of others who were buried in the graveyard of the Unitarian church which stood close by. The building was demolished and a new church erected in the vicinity of Sefton Park.

A stroll of five minutes up Renshaw Street (which continues the line of Lime Street) past the newly renovated Central Hall brings us to crossroads. Here is the ruin of St. Luke's Church, a poignant memorial of the 1939–45 war when it was gutted by incendiary bombs. It is surrounded by a garden which is always immaculate and a favourite place for lunchtime relaxation on any fine weekday. The Inner Motorway to be built round the fringe of the downtown area will one day remove part of the nave and a slice of the garden; but the fanciful gothic tower, erected in 1831, will stay to remind future generations of the Maytime hours of horror when so much in the city was destroyed.

We turn our backs on the skeleton tower to walk down Bold Street, but then leave this by the first turn left, which is Colquitt Street. On the right of this we see the Royal Institution, a pioneer venture in adult education when it was founded in 1817, largely through the endeavours of William Roscoe notwithstanding his financial predicament at that time. It has served cultural causes in Liverpool ever since and is now the property of the University, being used for extra mural lectures as well as a meeting place for various societies. A gracious Georgian building, it has a dignified entrance hall where there is a bust, by Francis Chantrey, of Roscoe. The lecture theatre, its seats steeply raked, has elegance.

Back in Bold Street we stroll towards the centre of the city, perhaps window shopping. For many years this was a street of superior shops—'our Bond Street', Liverpudlians liked to call it—and, to some extent, this is still the case, a number of the exteriors having architectural merit. That a City Council's decision in 1970 to turn it from a congested two-way traffic route into a pedestrian precinct, against the vociferous opposition of the shopkeepers, was wise I believe has now been shown.

At the lower end of Bold Street, by Central Station, is another building of considerable interest in the classical style, that of the Lyceum Club. This was built in 1803 to the designs of Thomas Harrison and presents an impressive portico, supported by four columns, when viewed from the opposite side of the street. From the year it was completed until 1941 it was the home of the Liverpool Library.

This could be said to have had its origins in a collection of books, mainly theological, bought with £15 given by a master mariner and housed in a church where the volumes were secured with chains; but the first general library was that of a club which met at the home of a schoolmaster and published a catalogue—of 450 volumes—in 1758. Less than half a century after its removal to the Lyceum it contained nearly 40,000 books; but the Corporation then formed a public libraries committee—the first, in the country—and the use of the subscription library at the Lyceum gradually declined. The building continues as a most agreeable club with a pronounced literary flavour and in handsome surroundings. There is an element of doubt, at the time of writing, about the future of this building; but it will be a great shame if it is not assured of permanent life and, moreover, given neighbours of respectable appearance after Central Station's buildings are pulled down.

From Bold Street's corner with Ranelagh Street and union with bustling Church Street, we turn, opposite the Lyceum, into Hanover Street, noting the attractive Georgian-style frontage of an hotel on the left. Almost facing this is the entrance to lifts up to the Neptune Theatre where local dramatic and operatic societies perform. The entrance is at the corner of an alley (School Lane) that looks far from prepossessing but is nonetheless our route; for it contains one of the architectural gems of the North of England.

We come upon it so suddenly that the effect is almost theatrical;

and, indeed, there is a touch of the stage set about the Bluecoat Chambers with its cobbled forecourt—a set surely for a Mozart opera, say *The Marriage of Figaro* or the first acts of *Don Giovanni*. The building occupies three flanks of the forecourt, the fourth side being cut off from unlovely School Lane by iron railings and gates, the cobbles at the entrance dappled in summer by sunlight streaming through the foliage of guardian trees.

On Saturdays when the weather is fine the railings become the open-air gallery of numerous Merseyside part-time artists, who hang their paintings and drawings here for sale. They draw a generous attendance, though not necessarily of buyers. The alfresco exhibition has become a most attractive facet of Liverpool life, and there could not be a more charming background for it than this legacy in pure Queen Anne, which is, in fact, one of the modern centres of the city's artistic activities and contains both a concert hall and a concert room, an arts and crafts shop, offices of musical, dramatic and other societies and the studios and workshops of painters, potters, sculptors and musicians, one of whom makes harpsichords and clavichords here so that the visitor can often hear sounds wholly appropriate to the building's period.

'The Bluecoat'—as all Liverpudlians now call it—was built, as was explained in Chapter Three, as a school, an act of philanthropy made possible by the profits from merchant adventure, slave-trading and privateering. The school—for both sexes—remained in the building through two centuries, the children wearing distinctive costume, that of the boys resembling the uniform of Christ's Hospital scholars. The school departed in 1906 when the boys moved into a large new building at Wavertree where it is still known as the Blue Coat (two words, be it noted, as against the one used for the Chambers).

The first tenants of the School Lane building after 1906 were the Sandon Studios Society, a group of artists and musicians who, up to that time, had studios in the neighbourhood of the site chosen for the Anglican Cathedral and who included, during his Liverpool years, Augustus John. The society is still among the Bluecoat occupants and there is a pleasant bar beneath the level of the forecourt with dining rooms above.

Three years after the Sandon's arrival, Mr. W. H. Lever (who became the first Lord Leverhulme) agreed to rent the former school and he re-named it Liberty Buildings. Liverpool University's School of Architecture then became tenants and a committee was formed to press Mr. Lever to buy the building, renovate it and hand it over to trustees for use as the headquarters of a Lancashire Society of Arts. Purchased it was—for £30,000 in 1913—but the society was a First World War casualty. Then the School of Architecture moved out and prospects of the building's survival, with its fabric rapidly deteriorating, looked doubtful. For a period it served dejectedly as a car showroom.

Matters came to a head in 1926, the year after Lord Leverhulme's death, when it was advertised for auction as a building site. Hurried attempts were made to have it scheduled as an ancient monument and to persuade the Corporation to buy it. When these failed a committee was formed to launch a public appeal for £40,000. One of the first donations was £1,000 from 'Lover of his Native City'.

Early generosity was not sustained, and on the day before the auction only £10,000 had been raised. After an emergency meeting there was a further gift of £2,000, but it was reckoned that at least another £18,000 was needed within eighteen hours if there was to be any hope of saving the wonderful old building. It was a moment for a miracle—and, as it happened, there were two.

The first occurred on the fateful morning in the unlikely setting of a Liverpool-bound train on the Mersey Railway and involved 'Lover of his Native City' and Mr. Ernest Hope Prince, then the Editor of the *Liverpool Echo*. 'Lover of his Native City' borrowed Mr. Prince's copy of the *Liverpool Daily Post*, the morning paper, and read the report of the committee's quandary. He questioned Mr. Prince about the situation and learned that it was no more than the truth that unless £18,000 was raised that morning the building would be lost. 'Ernest,' he said, 'you'd better come to my office straight away'. At the office he handed a draft for £18,000 to Mr. Prince, who immediately began telephoning members of the committee and organising purchase.

But meanwhile there had been the second miracle. For reasons which never became clear, the sale was quite unexpectedly postponed for three weeks. Before the day was over negotiations were in hand to buy Liberty Buildings. It was some years before Mr. Prince was authorised to disclose that 'Lover of his Native City' was Mr. W. E. Corlett, a solicitor and a philanthropist who had supported numerous causes but always anonymously because he abhorred personal publicity.

In 1937 the Bluecoat Society of Arts was formed, and they found it very hard going. The turning point came when Professor Reilly, of the School of Architecture, who had worked for more than twenty years to save the building, arranged for Epstein's *Genesis* to be shown by the Sandon Society. In four weeks more than 55,000 paid to see the massive sculpture, and with the funds thereby raised and the interest thus stimulated the society began to make real headway at last. But then came the war and 1941 bombs that seriously damaged the fabric. Once again an appeal had to be made; and there has been a further call on the public since then. Today the Bluecoat flourishes as will be seen from a later chapter devoted to the arts in Liverpool.

Before we leave the enchanting—and now well-maintained—building let us take a look at the garden behind the central block. This was largely the handiwork of Mr. H. Tyson Smith, the sculptor, examples of whose art we saw on the former head-quarters of Martins Bank. He planted the garden's trees; and one of them is somewhat exotic, a *Ginkgo biloba* ('maidenhair tree')—a living retort to all those who have claimed that only the London plane will endure in the centre of Liverpool. Scores of trees were planted in the central area of the city in 1970 and 1971.

School Lane leads us to Paradise Street (of 'Blow The Man Down' and other sea shanties), and we cross it to reach a site that has been ripe for development since 1945 and which Graeme Shank-land schemed as a shopping centre with a bus station and towers of high rental flats. From here, I hope, you will see how (as was outlined in the first chapter) Lord Street could have been greatly widened as the first phase of a magnificent shopping street eventually running from Mann Island to St. Luke's tower, with the Bluecoat Chambers open to it instead of being shoved away out of the sight of mainstream shoppers.

We reach South Castle Street, cross it and hunt about between more parked cars for iron gates bearing the name 'Chapel Walks'. The gates (locked every night) are at the only entrance to three cloistered blocks of two-storey offices, the quietest in the heart of the city, the pathway winding round them used only by those on foot whose business takes them to this little precinct. Precisely when the buildings stopped being houses (if they ever were) and became offices is not known because early deeds were lost; and why some of them have very large vaults is also unexplained. They were certainly counting houses more than a century ago.

They were much ravaged by bombing but carefully rebuilt when the present owners bought them and now have all modern conveniences as well as seclusion and character. Yet they are marked down for destruction during the seventies, presumably to make way for yet another towering giant like the one (with a frontage on James Street) which started to stare down on them in 1969. Part of their immediate neighbourhood is occupied by ugly or decaying warehouses and no plea is entered for these; but the Walks (they bring to mind a naval shore station though they were never used for this purpose) should surely be reprieved.

From the look of the one frontage that escaped serious bomb blast, the buildings are Georgian in origin. The Walks certainly got their name from a dissenters' chapel built in 1726. This became the Unitarians' church and William Roscoe and the Rathbones worshipped there until the church in Renshaw Street (mentioned earlier in this chapter) was opened and the building by the Walks sold to Methodists. Close by is the city's music library.

At the time of writing, South Castle Street is a neither-my-eye-nor-my-elbow thoroughfare. Part of it is a survival from the era of Yankee clipper ships and is obviously ripe for demolition if only to show off the large block completed in 1970 on the Canning Place site of the old Customs House.

This has a breezy, elevated concourse—a jacked up version of Exchange Flags, it has been called—reached from waterfront streets by ramps. The buildings on three sides of it are named after Thomas Steers, the port's first dockmaster, and contain a pub which has a downstairs saloon designed to represent the interior of a submarine, complete with periscope which provides views (on slides) of the Mersey and shipping. It has make-believe bulkheads and watertight doors; and in an upper room there are photographs of Second World War submariner V.C.s and a large mural depicting the surprisingly long history of underwater craft. Proudly displayed, too, is a 'golden rivet' (a joke both ex-ratings and shipyard workers appreciate because most of them were sent to find one in their youth).

Merseyside ex-submariners hold their meetings in this pub which is perhaps a little chi—but much less so than another let's-pretend bar in the city called 'The Captain's Cabin' and with portholes, scuttles and lifebuoys, a loo reserved 'for lady passengers' and a notice warning 'midshipmen' that if they are under 18 they will not be served. Moored at the dockside a brief distance from the sub-in-a-pub (where only pints are sunk) is a landing craft converted into an excellent club and restaurant.

South Castle Street joins Lord Street at Derby Square, where Queen Victoria, in a monster gazebo, has an expression that seems to indicate her distaste at being obliged to stand next door to entrances to public lavatories and with only utilitarian privet otherwise to look at. She and her temple are on the site of Liverpool Castle which, from 1734 to 1897, was occupied by St. George's Church.

One building in Derby Square deserves more than a passing glance and that is Moat House, built as offices for the London Life Association towards the end of the last century and with a handsome pediment and restrained decoration.

From Derby Square, James Street returns us, under the first walkway bridge, to Mann Island and the point where our walk began. We have not, by any means, seen everything that the downtown area has to offer, but I think it can be claimed that we have seen nearly all the best.

SEVEN

CATHEDRALS IN CONTRAST

I TOILED up stairs that spiral as in a medieval fortress to reach one of the two consoles of Liverpool Cathedral's organ, there to chat with an American, who, having completed a recital tour in this country, had made a special journey to play, solely for his own pleasure, one of the world's most majestic instruments; and also to see how closely the world's largest Anglican church resembled a picture he had in his mind from often studying a postcard view he received as a boy. He told me that he had been staggered that morning by the colour, having assumed from the black and white postcard that the stone was grey. But what, he appealed, *was* the colour? A sort of tawny pink, I suggested. He was not content with that, neither was I. The truth is that, although the colouring of the stone from the Cathedral's quarry at Woolton invariably draws exclamations from those making a first visit, it is exceedingly difficult to put a name to it when it is seen in daylight diffused by stained glass and reflected from the light grey marble floor. It also depends upon whether the sun is shining and from what direction.

My American acquaintance—a church organist at Shreveport, Louisiana—acknowledged that he had also been astounded by the proportions of the Cathedral even though he had arrived primed with the measurements: the main building's length, 576 feet, the maximum width, 214 feet, the height of the tower, 347 feet, and of the Under Tower vault, 175 feet (so that the Cathedral could accommodate Nelson's Column). To see matter-of-fact paper figures in terms of awesome stone had been a memorable experience for him. When I left him I had an experience myself, quite unexpectedly, of the size of the Cathedral. There are several ways in and out of the room behind the organ console and I had forgotten which of them led to those spiralling stairs. The process of elimination led me along walls of the Choir and of the North Choir Aisle, during which I tried several doors, all of them locked save one. This opened to a giddy drop, through trees, to the ravine of St. James's Cemetery, once a quarry.

Nearly 60,000 were buried in this ground, which for many years was a wilderness of summer weeds, an unauthorised adventure playground for generations of boys, many of them from the crowded tenements of nearby Toxteth. It had a melancholy air that some people found so appealing they wanted the place to stay in a state of neglect. But the position had become such that, with the continuous vandalism, many memorials of considerable interest were in imminent danger of disintegration, among them the circular temple which is the monument to William Huskisson, the M.P. killed by Stephenson's Rocket. This domed memorial, containing a statue of Huskisson, has become a main feature of the renovated cemetery, which has not been turned into a parade ground for guardsmen geraniums or made riotous with municipal tulips as certain Liverpudlians had feared (thereby doing the parks landscaping staff an injustice since there is ample evidence in the city of their appreciation of the appropriate in planting).

The cemetery has been termed 'a valhalla for sea-dogs' because so many ships' captains lie there. One of them, Captain John Oliver, was an officer under Nelson and lived to be 102; and another was Captain Lindsay Halsey, the headstone stating that he was of Charleston, South 'Carorlina' and 'came to an untimely death aboard the *Thomas Bennett* in the Bay of Biscay' in 1844. What happened was that Halsey was stabbed by the ship's cook, John Kent, of Great Howard Street, Liverpool (and therefore perhaps a neighbour of the notorious Paddy West), who convinced a jury that he acted in self-defence.

Here, too, is the grave of Kitty Wilkinson, the heroine of the cholera epidemic referred to in Chapter Three, and also that of Sarah Biffin, an armless Liverpool artist of the last century, who painted water colours with a brush held between her lips and who had the patronage, so it was said, of four crowned heads. Judging from a self-portrait, she was a formidable woman.

The boundary of the burial ground that faces the steep, high bank on which the Cathedral stands is a stone wall some 40 feet high and more than 300 feet long, masking what was the face of the old quarry. There are hollows in it marking catacombs and it is criss-crossed by ramps which were used by coffin bearers to whom the steep descent must have been a sore trial, particularly on a frosty day. I have often thought what a wonderful setting this great wall and the ramps would make for an outdoor performance of *Aida* on a Cecil B. de Mille scale! At the top of the wall, high railings prevent cars and pedestrians tumbling into the quarry in fog from Gambier Terrace, designed by John Foster Junior for well-off residents and built immediately before Victoria's accession. Part of it is embellished with an imposing colonnade and former houses now serve as a Merchant Navy residential club. The front windows command the most spectacular of all the views of the Cathedral, looking towards it over the ravine of the cemetery. They also have a vista of a miniature temple (more of the younger Foster's work), the mortuary chapel of St. James, which stands near the brink of the gorge.

At the foot of the great wall water flows from a chalybeate spring, and this was confidently commended in 1773 as a remedy for bad eyes, rickets, rheumatism and stomach upsets. Until the 1969 restoration the elixir splashed from a rusting drainpipe into a nearby gutter, but even so it was the daily practice of a physician with consulting rooms in nearby Rodney Street to visit the spring daily for a draught.

Rodney Street is a pleasant approach route to the Cathedral. For the most part it is still graciously Georgian, a number of the houses balconied and with imposing porches reached by steps with curving metal guard-rails. It has been allowed to keep the street lamps that used to be lit by gas, but traffic signals and parked cars rather spoil the effect. If we enter it from Mount Pleasant we see, on the left, another of the younger Foster's temples, the somewhat overpowering St. Andrew's Church of Scotland with twin domical towers and an Ionic façade. The future of this, the third largest Scottish church south of the border is gravely uncertain. There is no longer a congregation living within reasonable reach of it, and the church authorities, seeking to rid themselves of the increasing burden of its upkeep, proposed to pull it down and sell the site. Preservationists lodged objections, and at the time of writing the matter stands unresolved.

Continuing along Rodney Street we pass the birthplace of

Gladstone, identified by a plaque and now occupied by Toc H. From this point we come under the domination of the Cathedral's Vestey Tower (named after the family whose gift it was), though there is some distance to go, up a gentle incline, before we reach the end of Rodney Street and are able to appreciate the positively theatrical siting of the mighty church, shabby streets falling away from it quite steeply towards the river.

Yet this was not the place originally selected for it. Five years after the diocese was formed in 1880, Parliament authorised the erection of a cathedral on the west side of St. George's Hall and plans for a domed, gothic building were provisionally approved. By good fortune—because this site was thoroughly unsuitable—insuperable difficulties arose, and a subsequent proposal to build at the fork of London Road and Pembroke Place, near the Royal Infirmary, was also discarded.

St. James's Mount, Liverpool's earliest public pleasure ground, then became the choice, and in 1903 the architects R. Norman Shaw (whose work we saw near the Pier Head and in Dale Street) and G. F. Bodley were appointed assessors for a competition. Sensationally they recommended that Giles Gilbert Scott, aged 21 and a Roman Catholic, should be the architect because his design had 'the power combined with beauty which makes a great and noble building'. Uneasy about Scott's inexperience, the committee made Bodley joint architect, but the partnership, never a happy one, ended in 1907 with his death. The beautiful Lady Chapel, consecrated in 1910, is partly Bodley's work.

The Cathedral's foundation stone was laid by Edward VII in 1904, and the building is due to be completed in 1975 to a simplified plan for the west end that was approved in 1967. There are emphatic differences from the building that Scott originally designed. Through his life he made many modifications, some of them quite drastic; and that the committee agreed readily to the many changes is really a greater tribute to their farsightedness than that they entrusted the immense undertaking to an architect so young.

We enter the Cathedral, as do nearly all visitors, after climbing the steps that lead to guardian gates of the Rankin Porch on the south side. The porch, given in memory of a shipowning family, was opened by the Queen, then Princess Elizabeth, in 1949, and it

The Metropolitan Cathedral nearing completion amongst litter-strewn wastelands, now reclaimed

contains statues of her royal grandparents—who attended the consecration of the Choir and east transept in 1924—and also of her parents. These figures are by Carter Preston, of Liverpool, the contributor of much of the sculpture in the Cathedral. From the porch our way is through the Baptistery, where the font, a work of splendour, is crowned by an elaborately carved oak canopy more than 30 feet above a surrounding pavement in which various marbles are patterned to represent fish and waves. Nearby are steps to the Radcliffe Library (named after a former president of the Cathedral committee) which contains an illuminated manual of prayers and hymns associated with a Princess Elizabeth of the fifteenth century.

It is best to make for the Nave Bridge, a semi-circular arch which has an overhanging gallery of richly carved oak. From the height of this the glory and the magnitude of Scott's masterpiece are overwhelming. The view extends the length of the Cathedral, across the immense Central Space and through the choir to the gilded red sandstone of the reredos and the compelling Te Deum window. Here are soaring hosannas in stone, magnificence and simplicity marvellously blended by an inspired architect and by dedicated craftsmen.

I heard Mahler's Eighth—'The Symphony of a Thousand'— performed here by two large orchestras and hundreds of voices, and I count it as the most moving musical experience of my life. The problems in acoustics this presented, with an echo of several seconds in the vast cavern of the Central Space, were exceedingly complex; yet I have heard the unaccompanied violin of Yehudi Menuhin in this place when every note of a Bach partita rose larksong clear into the mists of the Under Tower's vaulted roof.

Above this roof is the highest (219 feet) and heaviest (31 tons) ringing peal in the world. There are thirteen bells, one extra to the main peal with 479,001,600 changes possible. The bourdon, named Great George after George V, weighs over 14 tons and is 9 feet 6 inches in diameter. The bells hang from 200 tons of steelwork held within a concrete girdle of more than 600 tons; and they were heard for the first time, ringing out over a hushed city, on a November day in 1951.

At the northern end of the east transept is the War Memorial Chapel with a cenotaph of carved marble. Upon this, inside a glazed case and standing on a cloth of gold, is a roll of honour

Interior of the Metropolitan Cathedral

M

containing 40,000 names and autographed by George V. At one side of the chapel's reredos is the figure of a soldier, at the other that of a sailor; and these were executed with great delicacy to harmonise with features of other periods, including the Renaissance. Twenty-six Colours hang from galleries, all but three of these carried by battalions of the King's Regiment (Liverpool), which was amalgamated with the Manchester Regiment in 1959. At the Chapel's entrance the ship's bell of the cruiser H.M.S. *Liverpool* hangs as a memorial to those who died in the Battle of the Atlantic. The two Commanders of the Western Approaches during the last war, Admiral Sir Percy Noble and his successor, Admiral Sir Max Horton, are remembered by tablets elsewhere in the Cathedral.

East of the War Memorial Chapel is the Chapel of the Holy Spirit, the reredos here showing, in alabaster, Christ praying in solitude. A figure of the Virgin, kneeling in adoration, is believed to be by Giovanni della Robbia. From this chapel we can walk, via the North Choir Aisle, to the Ambulatory, which runs between the octagonal Chapter House on the north side and the Lady Chapel, this extending to the east beyond the main building. It can be entered from the street by the charming Children's Porch, where there are sculptures representing David as a boy, the Good Shepherd with children, and other subjects appropriate to the title of the porch.

It is not possible to exaggerate the loveliness of the Lady Chapel, grace and consummate artistry wherever the eye alights, on the superb carvings of the galleries and choir stalls and on the reliefs, in carved and painted wood, adorning the reredos and representing the Nativity and the Baptism of Jesus. In the windows are represented female saints and also women of saintly deeds, among them Kitty Wilkinson, Josephine Butler (mentioned in Chapter Three) and Anne Clough, who was the sister of Hugh Clough, a poet, and was born in Rodney Street. She was a tireless campaigner for higher education for her sex, and her efforts led to the foundation of Newnham College, Cambridge, where she became a beloved principal.

All the windows of the Lady Chapel were shattered and part of the fabric damaged by one of the first Second World War bombs to fall on Liverpool—this was in September 1940. Early in the following year a high explosive bomb penetrated the roof of the south-east transept of the main building but miraculously ricocheted off a traverse arch above the vaulting and fell into the street. By no less a miracle, the Cathedral was spared further damage during the blitzkreig of May, 1941; and two months later, in the presence of some of the thousands in Liverpool then mourning relatives and friends killed by bombs, a section of the building that had been under construction for sixteen years came into use for the first time. George VI visited the Cathedral after the bomb attack in 1940, and his words on leaving were: 'Keep going whatever you do, even if you can only go a small way.' His counsel was followed.

From the Lady Chapel we take the South Choir Aisle and the steps leading from this into the Choir, thus reaching the Bishop's Throne. This is in Woolton stone and so, in effect, is part of the fabric. The stone is intricately carved in the upper parts and bears the arms of the see. From by the throne we are able more fully to appreciate the beauty of the reredos, its relief panels depicting principal events in the life of the Saviour. The panels were created by W. Gilbert and L. Weingartner, who made several other notable contributions, including the figures of the soldier and sailor in the War Memorial Chapel. Behind the reredos is the Te Deum window, almost 1,800 feet of stained glass, its dominant feature the figure of Our Lord in Majesty. Also depicted are the apostles, prophets, martyrs and representatives of the Holy Church throughout the ages.

Bronze rails on uprights decorated with figures symbolic of the Ten Commandments separate the Sanctuary from the Presbytery. The altar, seen against a gradine of black marble, is of panelled oak, its top being a single piece of wood. The choir stalls must surely be among the outstanding examples of hand-carved oak this century has produced anywhere in the world. They stand on plinths of black marble and some are recessed under stone canopies beneath the organ galleries and sumptuously carved organ cases.

The organ, reputed to be the largest of any in a cathedral, was overhauled in 1958-9. It has five manuals, 145 speaking stops and nearly 10,000 pipes. The Cathedral's organist, Noel Rawsthorne, is a former chorister who, at the age of 19, was appointed assistant to the celebrated Dr. H. Goss Custard and succeeded him six years later. He has now an international reputation.

In the South Choir Aisle are memorials to two Bishops of

Liverpool, John Charles Ryle (1880–1900) and Francis James Chavasse (1900–23). Bishop Ryle is represented by a recumbent figure beneath a projecting canopy (this was the first work of Carter Preston to be placed in the Cathedral) and Dr. Chavasse is shown at prayer at a faldstool. Another notable memorial in this aisle—and it is again by Carter Preston—depicts, in high relief, the Cathedral's first Dean, the greatly esteemed Frederick William Dwelly (1931–55) with one hand upon the shoulder of a boy chorister.

In the south-east transept stands the first memorial to be erected in the Cathedral, that of the tenth Earl of Derby, for a number of years president of the committee. It was designed by Sir Giles Scott and shows the Earl lying in his Garter robes which are spread upon the outstretched wings of an eagle. At the head of the memorial angels support a model of the Cathedral, its un-completed west end hidden beneath a veil.

The craftsmanship of the highest order, in stone and in wood, so abundantly in evidence, has been that, very largely, of local men who served ordinary apprenticeships—like those carpenters who embellished richly the interiors of the city's Edwardian pubs. Here, in the Cathedral, is substantiation of Arthur Dooley's insistent claim that inside the average Liverpudlian is a craftsman waiting for the opportunity to use hands and mind. It must be added that this is not an exclusively male characteristic as the gorgeous frontals, hangings and burses in the Cathedral show. The embroidery was worked by an association formed in 1903. For three days in 1970 more than 250,000 blooms, arranged by 520 women, decorated the Cathedral—an inspiring spectacle seen by 50,000 visitors.

Much of the wood, seasoned over several years, was carved in Liverpool workshops, and all the masons are Merseysiders, some of them employed on this single undertaking since their youth. The stone was dressed wholly by hand until 1953, when, in order to reduce costs, planing machines and compressed air tools were reluctantly introduced, though the finishing has remained a manual operation. By 1975, when the last stones are due to be laid, Tom and John Rowbottom will have been Cathedral masons for nearly half a century. Their father, killed in the First World War, laid many of the stones of the Lady Chapel; and a great uncle, who was nicknamed 'Old Gothic', worked on the masonry of Central Station buildings. Tom Rowbottom has said: 'Sir Giles used to tell us that he had designed work impossible for the masons but we kept proving that he was wrong.'

Soon after his design won the Cathedral competition, Scott said in a lecture at Liverpool University's School of Architecture that time alone would show whether his building was 'the last flare-up of the gothic revival'. Well, seventy years afterwards, it seems that it was.

Between Cathedrals let us turn from Hope Street into Mount Street for a few yards to look at Liverpool Institute, which has a Greek façade. The building was opened in 1837 as the consequence of a movement, begun some twenty years earlier, to provide evening instruction for journeymen and apprentices. After it had been used for a period as a boys' school by day and an evening institute for adults by night, a department was added to meet the demand for studies at university level from the lower middle and working classes. Thus the Institute was the forerunner of Liverpool University.

In the small but good-looking entrance hall elaborately designed wrought-iron gates stand between Ionic pillars and above these are the words 'That the soul be without knowledge is not good.' Beyond the gates is an entrance to a semi-circular and galleried assembly hall with sculptures in lofty alcoves and an organ which was installed in 1844. That was the year when Charles Dickens addressed a soirée in the hall and it has changed very little since. Several of the classrooms have a Dickensian appearance, too; yet this is a thoroughly up-to-date school with a splendidly equipped gymnasium and science wing. Proposals to move it to near the breezy esplanade of Otterspool have been firmly resisted by a force of old boys. The late Sydney Silverman M.P. was educated there, so were Sir Alfred Jones (a principal founder of the Liverpool School of Tropical Medicine), Lord Mersey, Lord Justice. Morris, James Laver, John McCabe, the composer, and Paul McCartney, the Beatle.

Having returned to Hope Street, we see on our right the Liverpool Institute Girls' School, opened in 1844 in the former home of an eighteenth-century mayor. On the same side of the street, in a modern four-tier box with a distinctive frontage, there are permanent exhibitions of building designs, furnishings and domestic equipment; and next door to this is the Philharmonic Hall, one of the last commissions of Herbert Rowse, architect of the India Building. It is on the lines of a super cinema of the thirties and therefore of small merit externally; but inside the unimpressive shell is a concert hall seating nearly 2,000, which is still one of the most modern in the country, comfortable and acoustically excellent. Unlike halls used for concerts in most provincial cities it does not have to accommodate dancers, trade exhibitions and all-in wrestling but was purpose-built for music (though it does, of course, serve for meetings, school speech days and the like). The hall replaced one that was also designed exclusively for concerts and which was destroyed by fire in 1933, a few years short of its centenary.

From this point every building ahead of us is subjugated by the colossus of the Metropolitan Cathedral, its enormous, hoarding-like forepiece of concrete staring into Hope Street. This compelling frontal is etched with a pattern of straight lines and has four apertures, two oblong and two triangular, in which hang Matthew, Mark, Luke and John, the bells that ring from 80 feet above the street.

The Church of Christ behind us is an epilogue to an ecclesiastical style as expressed by a Roman Catholic. The Church of Christ the King before us is a preface to an ecclesiastical style as expressed by a Nonconformist. But Sir Frederick did not deliver a retort to Sir Giles Scott, he composed a countersubject. At Hope Street's east end is the sublime, at the west end a sublimate.

Work on a Catholic Cathedral began at Everton in 1856, six years after the See of Liverpool was created. The Lady Chapel was completed, then money ran out; and it was not until 1921 that a second building fund was established. Twelve years later the foundation stone was laid of a Byzantine cathedral designed by Sir Edward Lutyens that would have been second in size only to St. Peter's, Rome, would have held a congregation of 10,000 and would have contained more than fifty altars. By 1939 three chapels of the crypt had been completed and these remain the souvenirs of a stupendous project that would have cost an astronomical sum.

An attempt to scale Lutyens down came to nothing, and in 1959 a competition was held for a cathedral costing not more than a million pounds. 'This figure restricts your choice of materials,' the 300 entrants were told by the Archbishop, Dr. (now Cardinal) John Heenan, 'but this should not dismay you. New cathedrals need not be inferior to the old. You can use techniques that were not available to those who built the splendid cathedrals of the middle ages.' Frederick Gibberd, starting from a shape he sketched on the back of an envelope, met this challenge as unequivocally as he did the condition that the altar should be both within the sight and easy reach of every member of the congregation. His cathedral cannot be said to be either inferior or superior to one of the Middle Ages because there are no points upon which a reasonable comparison can be made. It meets requirements beyond the imagination of the Middle Ages—for example, an underground park for 200 vehicles, a pedestrian precinct, underfloor heating and well-appointed lavatories.

Basically, it is a tapering cylinder of glass and concrete set upon an aluminium clad cone that roofs a circular arena surrounded by sixteen buildings, ten of these chapels, one the Baptistery which are separate constructions yet components of the grand design. It is a compound of 29,730 tons of concrete, 1,480 tons of steel, 1,800 tons of Portland stone, 500 tons of stained glass, 1,500,000 bricks and such materials of the sixties as fibre glass and polyester resin; and the sublimate of these substances has a dynamic energy, a muscular elegance and—here is the marvel to me—both majesty and an expression of compassion.

It was exciting to watch it evolve, with new methods and new machines, over five years, to witness the emergence of grace and then of fervour, silencing those coiners of such nicknames as 'Paddy's Wigwam' and 'Coggers' Circus'. The building was consecrated in May 1967, and a few days later there was a Mass to Musique Concrete by Pierre Henry, which sounded apt in an edifice that belongs to the future rather than the present. No doubt it will be copied in the years to come, but for the time being it is in several ways unique.

We reach it by a ramp that joins a piazza, part of a promenade ringing the building like the outer ward of a fortress and elevated so therefore presenting a view over the Mersey and Wirral into Wales. The promenade is a circuit of the podium upon which the giant and its sixteen satellites stand and which extended the roof of the Lutyens crypt. The entrance suggests a concert hall foyer rather than an ecclesiastical porch yet this adds to the dramatic impact when one steps inside the vast circle for worship to which it leads. In the centre of this circle, which is 220 feet in diameter, stands a high altar of snow white marble, a 19-ton block found at Skopje after a search that lasted two years. Upon this stands a crucifix in bronze by Elizabeth Frink, Christ suspended from a slim metal rod, modernistic in concept and therefore unacceptable to many, yet looked upon by others as an outstanding work of art. High above the crucifix floats what may be the world's biggest baldachin, a circle composed of many shining metal tubes, so different from those filigree-joined poniards pointing up from the lantern head and yet also suggesting a crown of thorns. Soaring skyward from above the baldachin is the lantern tower of sixteen windows. This weighs close on 1,000 tons and contains 25,000 separate pieces of glass—which came mostly from France and Germany—and is in 156 panels.

The sixteen windows were designed by John Piper and executed by Patrick Reyntiens, and for a time they borrowed Henley Town Hall to work in. The windows are 65 feet high and each one is 12 feet wide. Their design produces bursts of white light, representing the Trinity, during a progression through 300 shades from blues in the east to the reds in the west that are so marvellously illuminated by the dying sun. I was here in the evening of a bright June day for a concert and could hardly listen to the music for watching the kaleidoscopic effects produced through this magic lantern tower as the sun moved west and set. To the brilliantly glowing reds bathing the entire circle of the Cathedral was added the vivid cobalt blue from narrow windows that outline the height and breadth of chapels and other adjoining buildings.

This fascinating play of light heightens the colouring of the pipes of the four manual organ, which are an integral part of the interior design, clinical in simplicity. There are 5,000 pipes ranging in length from a fraction of an inch to 32 feet. I remember discovering with astonishment that I could walk from my seat to the console of the organ in less than a minute. I remember also noting that it had a telephone.

In the Chapel of the Blessed Sacrament the reredos has abstract patterns, painted by Ceri Richards, in tones of yellow and blue with white. The Lady Chapel—at, as it were, ten minutes to six when looking into the circle from the main entrance—has a striking ceramic statue representing the Virgin and Child. Because this is stated in modern terms (by Richard Brumby) it does not appeal to some worshippers; and yet how incongruous a sculpture on conventional lines would look in this setting.

Too stark, too sombre—these are criticisms most frequently heard of this extraordinary building. They are, indeed, the criticisms of Arthur Dooley, whose opinions are of more value than mine. I think, though, that they have validity only on a darkly overcast day. When the sun shines, particularly after midday, the raiment of the Cathedral's interior is of a splendour that seizes the breath; and, in the formalism of concentric circles ringing the high altar and in scores of straight lines on the floor that shoot like arrows towards it, there are influences I find almost mesmeric.

Liverpool has no venerable churches. The Parish Church, as was seen during our downtown tour, was restored after the destruction in the last war. St. Mary's, Walton, the parish of which contained the whole of Liverpool until the end of the seventeenth century, was also reduced to a shell by bombing. In the rebuilt church hang bells first cast in 1736; and a Saxon font and cross, shattered by blast from high explosives, were painstakingly pieced together again.

Walton and Woolton argue as to which has the oldest school house (both date from the seventeenth century). West Derby, which once had a castle, still keeps a seventeenth-century court house. In Childwall's postwar suburbia survives a small, countrified enclave consisting of the remnant of a hall erected at about the same time as the eighteenth-century pub and stables, these looking upon a church rebuilt in the nineteenth century but Saxon in origin. In Aigburth, Stanlaw Grange, with a history going back at least 800 years, has been restored and is lived in.

But these are little more than minutiae from the past. The treasures in Liverpool's architectural trove have all been gathered in 250 years and the jewels to be mostly highly prized are of our own time and at the ends of the Street named Hope.

EIGHT

NO DREAMING SPIRES

HAPPY accident placed the Metropolitan Cathedral in the ambit of the University Precinct, where several of the buildings went up in the same years as Sir Frederick Gibberd's church-in-the-round, their architects also using concrete in challenging ways. A prime example, only a few yards from the Cathedral, is the Sports Centre, which is appropriately brawny in physique and uncompromisingly functional in pattern.

Some Liverpudlians have likened it to a dock shed or a hangar and have complained that other buildings of about the same period look more like factories and office blocks than academies. Their only common tie is modernity, but it is claimed that the heterogeneity of the Precinct is in keeping with the diversity of nineteenth-century architecture in the downtown area. Certainly it is impossible to be indifferent to the appearance of the Sports Centre, to the raked, concrete mass of the Medical School's lecture hall, to the morose visage of the Dental School or to the round-hatted, whitefaced Senate Room. These are buildings that demand opinions from every passer-by.

Yet these sinewy seminaries of the sixties, striding across a hilltop, embosom a square of pre-Victorian graces, lawns, trees and flowers looked upon from Georgian windows that are of the University but were here long before it was conceived. The square, named Abercromby after the general who landed troops from Nelson's ships at Aboukir, became associated in our own century with an Abercrombie—the Sir Patrick of that ilk who was the second professor to occupy the Chair of Civic Design in the oldest department of town planning in the country. This department, fittingly enough, occupied the first of the post-1945 buildings and still has a view of the square. So, through Georgian windows, has the School of Architecture, founded in 1895, the first at an English university and for a time an occupant of the Bluecoat Chambers.

One side of the square is taken up by a building completed in 1969, the Senate House, centre of the University's administration. This is an architectural achievement, the least assertive of all the newer buildings, keeping the roofline and scale of the Georgian terraces on the other three flanks of the square and yet in no way aping their period in style. Trees in the square helped to soften the impact of new brick amongst the old; but nevertheless the way in which the Senate House complements—and compliments —frontages from so different an era is quite remarkable. Even the abstract by Barbara Hepworth—two holes in sculptured stone—in front of the new building looks right. The round-capped Senate Room, though it adjoins the Senate House, is not in sight of the square and therefore cannot be out of countenance with it.

A bridge between the Senate House and the Oliver Lodge Laboratory (Sir Oliver was for some years Professor of Physics at the University) in effect cloisters the square. It spans one of the borders, Oxford Street; and the parallel street is called Cambridge. But this Oxbridge instrusion into redbrick is adventitious because the names were given to the two streets many years before there were thoughts of a university by the Mersey. These were generated in the early 1870s when the port was still gripped by poverty in massive proportions, though recovering from the effects of the American Civil War. In 1878—two years before Liverpool became a city—a meeting of citizens decided upon a university, and a Royal Charter came three years later. Since that time the commerce, local authorities and individuals of Merseyside have subscribed millions to the University's development.

The initial component, the Victoria Building—which stares (I like to think without hostility) at the Metropolitan Cathedral— was designed by Alfred Waterhouse and is gothic in glazed red brick; and he gave it the only two spires to be found in the present-day Precinct. An elastic imagination would be stretched to snapping point to see these as dreaming spires—it is easier to suppose that the clock faces beneath the larger of the two are still mouthing an 'O' of astonishment at the transformation they have witnessed between 1962 and 1970. Before this period their view was of a dreariness relieved only by the distant prospect of the Anglican Cathedral and the close-up view of Professor Charles Reilly's Students' Union building which has a touch of the early nineteenth century in its bowed, balconied and pillared front.

Eighty-five acres, farsightedly allocated by the Corporation in 1949 for the Precinct, then consisted largely of run-down houses, once occupied by the well-to-do, out-and-out slums and exceedingly dreary commercial property partly devastated by war. There were deep railway cuttings and also tunnels, some devised by Joseph Williamson, the 'mad king of Edge Hill' in the first half of the last century to provide labour for the unemployed but to serve no other purpose. Since 1950 more than £35 million has been (or is being) spent on the 85 acres and the sector immediately around it, the projects including a multi-tiered teaching hospital covering 19 acres and a 2,000-pupil comprehensive school as well as some thirty University buildings.

In 1970 the area still had on its periphery wide open spaces left by bulldozers, these tracts to be occupied eventually by municipal housing and broad highways. It is considered that, because of these local authority schemes, the University's growth will be restricted to about 10,000 students and that this limit on numbers (an increase of 3,000 on the 1970 total) will be reached before the end of the present decade.

If we begin a tour of the Precinct from the entrance to the Metropolitan Cathedral and head towards the Victoria Building, we pass on the right the greatly extended Students' Union (embracing the Reilly building). A criticism of the extensions is that they have the appearance of a bus terminal; but since the Union has to accommodate a rush-hour influx (5,000 lunches can be served here) there was obviously method, not idiosyncrasy, in the design. Within the extension is the Mountford Hall (named after Sir James Mountford, a former Vice Chancellor), which seats 1,200.

Close to the Union is the Alsop Centre, which has a concourse, shops, a bank and a pub—happily named 'The Augustus John'— and these are on the side of Brownlow Hill opposite that occupied by the Victoria Building and two of the arms of the Faculty of Engineering Science—electrical engineering (completed in 1965) and mechanical engineering workshops and offices, with a seven-storey tower, built over a railway cutting in 1966, its construction posing some intricate problems.

If we walk along Ashton Street, its entrance from Brownlow Hill facing the Students' Union, we pass the Harold Cohen Library, opened in 1938, containing more than 350,000 volumes and seating 500 readers. We are then between the Medical School and the Royal Infirmary, which was also designed by Waterhouse but in a style much more sombre than that of the Victoria Building and now clad in soot. We have reached Pembroke Place and face the disagreeable (to me, anyway) mien of the Dental Hospital, completed in 1968. This adjoins the newer School of Dental Surgery and frowns across the road at the raked lecture hall of the Medical School, which has two concrete walls fretted and another embossed with the University's arms in king-size. On the rising ground beyond the School of Dental Surgery is the towering Teaching Hospital, which, planned and re-planned over twenty years, is due to be completed by 1974 and, as well as accommodating University clinical departments, will have 850 beds, replacing three of the city's general hospitals, one of these the Royal Infirmary. Close to the Teaching Hospital is the most up-to-date of the fourteen regional centres of the National Blood Transfusion Service.

We must walk the length of the Infirmary's frontage to reach the School of Tropical Medicine, extended in 1966 and at no time since its establishment sixty-eight years before that a charge upon the State but maintained by Merseyside, individual benefactors as well as firms, with the help of the Nuffield and Wolfson Foundations. It may validly be contended that this was no more than tropical Africa's due from a port that made fortunes out of slavery; but it can be argued, at least as reasonably, that Liverpool's debt to Africa has been paid and that all other areas of equatoria have also been substantial beneficiaries. On my last inquiry sixty-five students from twenty-five countries were at work there.

The school's earliest professor of tropical medicine was Sir Ronald Ross, the first man to recognise the connection between the mosquito and malaria. Its opening mission was to Sierra Leone in 1899 and by the start of the present century expeditions were equipped and maintained in Brazil, Mexico, Nigeria and Malta, all these at the expense of Merseyside business and co-ordinated by a committee under Sir Alfred Jones, shipowner. The activities constantly increased, and it was sometimes a critical struggle to make ends meet.

To review the manifold fields of research and of discovery over seventy years and to assess the alleviation of human misery and extension of life expectancy in the tropics due directly to the school's research would require two or three volumes. I will limit myself to a single instance of the school's work which may interest readers who served in the tropics during the last war and took daily the little yellow tablets containing mepacrine as a safeguard against malaria. The drug was developed between the wars by the Germans, and by 1939 they had large stocks of it. Britain and the United States, however, were almost entirely reliant on quinine, 97 per cent of this coming from Java.

Professor Warrington Yorke, of the Liverpool School of Tropical Medicine, saw how catastrophic to the Allies it could be if Japan entered the war and overran Java. He agitated first in Britain and then in America for the manufacture of mepacrine on a massive scale. Fortunately heed was paid to him at, as it was to turn out, the last moment. Yorke's energetic campaign led to a malarial unit being established and this, a year after his death, developed paludrine which, following clinical tests at the Liverpool School, became the most powerful of the anti-malaria measures.

The school's 1966 extension enabled the intake of post-graduates, mostly from tropical countries, to be increased. Its warfare against leprosy, beriberi, elephantiasis and other dread diseases of tropical countries is unremitting. Progress is being made in the relief of schistosomiasis which afflicts almost two-thirds of the population of Egypt and millions in other countries in Africa and in South America and the Far East. Merseyside commercial interests are largely represented on the school's governing body together with the Council and Senate of the University, and the secretariat is provided by the port's Chamber of Commerce.

If we now retrace our steps past the Infirmary to the Medical School and then turn along Crown Street from Pembroke Place we see, on the left, rising high above the large comprehensive school, the ten storeys of the Life Sciences building, opened in 1969 and the dominant feature of the northern end of the Precinct. It is, in my opinion, too dominant and, indeed, the least pleasing of all the University's seminaries; so I was gratified to read in a report published early in 1970 of practical, if not aesthetic, objections to any further erection above four floors in height.

Where Crown Street joins Brownlow Hill we have a view of the several buildings of the Faculty of Veterinary Science, which have murals of farm animals on the street-side walls; and there is a way out of the street on to the tree-dotted campus—known as The Lawn—flanked on one side by the large, winged building of inorganic chemistry and by the physics building on the other. This route returns us to Abercromby Square, and on the opposite side of this, behind the Georgian façade of Cambridge Street, there is another campus shared by the Faculties of Arts and Law. Points of the U-shaped buildings containing a reading room and lecture halls face the premises occupied by Modern Languages; and close by is the Law Building (completed in 1965) which is of an interesting pattern, its main rooms being interlocked. One of these is the Moot Room, with timber-faced walls and designed for mock trials. Hereabouts are a few sad relics of Myrtle Street in an otherwise empty space waiting to be turned into a wide highway. Myrtle Street was for long a shopping place with something of the dirt-stained colourfulness of an eastern bazaar, and I heard about it on my first evening in Liverpool in 1952 from my landlady, who ended a quick rundown of the amenities of the city with: 'An' if you want to shop why then go to Myrtle Street, things is coppers cheaper there than anywheres else in the 'Pool.' Something of its character is still found in Brunswick Road, on the other side that big new hospital, but here, too, shops are under the shadow of death. Myrtle, Vine, Mulberry, Peach and Walnut, the names of these neighbouring streets serve as reminders that the houses in them were built on that Botanic Garden in which William Roscoe found so much pleasure and which was moved to the other side of Edge Hill in Victoria's Coronation year. Now the site awaits a third life, many of the houses felled.

Falkner Square, also on the edge of the Precinct, clings to some of the grace it had until after the Edwardian era. It may continue to do so for it has the protection of a preservation order; but the grassy carpet of the little park in the middle has worn threadbare under scampering children's feet. The square has also the misfortune to be in the vicinity of streets recognised for years as good pull-ups for prostitutes, so that a respectable girl venturing into them at night is subjected to the embarrassment of kerb-hugging, loitering cars and propositions. Thus, in Liverpool, is lust paraded outside the palisades of scholarship. There are also spots in this polyglot part of the postal district of Liverpool 8 to which visitors from outside Merseyside, as well as those who live in the region, are lured by the promise of vice in various forms. It is not unusual for their quest to end in a hospital bed after their spare cash has been removed.

Before we leave the Precinct's area, mention must be made of two buildings close to the Metropolitan Cathedral. Both are in the Greek Revivalist style and one of them, built in 1815, has found a useful new life as a centre of Irish social life in the city. The other, standing almost opposite, has a frontage with six imposing pillars which follow the curve from Oxford Street into Mount Pleasant. This is the Liverpool Medical Institution, opened in 1837 and discreetly extended in recent years. A library of outstanding interest is housed for the most part in Georgian-style rooms of considerable appeal, and the 40,000 volumes include a 1532 Hippocrates and Thomas Raynalde's *The Byrth of Mankynd* (1545), the first book on midwifery to be printed in English. The Institution, which today has more than 1,000 members, is a reminder of the city's long association with medicine. Four of the original Council of the British Medical Association were Liverpool men.

Notable contributions to medicine have been made. One of the most recent was the development, in 1966 (its announcement coming in the same week as the first heart transplant operation in South Africa) of a vaccine to eliminate the critical anaemic condition which can occur in the Rhesus Positive baby of a Rhesus Negative mother. The importance of this discovery is indicated by the fact that, up to 1966, one birth in about 200 was affected by this condition. The successful research was by the Nuffield Unit of Medical Genetics at the University, a team of seven doctors under the direction of Professor C. A. Clarke. Twenty four anonymous volunteers (all men, all Merseysiders) took tests over a period of several years, readily accepting the risk of jaundice. Later they were joined by women volunteers. The men called themselves 'the Pregnant Dads'.

A second University precinct—this one residential—is in park-land on the rump of Mossley Hill where stood Carnatic Hall mentioned in Chapter Two. The name has been preserved in one of the two groups of halls of residence and the other group contains the handsome former home of the Rathbone family.

Aerial view of the University Precinct

There are seven halls in the two groups and two others (both for women) in other parts of the city which it is proposed to close; but the development of the undergraduate village has been re-tarded—like the growth of the Precinct embracing Abercromby Square more than three miles away—by lack of money.

Many people feel that it was a mistake to put the University's residential wings at such a distance from the lecture rooms. They say that, apart from the cost of the time-wasting travel imposed, students are deterred from participating in the social life of the centre of the city and from returning to the University after their evening meal, so that the amenities are under-used and the buildings almost as de-populated at night as nine-to-five office blocks.

It must be borne in mind, however, that only 31 per cent of the students are in halls. Almost as many live with their parents in and around Merseyside and the remainder are either in lodgings or have their own flats, most of these in walking distance of Aber-cromby Square. Students do, in fact, have a notable share in social work in the poorer areas of the city. If their participation in the cultural activities of Liverpool has been disappointingly limited this is probably because those who live on grants have little enough money to spare for concerts and theatres even when they live on the doorstep.

The city has benefitted from the development of the under-graduate village on Mossley Hill because this has ensured the future of an important segment of the green belt beginning at Sefton Park and extending, with two minor interruptions, to Woolton. This is discussed in the next chapter.

The University's Carnatic Hall of Residence, Mossley Hill

N

NINE

ELBOW ROOM

WITH 130,000 more inhabitants, Liverpool covers 28 fewer square miles than Sheffield and is nearly that much smaller in area than Leeds yet has a population greater by 160,000. Elbow room is thus at a premium on the Lancashire side of the Mersey, but almost a twelfth of the land within the city boundaries is for recreation.

In 1843—the year that England's first municipal park was laid out in Birkenhead to the designs of Joseph Paxton—Richard Vaughan Yates paid £50,000 for 44 acres at Toxteth, giving the public access to most of them but leasing land on the periphery for building large villas, rents from which paid for the upkeep of the open space. This well-timbered estate, which became Corporation property, is known as Princes Park (no apostrophe!) and is 2 miles from the centre of the city, approached from a wide boulevard of two carriageways which were made before there was motor traffic. The boulevard is flanked by terraces of tall houses, a number of them now noticeably the worse for wear, between churches and chapels (one of which bears the coloured Christ referred to in my first chapter).

Princes Park is in the postal district of Liverpool 8, mentioned in the previous chapter, which has so often been portrayed by newspapers and TV as slum-ridden and having an artistic enclave *à la* the Paris Left Bank. There are bare bones of truth here but such pen and camera studies invariably ignore the park and the substantial houses that overlook it (in one of them Fritz Spiegl keeps a remarkable collection of antique organs). In emphatic contrast to slums still remaining in this district and to a deal of dreary postwar housing built there by the local authority,

Princes Park offers a view across the lake and trees to a large block of apartments that brings London W.1. to mind.

A quarter of a century after Princes Park was opened, the Corporation laid out Stanley Park (100 acres) in the congested north-east of the city, Newsham Park (149 acres) in the east and Sefton Park (269 acres), bought from the Earl of Sefton and practically adjoining Princes Park, in the south. Sefton Park, given a high grade residential surround, was superbly landscaped by a Parisian who provided a lake and a glen through which a stream hurries, reflecting in late spring the colours from rhododendron blooms. Ornate lodges were built, and soon after the turn of the century a Scottish firm erected a domed palm house, 70 feet high and 100 feet in width. It has stayed a focal point and is furnished with a range of conservatory plants. In the park is the only replica of the Piccadilly Eros, and there is also a charming statue of Peter Pan.

By erecting high blocks of flats on the hem nearest the city, the Corporation destroyed in the sixties an illusion, from the centre of Sefton Park, of being on an estate in the heart of the country. Luckily for Liverpool this blunder was not repeated on the opposite boundary, where a sweep of forest trees merges with the fourteen acre Greenbank Park (which also has a lake), with the woodland adjoining university halls of residence on Mossley Hill and with the playing fields of Liverpool College, a boys' public school founded in 1840. A road through Sefton Park makes a pleasant interlude for many who live in the south of Liverpool on their way to and from work by car. There is a speed limit of 20 m.p.h. (it used to be 10!), which is blandly ignored by one and all.

Two or three hundred yards from Greenbank Park is the entrance to Wavertree Playground (108 acres)—'The Mystery'—where Liverpool Show, instituted by the Corporation in 1949, is held on three days every mid-July and, given good weather, draws an attendance of well over 100,000. Neighbouring the university halls on the Carnatic site is the public park (29 acres) surrounding Sudley, a former mansion turned into an art gallery; and on one side of this are the timbered grounds of the I. M. Marsh College of Physical Recreation, a tower block, run by Lancashire Education Committee and drawing young women teachers from countries both in and outside the Commonwealth. Sweeping downhill from Sudley are the University's extensive playing fields graced by a pavilion of outstanding attraction, designed by Gerald Beech and decked like a ship. Only a narrow ribbon of houses separates the playing fields from 500 acres of mature parklands beginning with the Botanic Garden.

Long ago these lands were the estates of the Perceval family. They then became the private pleasure grounds of captains of commerce who garnished them as settings for fine mansions. Now they belong to the citizens at large who, as well as sauntering through them, play golf, football, cricket and bowls, ride horses, watch open-air Shakespeare, listen to military bands and pop groups—and even catch fish.

The Botanic Garden was transferred to parkland previously known as Harthill during the 1950s from Wavertree Park, where every greenhouse had been flattened by bomb blast. The main entrance to them is the imposing gateway built for Harthill and graced by statues representing the four seasons. From this runs an avenue shaded by 100 limes planted at the time the statues were installed; and to one side of the lime grove a host of cherries and crabs produce a spectacular display of spring blossom. In the midst of this orchard is a chunk of granite which was a sample sent to Jesse Hartley when he was building the Liverpool waterfront.

On the opposite side of the limes are glasshouses covering well over an acre and the home of the municipal collection of orchids, which includes numerous varieties raised here and given the names of Liverpool parks. The nucleus of the collection came long ago from shipowners with interests in South America, who supported plant collecting expeditions in Amazonia and the rain forests of Brazil. There is a wealth of other tropicana under the Botanic Garden glass, and selections from it are made for display at Chelsea Show.

The conservatory area is entered from a hexagonal vestibule in which stand the Calder Stones, thought by some to be relics from prehistoric times. From the vestibule runs a broad corridor, lined with sub-tropical shrubs and climbers, and this is the spine for sixteen glasshouses of varying height and width and with differing temperatures, half of them open to the public. Two fern houses, one of them for tropical subjects, are of particular interest and they lead to a sun walk running the length of the conservatory area. The walk is roofed but open-sided. Here camellias contribute to the annual spring banquet of bloom, and the walk looks across a large rose garden to a belt of forest trees that mask the houses beyond.

Calderstones Park, adjoining the Botanic Garden, has few equals in the North-west of England, yet there was a great fuss when the Corporation bought it at the beginning of the century for £43,000 from the founder of the shipping company that eventually became Cunard. This was £9,000 less than he paid for the 94 acres some thirty years earlier, but numerous Liverpudlians considered it to be nevertheless a prodigal waste of their money. Time has shown how hopelessly wrong they were.

The former mansion is used as offices and as a café and close to it is a stage for summertime concerts. Rhododendrons in a comprehensive collection bloom beneath towering beeches, and there are many other noble trees including a superb liliodendron and an oak reputed to be 1,000 years old. The park has old English and Japanese gardens a rockery constructed of Woolton stone, and a 7-acre lake, with a wooded island, where geese and duck sail. From the lakeside a path winds through a water garden, crossing and re-crossing a stream strewn with marigolds and swept by branches of weeping willows. This route crosses a leafy road and then climbs past the playing fields and wooded grounds of a domestic science college (which has a number of overseas students) to reach two municipal golf courses (one of eighteen, one of nine holes) which are parklike in character and have more splendid trees in their 150 acres. From the highest part of the larger course there is a view over the treetops of every park I have mentioned to the Liver Building 7 miles away. From this vantage point the sturdy tower of Mossley Hill Church (close to the University's halls of residence) appears to rise from an unbroken stretch of forest.

Next in line in this pride of parks is Allerton Tower, its 78 acres offering both the formality of broad lawns and the caprice of shrubby alcoves which, in several instances, spring a surprise view of a Welsh hill. There are a few remnants of the big house that gave this park its name and which was designed by Elmes, the architect of St. George's Hall. A double boulevard separates Allerton Tower and adjacent grounds of Allerton Priory School from Clarke Gardens, the 41-acre estate of eighteenth-century Allerton Hall, where William Roscoe lived stylishly until his bankruptcy. Now it is a cafe, and Soay sheep, the primitive breed from remote St. Kilda, scamper through the trees close by.

From here expansive grassland, planted with groups of trees, sweep downhill to Garston; and in the opposite direction are playing fields, some in a stream-fed valley, others on the slope of Camp Hill which is crowned with gardens and presents views of industrial Lancashire—the 'mucky mountain' of Cronton Colliery a prominent landmark—as well as of rural Wales and of the Mersey in its maximum width. A tree-lined walk leads to the beeches of Woolton Woods, a 62-acre park where a floral cuckoo clock has long been a summer attraction. Next door are ample grounds of a nurses' training school, and there are three other parks within 2 miles.

Add Otterspool and Speke Hall (both described in Chapter Five) to the list and it will be seen that the southern districts of the city have recreation space almost on a lavish scale. Other quarters have been less generously served, though they share more than eighty parks including Walton Hall, of 130 acres, where there is a lake. Stanley Park, between the stadia of Everton and Liverpool Football Clubs, has a palm house.

It may wrily be observed that, with scores of acres blitzed by bulldozers, the older parts of the city do not want for elbow room, even if these badlands do make desperately poor playgrounds. Some parts of them are going to be landscaped and planted, but the Westminster brake on municipal spending has made progress painfully slow.

The estates of Knowsley Hall and Croxteth Hall had rarely been seen by the public until 1971 but provide essential zones of greenery to relieve the vast spread of municipal red brick on and beyond the city's boundaries in what amount to new towns. Knowsley now has a £750,000 safari park (it had a zoo in the nineteenth century) so Liverpudlians are now able to see a little of the hall, partly of the seventeenth century, where the Earl of Derby no longer lives, having built a house on the estate that is easier to manage. Croxteth Hall, also partly of the seventeenth century and restored after a serious fire in recent years, continues to be the home of Lord Sefton and, immediately outside its walls, provides a vast and otherwise unattractive housing estate with a leafy, almost rural, lane.

Obviously North Wales has powerful weekend attractions for

Liverpool families many of whom have cottages in the hills or
caravans among the thousands that stand ever immobile by
beaches. But the coast at Formby, which is under National Trust
surveillance and therefore protected from invasion by caravans if
not from erosion by the sea, is also popular and easily reached by
electric train. Adjoining the beach here is a nature reserve of
1,200 acres and consisting partly of pine woods, partly of wet
slacks and heath and partly of marram-clad dunes. This contains
much plant and animal life of interest and is the haunt of the yellow
natterjack toad.

At fine weekends, when low tide is at a convenient time, there
is a procession across the sands of the Dee estuary to Hilbre to
watch Atlantic grey seals and a great variety of seabirds; yet this
rocky islet is sufficiently cut off from mainland life by the tides
for the Duke of Edinburgh to have spent days there photograph-
ing birds without being photographed himself. Three miles away
and running down towards the Dee marshlands (treacherous for
all but wildfowl) are Liverpool University's Botanic Gardens,
which are open to the public at all times. They were planted by a
Liverpool cotton broker and were given to the University in 1949.

The most stimulating prospects of additional elbow room were
presented by meadowland at Aintree within the circuit of the
Grand National course. But in mid-1970 negotiations to buy the
racecourse, with the help of the Government and racing interests,
came to an end. The Corporation refused to pay more than
£1,250,000 and this figure was hundreds of thousands less than
the price sought by the owners, Tophams. In 1971 came a £10
million plan by a private developer to build on part of the
meadows but preserve the course. But the future of the great race
is far from assured.

TEN

SOCCER CITY'S STEEPLECHASE

TIME was when the morning of Grand National Day filled the heart of Merseyside with excitement, streets colourfully thronged, the overnight boat from Dublin jam-packed, as in the period of immigrant ships, and names of horses on everyone's lips and in everyone's mind as all but the halt made for Aintree.

It is still a big occasion at the Adelphi Hotel, where a banquet follows the race; but elsewhere in the centre of Liverpool the event now means less, in terms of crowds, than normal Saturday afternoon worship at either Anfield or Goodison, the shrines of soccer city; and people no longer talk very much about the race in pubs and on buses in the week preceding it. Standards of 'the greatest steeplechase in the world' have not declined, and the way in which it is run has not become less spectacular; but through the eyes of television cameras mounted on vehicles that keep up with the horses by using a motor-racing track, laid inside the steeple-chase circuit in the 1950s, the National can be seen in infinitely more detail from the fireside than from any point on the course. So, although the race has a multi-million audience round the world, numbers in the stands and on the banks have declined, the Irish invasion has dwindled and, in consequence, the day has lost a deal of the old pageantry and ebullience.

Some of the anticipatory fever disappeared with 'Jump Sunday' in 1959. It had for many years been a tradition for Merseyside families to walk the course on the Sunday preceding the race (which used to be on a Wednesday, then a Friday) and, with the coming of the car, they were joined by thousands who journeyed from farther afield. Hucksters, and tipsters were there so that Aintree on 'Jump Sunday' had the fairground atmosphere of

Epsom Downs on the eve of the Derby. The cost of clearing up the mess put a stop to this custom.

Since 'Jump Sunday' ceased there have been more 'last' Grand Nationals than farewell performances by the most reluctant-to-quit prima ballerina. 'Thank U very much for the Aintree Iron' sang The Scaffold—that gifted Merseyside group who compound pop, parody and satire—in a tune that climbed the charts as surely as their 'Lily the Pink'. The story of the National in the sixties might have been titled 'The Aintree Irony'.

In 1964 it really did look as if the great race was doomed and that the course would vanish under houses, but then a prolonged High Court action ensued. In 1970, as explained at the end of the previous chapter, the future looked even bleaker than it did in 1964. It is another of the ironies of Aintree that the Corporation put up the purse for the first races (on the flat) there in 1828 but withdrew the following year.

In all the disputation since 1950, the conflict over broadcasting copyright and then about the future of the course, the forceful personality of Mrs. Mirabel Topham, once a West End actress, has been dominant. She became chairman and managing director of Tophams Ltd. in 1938, ninety-nine years after the first steeplechase at Aintree and the arrival there of Edward William Topham, a Yorkshireman, whose skill as a handicapper earned him the sobriquet of 'The Wizard'.

The Liverpool Steeplechase was inaugurated at Maghull, next door to Aintree, in 1837 by William Lynn, who had a pub near the Lyceum Club and whose grave is in that cemetery close to the Anglican Cathedral. Two years later, as the Grand Liverpool Steeplechase, it was run at Aintree and won—fittingly enough, for the race that was to become the chanciest of all—by Lottery. Captain Becher, having remounted Conrad at the third fence, came a purler at the brook which has, ever since, born his name; and perhaps in that year, but certainly in 1840, a horse named Valentine ran and bestowed a title on another of the watery hazards. The race was 'nationalised' in 1843 and five years later 'Wizard' Topham leased the course from Lord Sefton.

The story since has been laced with drama and well-seasoned with romantic triumphs by horses of humble pedigree. Abd el Kadir, the winner in 1850 and 1851, was out of a mare that pulled a stage coach; and another to win twice, The Lamb, had been given as a weedy foal to the Irish breeder's small son for a pet. It was known as The Lamb not because it was grey (a colour ever suspect at Aintree) but because it was unusually docile, perhaps through the influence of the boy. When he died, the horse was sold for £25 to a Dublin vet, who leased it to Lord Poulett for whom it won the Nationals of 1868 and 1871—the second time when in competition with The Colonel, victor in 1869 and 1870, which had Exmoor pony in its blood.

Cloister, twice in second place, won the 1893 National carrying 12 stone 7 pound by forty lengths; and Manifesto bore the same daunting weight in 1899 when scoring a second victory. Grudon won the 1901 race in a blinding blizzard with its hoofs plastered in butter to prevent snow balling under its shoes. Glenside, aged 19 and bought for a song by Frank Bibby, a Merseyside ship-owner, was the only survivor of thirty-two runners two fences from home in 1911 but was in such poor shape that bets were being placed on whether it was capable of finishing. According to a report, the horse 'staggered past the post as though drunk'.

Tipperary Tim, no better suited physically than Glenside to the Aintree conditions, was the only runner to finish in 1929; and doubtless its demonstration that any sort of horse could triumph in the National given lots of luck, resulted in the record field of the following year when sixty-six took part in the cavalry charge to the first fence. Easter Hero—whose refusal at the Canal Turn first time round in 1929 caused the elimination of twenty-one horses—appeared to have victory in sight in 1930 but then spread a plate, and Gregalach won at 100 to one. Nickel Coin, which did not race until 7 years old, won the sensational National of 1951, when eleven of the thirty-six starters came to grief at the first fence and only three completed the course.

Yet the most dramatic of all the Grand Nationals was surely that of 1956 when the Queen Mother's Devon Loch flopped on to its belly a hundred yards from victory. Several theories have been advanced for this astonishing collapse: it has been suggested that wild cheering for an apparently certain royal win unbalanced Devon Loch; others have said that the horse attempted to leap a water jump that wasn't there (the obstacle occurs only on the first circuit and Devon Loch fell when parallel with it).

Peter Simple, Ally Sloper, Reynoldstown (only horse twice to win the Aintree race this century), Russian Hero (but a genuine

Russian entry was a flop), Kellsboro' Jack, Highland Wedding—
these are a few of the names that have been toasted at that Adelphi
dinner on Grand National day. One that wasn't was Tom Scott,
whose son became a mayor of Bootle; but he should be remembered as the only man to have jumped the National course
without a horse (that was in 1870). Perhaps it might be an idea to
hold a pedestrian race over the fences on a resuscitated 'Jump
Sunday' if, against all the signs of 1970, the great race continues
at Aintree.

There is a colour problem in Liverpool, but the colours are not
black and white or orange and green. You could enter the
Metropolitan Cathedral wearing an orange jumper and little
would be said; but try standing on the Kop when sporting a Royal
blue sweater or going to the Gwladys Street end of Goodison
flaunting a scarlet scarf and listen to the comments. Red is for
Anfield, blue for Goodison, and when the twain meets tumult
results; but it is a vocal tumult, nothing more. It is a long time
since these jousts between rivals were marred by incidents
unhappily commonplace in Glasgow when Rangers and Celtic
collide.

There is no connection between orange and green and red and
blue. Influences that determine a Merseysider's football allegiance
are as mysterious as those which selected W. S. Gilbert's little
Liberal and little Conservative. 'Yes, there are two teams in
Liverpool,' the native agrees with a grin, 'Everton and Everton
Reserves' (or, of course, 'Liverpool and Liverpool Reserves'). I
recall an afternoon at Goodison when, in the second half, there
was a joyous cheer at the Gwladys Street end. As there was
nothing occurring on the pitch to cheer about, I was mystified;
then it transpired that news that Liverpool were a goal down in
an F.A. Cup quarter-final had come over portable radios.

The rivalry is, on the whole, good-tempered but it is implac-
able. Those who go to Goodison one week, Anfield the next, are
in a tiny minority and usually settlers. 'I wouldn't go to Goodison
(Anfield) without the Reds (Blues) for fear of being took sick.
Just think of the shame of being seen dead there!'

There was a rare period of relative accord at the end of the
1965–6 season when the F.A. Cup crossed Stanley Park to Goodison to make way for the League championship trophy at Anfield!

Everton (the older of the two) were champions in 1963–4, Liverpool in 1965–6; Liverpool won the F.A. Cup for the first time in 1965, Everton for the third time in 1966. Liverpool were League runners-up in 1968–9 and Everton became champions again in 1969–70. In 1971 Liverpool were Cup finalists. Small wonder it is called soccer city!

So much has been written and broadcast about the Kop, non-Merseysiders may be pardoned for assuming that Everton supporters, by comparison, praise their gods pianissimo. But it is largely a matter of architecture. Goodison is larger and more open than Anfield so that the vox pop spreads and disperses quickly— or at least this was the case before major alterations to both grounds were completed during the summer of 1971. Even when the Kopites were at Goodison in full cry (at the derby games or when the World Cup matches were held in 1966) the sound was several decibel points below the Anfield roar.

All the same, there is a special magic about the Kop and its 'choir'. It has a telepathic communication system so that a wise-crack apparently comes from thousands of throats simultaneously, not as an echo; and there is also its inventiveness—most chants and songs heard on the football grounds of England, from 'Ee aye addio' to 'You'll Never Walk Alone' came out of the Kop. Certain names are specially suited to the explosive chants. 'St. John' came like a flash of lightning and a thunderbolt—not 'Sinj'n' or 'Saint John' but 'Sntj*ohn*'. 'Roger*unt*' used to be a terrific sound, too. Goodison's Gwladys Street end turned 'Alex*young*' into a mighty hosanna and now achieves an equally exultant 'Aln*ball*'.

The incomparable Dixie Dean, the only player (up to 1970, anyway) to score sixty League goals in a season (he, in fact, netted a hundred counting all matches) is still a figure of some prominence on his native Merseyside. I was at a 1970 dinner when he convulsed the guests, and I decided that it was not so much what he said as how he said it, his timing as precise as a speaker as it was as a player. Also a guest was Kenny Campbell, then aged 77, who was one of a trinity of Liverpool internationals to inspire the club's telegraphic address, 'Goalkeeper'—the others were Elisha Scott (Ireland) and Sam Hardy (England). Kenny (a Scot, of course) is still spry, still in business as a sports outfitter on Merseyside.

He recalled at the dinner that Dean put one past him when,

near the end of his League career, he was keeping goal for Leicester City. 'So I feel nervous tonight,' he went on, 'because Dixie keeps on nodding at me.' Also at that dinner (Tranmere Rovers, 'over the water', were hosts) were Billy Liddell, for so many years an idol of the Kop and now a Liverpool magistrate; and Joe Mercer, who is a Merseysider (born at Ellesmere Port like Stan Cullis) and whose bandy legs twinkled at Goodison in those days when Dixie was king.

Goodison draws substantially more support than Anfield from the Wirral side of the Mersey where Dixie was born. It is unlikely that this has much to do with him—there is, in fact, no satisfactory explanation for it or for the North Wales preference for Everton blue. But Tunnel statistics and rail returns are conclusive proofs that Dixie's lot are tops in Cheshire and Cambria.

The city's youth produces a powerful football force, too. Liverpool Boys became in 1970 the first to win the English Schools Trophy three times in four years and presumably two or three in the team that achieved the third victory are destined to wear either a red or blue shirt professionally before they are out of their 'teens.

Much amateur soccer is played in Liverpool on both Saturday and Sunday (there is a large Sunday League). Ten miles only separate the Pier Head from Rugby League country, but the code has never really caught on by the Mersey; and Liverpool City, having tried for years to evangelise the diddyland of Knotty Ash, changed its name to Huyton R.L.C. and moved nearer to the converted. But Rugby Union thrives.

Though golf courses inside the city are not outstanding, some of the coastal links within half-an-hour's drive of it are—Royal Liverpool at Hoylake and Royal Birkdale at Southport, for example—so world champions are visitors as regular as Grand National jockeys. Championship tennis is played annually at Hoylake though county cricket comes but twice a year (sometimes only once). Two yacht clubs race the tricky region of the Mersey's mouth and there are two sailing clubs upriver, eight others within easy reach of it. There is also a rowing club.

So Liverpudlians do not languish at that time of the year when the turf of Goodison and Anfield grows idly lush.

ELEVEN

ARTS NEARLY ALL ALIVE

A MONTHLY magazine with the title *Arts Alive, Merseyside* is posted to more than 12,000 addresses. This publication—begun years ago by the Bluecoat Arts Forum of nearly forty organisations and now issued by the Merseyside Arts Association, which is financed by local authorities—is one measure of the strength of the arts in and around Liverpool, though not all branches are robust.

Music has far and away the strongest appeal, and such has been the case for at least a century. Mainsprings of this interest are the Philharmonic Hall, headquarters of the only symphony orchestra in the provinces not reaching in 1970 for a begging bowl; the University, which has a music department, an orchestra and choirs; the Bluecoat; and the two Cathedrals. The Philharmonic Hall, the Royal Liverpool Philharmonic Society ('Royal' since 1957) and its orchestra are all three called 'the Phil' by Merseysiders. Average attendances at the orchestra's concerts exceed 90 per cent, a high proportion of the seats being booked for the entire season at a substantial discount which makes music of the highest standard still relatively inexpensive, even though prices were raised in 1970. It is, of course, heavily subsidised and largely by the ratepayers of Liverpool; but substantial contributions from firms and individuals to a special fund enable the society (which has well over a 1,000 members) to bring the greatest of the world's virtuosi to the hall. Nearly 6,000 tickets for 'Industrial' concerts —these consist of a single programme performed on three consecutive evenings in each of eight months of the year—can only be obtained through works and offices, and in some the demand is such that they are drawn out of a hat.

The society, founded in 1840 so one of the oldest in Britain, had Max Bruch for a musical director, and then for twelve years shared with Manchester the services of Sir Charles Hallé, who conducted the last concert of his life in Liverpool in 1895. Following his death there was a breach between the two cities, Manchester preferring Hans Richter, Liverpool choosing Sir Frederick Cowen.

Every symphony that Sir Thomas Beecham (born at Huyton) heard until his late 'teens was performed in the Philharmonic Hall. When at the height of his fame he conducted in the hall on several occasions; but there is also a memory of him limping down the main aisle, through the pit and the stalls, in the Royal Court Theatre to conduct a performance of his beloved *The Bohemian Girl*, gout preventing him from using the door under the stage.

Sir Adrian Boult, son of a Liverpool shipbroker, was taken to the Philharmonic Hall for his first concert at the age of 7. As a youth he went through all the instruments of Liverpool Police Band with the bandmaster who was also a first violin in the Phil; and when the outbreak of war put musicians in the city out of work he found them employment by organising a series of concerts in the old Sun Hall (it seated 5,000), the prices of admission twopence to half-a-crown. He conducted the Phil for the first time in 1916 and still takes at least one concert a year.

From time to time Sir Henry Wood conducted the Phil; and Reginald Pound, in his biography of the maestro, tells how on returning to the Adelphi after one concert, Sir Henry wiped all the morning calls from the night porter's blackboard so that he could demonstrate his skill as a caricaturist with chalk to B. C. Hilliam ('Flotsam'). Whenever the two met afterwards that night porter's anguished cry of ''Ave a 'eart, Sir 'Enery!' was a stock greeting.

Sir Malcolm Sargent became the Phil's musical director in 1942 and the orchestra turned fully professional. It soon developed into a considerable musical force, giving London a lead in its encouragement of young composers. Benjamin Britten's now universally known *Young Person's Guide to the Orchestra* was heard for the first time in Liverpool, as were works by Gordon Crosse and two Merseyside composers of great promise, Malcolm Lipkin and John McCabe. Daniel Barenboim, making his first visit to this country, spent the evening of his thirteenth birthday playing with the Phil and treasures the copy of *Alice in Wonderland* he received. Gwyneth Jones sang with the orchestra when unknown, one year as a contralto, the next as a mezzo and the next as a soprano!

Since Charles Groves became conductor in 1963, the Phil has performed all Mahler's symphonies—possibly the only orchestra in the world to have done this in recent years—and has had three European tours. It caters, with the Hallé, for the whole of the North of England and Wales and a number of its members aid child and adult amateur musicians.

The Merseyside Concert Orchestra, its sixty or so members including both children and grandparents, plays periodically in the Philharmonic Hall, where chamber music recitals are held by the Rodewald Society established at the beginning of the century. Liverpool Mozart Orchestra, in which professionals, giving their services, combine with amateur players, put on concerts in the Bluecoat, where the Sandon Studios Society and the Lieder Circle hold recitals. There are two military and several brass bands.

Two large choirs, the Philharmonic and the Welsh Choral Union, blossomed because of Sargent's inspired encouragement, and they continue to rank with the best in Britain, tackling the unfamiliar as well as oratorios it is customary to sing in most large towns. The Cathedrals, of course, make notable contributions to choral music in the city, and there are a score or more other choirs, including three for young people, each more than a hundred strong. For a great many years the voice was the only musical instrument that the majority of Liverpudlians could afford and they still love to sing. Every seat is always sold weeks in advance of the carol concerts held in the Philharmonic Hall, as evergreen at Christmas there as the trees that traditionally decorate the platform; and carol services in the Cathedrals are packed.

The youth of the city is strongly involved in all this activity, partly because of stimulation from the education authority—which loans instruments to children who genuinely wish to play them—and partly because Liverpool is refreshingly free from the stuffiness and snobberies that afflict music in many towns. Fritz Spiegl does some healthy mickey-taking from time to time and the Phil have performed a symphonic version of a Beatles tune. No eyebrows are raised when youngsters hightail it from a

The Playhouse
Housing contrasts

Saturday night concert to the 'Cavern' or one of the other beat clubs for the rest of the evening. At the annual 'Youth Makes Music' concert, given by prizewinners in a festival that attracts 1,500 entries, it is customary to hear Bach and beat, fugues and folk. Three young men who have had the benefit of Liverpool Cathedral choir training and discipline are The Crofters, after the Cathedral's Croft.

From more than thirty school orchestras players are recruited for the Liverpool Junior Schools' and Senior Schools' orchestra, each of more than seventy players. A Youth Band (military) has eighty instrumentalists and there are numerous ensembles. The Merseyside Youth Orchestra, composed of more than a hundred players who come from both sides of the river, has ex-members in symphony orchestras in several countries. There is a Festival Youth Orchestra of sixty and a Merseyside Youth Choir.

The city rarely has an opportunity to see professional opera more than two or three weeks in a year, so it is not surprising that, despite efforts made by the Liverpool Grand Opera Company, the Opera Circle and (until its demise in 1970) the only Verdi Society in the country, interest flags—except in the 'pop' operas (*Carmen*, *La Boheme*, *Madame Butterfly* and so on) and Gilbert and Sullivan.

When I moved to Liverpool there were five professional theatres in the city. The first of them to go—and with no more than a whimper of protest—was the 'Pivvy' ('Pavilion'), a variety house that turned to the then new-fangled bingo and has stayed with it. The next to close its stage doors was the 'Shakey' ('Shakespeare'), opened in 1888 and described as 'the most beautiful theatre in Britain' and also as 'the tart of voluptuous Victorian architecture'. There was a great fuss about this and a reprieve came through two Americans, the actor-producer Sam Wanamaker and his backer, Anna Deere Wiman. Wanamaker, full of ideas and zest, restored glitter to the old theatre and brought back gusto; but in thirteen months the venture lost £120,000 and again the 'Shakey' closed.

It re-opened in 1963 as a plushy restaurant and club but within a few weeks was devastated by fire. Then it was admirably restored, the renewed plasterwork and sculpture providing yet more modern examples of Liverpudlian craftsmanship. It continues

Otterspool Promenade
Speke Hall
O

as a restaurant but with nightly cabaret so that live entertainment survives at the 'Shakey' even though it is not precisely a theatre.

While the Shakespeare was being restored, a Corporation-backed repertory company was established in a hall built, shortly after the Medical Institution next door, as a chapel for a fire-and-brimstone evangelist and subsequently used for lectures then as a cinema. It was given an apron stage and re-named the Everyman Theatre.

At the time it seemed to me an almost absurd waste of public money when the city already had a repertory company, the second oldest in the country, in a theatre of much attraction, the Playhouse. Time proved that I was quite wrong. The Everyman has cost the ratepayers many thousands, but its dedicated company, under the inspired direction of Peter James, blended talent with adventure, gradually gathering an audience of regulars, mostly young, and this partly because of its crusading performances for schools. In 1970 a new patron appeared in George Platt, who retired on the right side of 40, having made a fortune from patent firelighters. He put up £4,500 for a festival of experimental drama to which various avant garde groups contributed; and he enlivened the proceedings himself by standing in the foyer singing 'Land of Hope and Glory' after leftish happenings on and off the stage.

All this sounds fascinating; yet the Everyman, structurally, is a sow's ear that will never be silk. It is fine for those who like to go to the theatre in jeans and sweaters. The majority, though, still want theatre-going to be an occasion for dressing up. In a well-ordered place (such as Utopia) the Everyman's company would be in the 'Shakey'! The departure in 1970 of the gifted Peter James presented a problem but it seems to have been resolved.

Simultaneously with the Everyman's emergence as a theatrical influence, the Playhouse—under the shadow of the new Beacon—acquired a restaurant and foyer of striking architecture—cylinders of glass and concrete balanced on a single pillar—and was brought up-to-date backstage, with one of the largest theatre workshops in the country. All this cost £275,000, and once again Liverpool ratepayers' money was generously handed out.

The Playhouse is as near the ideal in repertory theatres as can be achieved, retaining Edwardian elegance but providing all mod.

cons. for actors and audience. It was originally a music hall and turned to repertory in 1911 with the great Basil Dean (then aged 23) as producer. John Masefield wrote an ode for the opening night. Through the years the company has counted among its members Rex Harrison (Liverpool-born and told in his season at the Playhouse that acting was not his vocation!); Michael Redgrave and his wife, Rachel Kempson; Diana Wynyard, Robert Donat, Flora Robson, Wyndham Goldie, Hugh Williams, Cecil Parker, Megs Jenkins, Cyril Luckham, Richard Briers, Gerald Harper, Robert Flemyng, Ronald Sinclair—and Brian Reece, Deryck Guyler and Rita Tushingham, who, like John Gregson, Derek Nimmo and Glenda Jackson are Merseyside born.

The Playhouse has become a component of the St. John's Precinct and so has the Royal Court, built just before the last war on the site of a theatre which began as a circus in 1826, was owned for several years by Carl Rosa and was burned down at about the same time as the old Philharmonic Hall. For a good many years audiences could see at the Royal Court plays, with star-strewn casts, before they were put on in the West End; and, seating 1,600 and with a fairly large stage, it has proved reasonably suitable for opera, ballet and musical comedy. But, in the summer of 1968, it turned to bingo for some weeks; and the following spring brought an announcement that it would be used solely for this purpose until sold. A storm of protest produced 37,000 signatures to a petition appealing to the Corporation to save the theatre.

As it turned out, a second summer of bingo was not very successful and the Royal Court re-opened with the theatrical pattern unchanged and with largely capacity audiences except for some performances by the Welsh National Opera and the Royal Ballet. A Christmas season show, headed by Liverpool-born Frankie Vaughan, did well. So it was a shock when Howard and Wyndham announced that the theatre would close permanently in the May. Those 37,000 petitioners of 1969 at once renewed their pleas to the Corporation.

Within a few days the report to the Arts Council on provincial theatres was published. This suggested that Liverpool should have, apart from the two repertory companies, one theatre and it listed the Royal Court with the Empire in parentheses. Presumably, therefore, the Royal Court was considered the best choice.

The Empire, one of the largest theatres in the provinces, needs 17,500 customers in a week if it is to be filled to capacity for six nightly performances and a matinee. To their credit, Moss Empires, the owners, have never once suggested that they proposed to close the theatre, though it has stood empty for many weeks on end during the last few years, except for occasional one-night stands by pop stars. Visits by Sadler's Wells in 1969 and 1970 were indifferently supported, though this was probably partly because of very limited publicity (on the second occasion, the public were asked to send a stamped envelope to the theatre to be informed of what operas were being performed and when!)

There, at the time this book was first printed, the matter rested —with the Corporation being pressed to buy the Royal Court. But the city's dwindling number of ratepayers are becoming a little impatient with the role of fairy godmother to the arts of all Merseyside. In a few years hundreds of thousands of pounds of their money has gone to the arts; and they argue—surely reasonably—that the theatres are for the whole of Merseysiders and all Merseysiders should help to pay for them. The Merseyside Arts Association, which draws financial support from fifteen local authorities has been trying hard to stimulate interest outside the Liverpool boundaries in saving the Royal Court.

The situation improved at the end of the summer of 1970 when, through the initiative of Ken Dodd, Bernard Delfont agreed to reopen the theatre for the Christmas season with a show starring the Knotty Ash comedian; and DALTA (Dramatic and Lyric Theatre Association), in conjunction with the Merseyside Arts Association, arranged 1971 visits by the Glyndebourne Touring Opera, the Scottish Opera and the Royal Ballet. A fund-raising Royal Court Theatre Club was formed, largely through the efforts of Neil Tierney, a *Daily Telegraph* music critic.

Another venture which has cost the Corporation a lot of money is the Neptune Theatre. This, once privately-owned, was re-equipped and given an apron stage, primarily for amateur productions. It is admirable—but again it is for the use of all Merseyside, not Liverpool exclusively. Amateur dramatic and operatic societies flourish in the region, though not all can afford the Neptune rent.

Experiments in drama and other arts go on behind the soot-coloured classical façade of a former church in what remains of Chinatown and are led by Bill Harpe (choreographer of a modern Mass at the Metropolitan Cathedral) and his wife, Wendy. They have taken the theatre on a lorry to back streets and housing estates and they have run 'Cultural Bingo' and other off-beat projects with shoestring support. The Scaffold plans to put some of the money made from 'Lily the Pink' and 'Thank U Very Much' into yet another centre of the arts for all near the Philharmonic Hall.

As well as the Corporation's Walker Art Gallery and its annexe at Sudley, art exhibitions are held at the Bluecoat periodically and permanently at a club in old sailortown called the 'Gazebo' and at a former pub in Woolton called the 'Black Horse'. The Woolton show is Arthur Dooley's Own, strictly for art 'by the workers' (but not, necessarily manual workers), and it contains from time to time stimulating creations, including paintings by a dustman, Alan Jones, and a process worker, Ian Pendleton. Some of them were exhibited in 1970 in a room at the House of Commons, thereby making contact with the Establishment which, in the beginning, the 'Black Horse' defied. I believe that it has elements for survival, perhaps modest prosperity.

Poetry is represented by a slowly widening circle influenced by Brian Patten, Adrian Henri, Harold Hikins and a few other writers less wellknown but showing promise.

To sum up: for music, except opera, the future seems entirely secure and full of promise; for drama, the outlook is healthier than in other large cities despite the doubts about the Royal Court; and, as for the other arts, seed of an exciting renaissance on Merseyside has been sown but whether it will fructify depends upon how thorough is the weeding that has to be done.

TWELVE

LOOKING FORWARD

How fair will be the future in Liverpool depends upon how soon Merseyside's perennial problem of poverty is removed. In May, 1971, there were 40,000 out of work (33,000 of them men) in the region, more than double the total in the same month in 1966—and this despite all the money poured into it as a Development Area where each new job has cost the taxpayer an average of £671. At the start of 1970 there were eighty industrial buildings—including two new factories—idle in the city.

The Cammell Laird catastrophe and redundancies at factories on the Lancashire side of the Mersey were further blows suffered by the area in the first few months of the new decade. Plainly there has to be a massive transfusion of new industry and commerce if the poverty that has dogged Liverpool for two hundred years is ever to be erased. But firms are reluctant to move to Merseyside despite the cash inducements its Development Area status offers; and this is because the labour force has a reputation throughout the rest of the country that—to use a blunt but not exorbitant word—stinks. Few days went by in 1969 and the first half of 1970 when the newspapers did not contain reports of unofficial strikes in the Liverpool area, and so often the reasons for them seemed trivial. Yet an analysis will show that the vast majority of these disputes occurred in one industry—the docks. In all other respects Merseyside was no worse, if no better, than other regions.

Though Liverpool was still Britain's premier export outlet at the start of the seventies, the Mersey Docks and Harbour Board lost £1,780,000 in 1969. Partly this was due to crippling interest charges (bear in mind the construction of Seaforth deep-water berths, and the improvements in the sixties on which even more was spent); but there were two other important factors: an inadequate labour force and strike after strike, nearly always unofficial, which cost the equivalent of the work of 600 men. An importer for whom a terminal had been specially built withdrew ships from the port after being obliged, because of a strike, to dump a million rotting bananas in the Irish Sea. The Mersey's reputation in the world gravely deteriorated; and at the end of the year the Director-General of the Dock Board declared: 'The Port of Liverpool is in jeopardy.'

Early in 1970 it was agreed that the port could recruit an additional 800 dockers. But the climate just before this decision was poisoned by a warning from the chairman of the National Docks Modernisation Committee of redundancies in the country's port labour. The Liverpool docker heard this voice and that voice, each apparently speaking with authority but saying quite different things. Which was he to believe? He was told that his port was to be nationalised. He asked: 'Does this mean yet another upheaval? Does it mean I get the chop?'

There were hopes that a wage agreement at the end of 1969 would greatly reduce strikes. It had not done so by the following summer. In the first half of 1970 there was scarcely a week in which work was not disrupted by a dispute. By the end of May there had been fifty-eight stoppages in 1970 and 38,333 man days had been lost. A strike by tugmen cost the Dock Board £280,000 in lost dues and charges. In June, 1970, the chairman of the Port Employers' Association warned: 'The port is in a crisis situation and nobody seems to care.' Then came the national strike; and in December, 1971, bankruptcy.

It was claimed that the strikes were being engineered by anarchists and other extremists and that dockers were their easy prey. But the dockers I know are not easy prey for any man. I think they have an inbred fear of losing their jobs and of the extreme poverty that afflicted their fathers, grandfathers, great-grand-fathers and so on back to the eighteenth century. The reasons why the Liverpool docker turns bloody-minded are in the third chapter of this book. Yet, until this attitude disappears the port will be in decline.

In future, freight by sea will very largely be in containers; and Liverpool has been losing this trade to Southampton. The crucial question is whether, when the docks at Seaforth are completed, it will be in a position to compete realistically with the Solent. In the first half of 1970 ships in the Mersey were subjected to serious delays and schedules were disrupted. Ships operating transatlantic container services had to be diverted from the port because of unofficial strikes. A vessel that would have inaugurated a new citrus fruit connection with South Africa was switched to the Continent after waiting three days in the Mersey for a strike to end. In a now highly competitive industry Liverpool simply cannot survive as an important port if it continues to lose goodwill in this way. Moreover, because of the extremely bad publicity that dockland strife brings to Merseyside as a whole, non-maritime industries will continue to be dubious about settling in the area and bringing the jobs so vitally needed. Somehow the canker that grew from the bitterness of scores of years of atrocious working conditions has got to be removed from the minds of dockyard workers. There were signs in 1971, that this surgery was at last in hand.

But there is another factor upon which the Mersey's maritime importance depends and that is the provision of a motorway from the quaysides to the M6 and across England to the Humber. In 1970 it was still not in sight. Without it Liverpool cannot hope to have an important role as a transatlantic port for Europe, assuming Britain enters the Common Market in 1973. The Clyde and the Solent are better placed.

The Government put the National Giro Centre and an important sector of the Inland Revenue into Bootle where the town council has shown notable enterprise. But this is not nearly enough. Parliament and Whitehall must prove that proclamations about moving departments of the Civil Service, and also industry and commerce, out of the overcrowded South-east are not just so many words. And regional planners must have powers as well as drawing boards.

Another vital question that has to be answered before Merseyside's future can be brought into focus is: how will it be administered? Within a few days of the return of a Conservative Government it was obvious that the Redcliffe-Maud Report on local government was a dead duck. This proposed that Merseyside should be a metropolis extending from the Dee almost to the

Ribble estuary and including Chester and St. Helens. There is a strong—probably majority—opinion in favour of a metropolitan council administering both sides of the river—after all, a Merseyside Passenger Transport Authority (which inherited a debt of £1m) already exists—but the general feeling is that the region designated in the Report was much too large. Not long ago Whitehall refused to accept that Widnes and Runcorn were indubitably Merseyside towns. Redcliffe-Maud went to the other extreme.

We now seem likely to get mini-Maud with a supra-authority ruling the towns that unequivocally make up Merseyside: Liverpool, Birkenhead, Wallasey, Bebington, Ellesmere Port, Huyton, Kirkby, Bootle and Crosby, together with Whiston Rural District and the borough of St. Helens, but not Widnes and Runcorn. If this happens Liverpudlians will have a minority voice in shaping their city's destiny.

Suppose that the present plans for central Liverpool are not disturbed. By 1980 the heart of the city will be partly ringed by a motorway, Church Street will be free of traffic, pedestrian walkways will crisscross shopping areas and there may be a civic centre, costing £10 million, near St. George's Hall, though initial designs for it worried the Merseyside Civic Society because of an appearance alien to the Victorian grace of the 'Forum'. An underground line will link the city's rail terminals; and an outer loop line may serve a number of suburbs and be linked by buses.

I hope that, by 1980, there will be a bridge across the Mersey in near prospect, if not in being, and that both this and the road tunnels will be toll-free, bringing those with homes 'over the water' back into the social life of Liverpool. When motorways can span miles of low-lying land by viaducts without a charge being made to use them, it seems to me to be quite illogical to demand an entrance fee to motorways that go under or over rivers. The Mersey tunnels should be part of the road system of the country and maintained by the State.

It is possible that by the early 1980s the tunnels, if not a Mersey bridge, will link with a new crossing of the Dee estuary bringing North Wales much closer to the Lancashire side of the Mersey (Rhyl would be only a forty-five minutes' drive away) for the weekend relaxation of Liverpudlians.

The blank spaces on the periphery of the downtown area will have streets and squares of new housing (but no towering flats). Yet will those depressing enclaves of tenements—the 'Bull Ring' of Brownlow Hill, the quadrangled 'Gardens' off Park Lane and between Scotland and Vauxhall Roads still be there? In 1971— with 12,000 names on the housing lists and despite warnings that the city might have more than 20,000 empty dwellings one day— I think they will. If they are then, inevitably, they will be a new strain of Liverpool slums, that is to say they will be accepted as homes only by the desperate.

By comparison with these matters, the future of flower ladies and barrow boys in the city may seem of slight concern. But it is of moment to me. At the time of writing there is a move to ban all street sellers from within half a mile of the St. John's Precinct. If it succeeds those Saturday open-air art exhibitions near the Bluecoat could go as well as the flower ladies. The hues and cries that can still make shopping in Liverpool a lively and stimulating experience despite all the new concrete and glass, are therefore in danger; and what alarms me (as it alarms Arthur Dooley and a great many others who want Liverpool to stay different from Manchester and Birmingham) is that minds which find no attraction in street sellers will also find no appeal in streets like Hackins Hey—or in a Punch and Judy theatre leaning against St. George's Hall. If ever these minds become dominant, if we are going to have only superstores, bier kellers instead of pubs and Anglo-American chi-chi instead of wacker gusto, then Liverpool will be lost and those two Cathedrals will be memorials to a warmly exuberant, salty and sometimes inspired race that created the singing city, gave it a rakish nobility and then vanished.

But I see so many young Liverpudlians, not those stone-throwing scruffs and tormentors of the infirm and the infant but those who are full of ideas and have generosity, humour, compassion, intelligence, vitality and a genuine taste for adventure. In their midst it is impossible to be despondent. The Liverpool of the future is in their hands. And I reckon they will make a good job of it.

INDEX